T.R.A.I.L.S.

Trail Riding Assessment and Informational Learning System

Buying and Training Fearless Trail Horses

By David McFadden

T.R.A.I.L.S.

Trail Riding Assessment and Informational Learning System

Buying and Training Fearless Trail Horses

By David McFadden

Pennington Books

Dallas

2020

For information about permission to reproduce selections from
this book: write to Permissions,
David D. McFadden,
5120 West Lover's Lane,
Dallas, Texas 75209
Visit our Web site: www.trails.horse

Cover and inside illustrations by Melina Inmon

Library of Congress Cataloging-in-Publication Data
McFadden, David D.
T.R.A.I.L.S. Trail Riding Assessment and Informational Learning System / David
D. McFadden
Includes bibliographical references and index
ISBN: 978-1-7348191-0-6

1. Horses-Behavior. 2. Horses-Training
I. Title

Printed in the United States of America

MP 10 9 8 7 6 5 4 3 2 1

Part One

"No hour of life is wasted
that is spent in the saddle."
– *Winston Churchill*

Dedication

This book is dedicated to Cisco (1999-2018), the horse that trained me.

Rescue Day (2001)

2003

2018

Contents

Introduction and Important Advice

The purpose of this book is to introduce horseback riding enthusiasts to the great experiences and enjoyment that awaits the weekend trail rider. From my years spent on the back of a horse, whether trail riding or in a paddock adjacent to my stable, I have come to value the close relationship that develops between horse and rider. I hope that this book conveys some of the benefits that result from time spent trail riding across beautiful terrain.

At the same time, I want to emphasize to the inexperienced or novice rider the importance of professional programs that teach basic horse riding skills, horse-care fundamentals, and the health and safety of both horse and rider. While horseback riding can be great fun, developing prudent safety habits should be priority number one! In addition, there may be federal, state and local laws which may directly affect your rights and liabilities regarding horse ownership. This book is not intended to take the place of a program of individualized instruction and training.

Before owning, riding or training horses, you should contact experienced and reputable horse trainers, instructors, and veterinarians to develop a program geared toward your individual skill level and your knowledge in the science, care, and management of horses.

I hope this book will inspire you to become safe, responsible, knowledgeable and capable horseback riders.

Website Access

In order to conserve resources, the printed copy of this book has limited images. The online version has the entire series of photographs for each chapter. This book purchase gives limited access to website content including photographs, videos, weekly training tips, a printable version of the scoring system template and our online horse community for information sharing, trail ride calendar of events and connections. In addition to our library of images and videos, you can search for training information, instructional videos and products online.

Full access, online membership is only $50 per year. With this membership you will have full access to our library of training images, product links and videos. Training techniques are much easier to understand and learn through videos. We highly recommend the online membership to maximize your potential from this method. New content will be added frequently.

WWW.TRAILS.HORSE

Introduction
Who Should Read this Book

Any horse owner or anyone looking to purchase a horse whose primary goal is to be a trail rider should read this book. This book will take you from pre-purchase to complete horsemanship. Far too often, the goal to fully enjoy the horse-owning experience falls short because people purchase the wrong horse or do not fully appreciate the importance of horse training with a purpose. The ultimate "purpose" is to experience "joy" while in the saddle. In this book, I define joy as "horse and rider safely traveling down a trail while the rider has a sense of overwhelming pride, satisfaction, and happiness."

My own horse-owning journey started out on shaky ground because I purchased the wrong horse. By this time, I was 38 years old and had ridden horses no more than six times in my life before deciding to buy one of my own. Five of these times were on dead broke rental horses that walked nose to tail without any drama. I had close friends, Barbara and Alan, who had moved to Dallas from Jupiter, Florida, with a Quarter Horse stallion named Bandit. We bought an investment property together and converted it to horse property. It was a three-acre property located a couple of miles from a nearby lake with 20 miles of horse trails. Barbara had grown up with horses and even trained Tennessee Walkers as a teenager. So, with Barbara as my guide, off we went to find a horse.

At this time, I had one profound memory of

horseback riding: bouncing around in the saddle. So, in our initial discussions about the purchase, Barbara had mentioned that certain horse breeds are termed "gaited." She informed me that these horses move in a way where you do not bounce in the saddle. I was intrigued because I remember how uncomfortable I was during the bouncing process. So, we looked online for gaited horses that I could afford.

Because Barbara had such extensive experience with Tennessee Walkers, we ended up visiting a Tennessee Walking Horse barn near Dallas. There were several horses for sale, and a trainer rode them all for us. I don't remember the exact reason, but we focused on a sorrel gelding named Sunny. I am mildly proud to report that I did not buy Sunny on the first visit. Instead, we went back for a second visit where Barbara and I rode Sunny in a round pen. Sunny was a retired show horse that behaved well in the round pen. They told us he was "willing" and "forward" moving. Being a hyperactive, fairly athletic person, this idea of a "willing" and "forward" moving horse seemed like a great match for me even though I did not know what either of those terms meant.

Like many horse purchases, it was the perfect storm, meaning all the factors were in place for me to make an impulse buy. Sunny was groomed to perfection and looked like a model horse. In and around these familiar surroundings, Sunny was a fairly calm horse. In retrospect, I now realize that the trainer who worked Sunny was a very accomplished rider, and that Sunny really had no choice but to obey this trainer's commands. When Barbara and I rode Sunny, we were in a round pen close to his barn and barn mates. Many of these "show horses" perform well in an arena or a round pen. I had no earthly idea of how much a horse's personality can change in a different setting, with different handlers, and without an Alpha leader.

By now, I am sure you can guess that I purchased Sunny. No one in my circle of friends had a trailer, so Sunny was delivered to our horse property. And, so, my adventure began. For the first couple of months, I was learning the basics of tack and horsemanship. My riding was limited to the small paddock near the barn and the extended yard within the 3-acre fencing. Sunny was fairly well-behaved in this setting. Again, in retrospect, he was never more than 100 yards from his barn and Bandit, who had become his friend. In spite of his good behavior, he was still way too much horse for me. My balance was poor, he was very responsive, tended to be skittish, and required firm bit pressure that I never got quite right. One day when showing my father and sister what an accomplished rider I had become (not!), I was encouraging Sunny to increase speed. Suddenly, I found myself in my first canter. Between my poor balance and Sunny's reactivity, we continued to gain speed until I lost my balance and fell off; this was my first unintended dismount. I did not land well, but my pride insisted that I jump up and declare myself "okay." I was sore for a week.

For the first few months, Sunny and I stayed on the 3-acre property as I did not have a trailer. In that time, I came to realize that Sunny's barn mate, Bandit, was a one-person horse and that it is not readily accepted to take a stallion to a public trail. Therefore, it was up to Sunny and me to blaze our own path to a future of trail riding. So, just before Thanksgiving in 2001, I purchased a used, two-horse trailer. I could barely contain my excitement as my new life as a trail rider was about to begin. On Thanksgiving Day, I planned to load Sunny and head to the Lake Grapevine Horse Trails for my first solo trail riding experience. I hooked up the truck, and the trailer, pulled to an open area of the paddock, haltered Sunny from this stall and walked down to the trailer for a glorious day of trail riding. Sunny had other plans. Specifically, Sunny fully intended to stay at the barn and enjoy his normal day with Bandit.

Our first approach to the trailer was moderately uneventful until we got within four feet of the opening when Sunny realized my intention. He stopped, planted his feet, and would not move. After 15 minutes, I asked Barbara to help. Barbara pulling from the front and me applying pressure from behind only agitated Sunny more. For a couple of hours, Sunny was far more determined to stay home than we were to load him. Towards the end of this endeavor, I lost my temper and decided to increase the pressure from behind. I moved closer with my hands waving at the same level as my head. When I got close enough, Sunny kicked and hit me in my right hand, just inches from my face. We immediately aborted the attempt to load Sunny on the trailer, and I never again entered the kick zone of a horse.

Not to be defeated, I decided that I would walk, ride, or lead him to the trails that were a couple of miles away. So, I walked him for about half a mile from the property, under a major freeway and north towards the trails. With each step, Sunny became more agitated about being away from the property and his friend, Bandit. Once we were away from the freeway, I mounted him to attempt to ride the remainder of the way on the road. Immediately, he made a detour up and over the grass culvert under a tree and continued to try to turn around to go back home. I made a quick dismount and decided that, for the second time that day, I would have to accept defeat and began walking him back home. Once past the freeway, I again decided to mount and attempt to ride him back to the property approximately one-quarter of a mile away. Another bad idea! For those of you who have experienced riding a shod horse on smooth asphalt, you can imagine my horror when he began sliding and slipping the entire way back home. If you haven't experienced this sensation, don't! At this point, I am simply a passenger as Sunny is frantically trying to rejoin his two-horse herd. This particular quarter-mile of road is slightly uphill to a crest and then downhill to a 90-degree left turn. About halfway up the hill, Sunny is calling to Bandit, who hears him and starts calling back. Bandit's response only excites Sunny more, at which time we break into a canter. I am pulling back on the reins as much as I can but to no avail. Not only is Sunny continuing to pick up speed, but he is also now on the yellow line as we approach the crest of the hill where oncoming traffic cannot see us. Very fortunately, when we reach the crest of the hill, there is no vehicle there to meet us. We slipped and slid down the other side without falling, but all I could think about was the corner and the uncertain physics of metal horseshoes, smooth asphalt, and a crazy, homesick horse on a mission to be reunited with his friend. Somehow, I survived, but I will never forget the absolute horror I felt that day as I had virtually no control of this 1000-pound animal in a perilous situation.

Sunny never did turn into a good trail horse. Many Tennessee Walking horses that are bred for and shown are not as sure-footed as we need for trail riding. There were a dozen other close calls I had on Sunny that could have turned out badly. I was very fortunate that my ignorance, lack of riding ability, and poor planning didn't culminate in serious injury or death. Far too many people make this same mistake when buying their first horse.

My second horse, a rescue named Cisco, should have been my first horse. He was everything that Sunny was not; no papers, kind, gentle, sure-footed, not herd bound and not afraid. Cisco made me look like a seasoned veteran from my first ride. Cisco had hundreds of riders over the years. What's more, he had an uncanny sense of being able to gauge the abilities of each rider and would vary his level of enthusiasm and degree of difficulty to match their skill level. If I could find ten more like him, I would buy them all.

Cisco died in October of 2018 from complications of Cushing's Disease. Up until weeks before his death, he was safely carrying novice passengers around my ranch. Upon his death, I posted a picture of him the day I rescued him on Facebook, along with about two dozen pictures with various riders. Many of my friends, family members, and ranch guests had ridden him over the years. While writing his short little eulogy, I teared up when I realized what I had just written: "Picture one is the day I rescued Cisco, and all the rest are the days he rescued us." You will be missed, old pal!

Unlike some beginners, I had the fortitude and tenacity to stick with trail riding in spite of some early setbacks. Not everyone can or will persevere past these challenges. My reward has been thousands of hours of pleasurable trail riding, making friends, and improving my knowledge of horses and horsemanship. My years of trials and tribulations have culminated in this book. I hope it will help you find and train your perfect trail companion.

As I write, I continue to remember the many riders who have come and gone from my ranch whose horse-owning experience was far less than what they had hoped. More times than I can count, these very well-intentioned horse enthusiasts had horse-owning failures to such an extent that they are no longer horse owners or riders. Two people, in particular, are Dawn and Donna. Their contrasting stories are quite appropriate to introduce this book.

Dawn's Story

I met Dawn through a non-horse related business. When she discovered I had a horse ranch, she was nearly ecstatic. At 40 years old, she wanted to recapture the joy she had as a teenage rider. We arranged a time for her to visit the ranch on a Saturday morning. Dawn enjoyed the tour of the property. She was dressed to ride and could

not wait to mount-up and go. I own Tennessee Walking Horses, and on that day, we rode Sport and Midnight. I will mention Sport numerous times in the book. For trail riding, Sport is the ultimate luxury sedan. No matter what speed Sport is traveling, he is as smooth as glass, very willing, and can make an intermediate rider look like a professional. So, wanting Dawn to have a great first experience, I put her on Sport. She had never ridden a gaited horse before, and almost from the first step, she was raving about him. The joy in her voice, body language, and spirit were palpable. And, so it went for an hour. Dawn gushed about Sport through email for days following the ride. Everyone who owns horses, pets, or has children knows the pride you feel when someone compliments you over their impeccable behavior. Of course, I was beaming with pride over Sport's performance but, even more so, the amazing experience that he provided for Dawn that day.

From this point on, Dawn began a daily pilgrimage to the ranch, driving 25 miles (each way) from downtown Dallas. She brought bags of carrots and spent hours per week visiting with and spoiling every horse in sight. She had her favorites, and I would get texts and emails detailing and summarizing her visits. I don't know if I have ever seen the word "amazing" used more in my life. She bonded with one of my mares named Gracie, that really enjoys human attention. Dawn and Gracie spent many an hour together. Dawn brought her entire family to see the ranch and meet her new equine friends. This went on for months. When time permitted, we would trail ride. She tried other horses and enjoyed them all.

Dawn's riding skills seemed fantastic, and I never perceived a moment where she was nervous or unstable in the saddle.

After a few months of this, she announced that she would like to get a horse. I knew this was coming, as she had mentioned this idea more than once. I offered to help her in her search. Dawn had a profitable business and plenty of money to spend on the horse, so I was mildly insistent that she take her time and find a GREAT horse.

She graciously acknowledged my offer but didn't seem interested in my help. She kept me abreast of her search progress, but the request for help never came. I had a very uneasy sense that she was going to make a big mistake and tried to intervene lightly as best I could, but to no avail.

Within the month, Dawn informed me that she had found an Arabian mare in Wisconsin from an online site. My worst fears were now starting to be realized. I asked as many questions as I could, but she was overcome with excitement and was unable to think rationally about the horse. She kept repeating accolades about the horse that the current owner had "told" her. I kept pleading with her to allow me to talk to the owner or, better yet, for her to fly up there to ride the horse or watch someone else ride it. She was so convinced that this was the perfect horse for her that she became a bit annoyed at my insistence. Shortly afterward, she announced to me that the deal had been done and that the horse was being transported that same week. Purchase price $8500, transport fee $1500. I was horrified but did my best to be excited for Dawn. I was very hopeful that she would get lucky, and this would be the perfect horse for her.

By now, I am guessing you know the rest of the story. Arabian horses are bred to be hot, and this was one scalding hot mare, bordering on fresh lava. If the mare had any training, it was minimal and was limited to an arena. She had just about every bad characteristic imaginable. The horse was not accustomed to being tied, was highly herd bound, and Dawn liked the *look* of leather halters. The combination of these three facts caused Dawn to buy about five leather halters because the mare, when tied, would struggle so hard that she would break each halter and run through hot-wire fences back to her barn. This was just the beginning of Dawn's nightmare. She attempted to ride the horse three times. Each of the three times, Dawn was bucked from the saddle, and the horse ran back to the barn. Two of the three times, Dawn had some bruises on her person and her pride. On the third fall, she broke some ribs. After the

third fall, she never rode the horse again. She was miserable, had buyer's remorse, and her spirit was completely broken.

We tried to shame the previous owners into buying the horse back, but they refused. Dawn considered a lawsuit but decided against it. She kept the horse for about another year, paying board all the while. All her attempts to sell it were unsuccessful. She ended up giving the horse to an Arabian breeder. Dawn has not been on a horse since. That was fourteen years ago. The only way her experience could have been worse would be if she had become paralyzed or had died. In the end, it was a harsh lesson to learn about buying the wrong horse. Eighteen months and $20,000 later, Dawn's dream had become a total nightmare. Watching Dawn go through this experience was the catalyst for my developing the T.R.A.I.L.S. system and writing this book. I am incredibly hopeful that it will help many people avoid Dawn's experience.

Donna's Story

Now, let's contrast Dawn's story with Donna's story. I met Donna and her husband, Bob, through the same non-horse related business. They are distant neighbors of mine, and shortly after we met, they came to see the ranch. Donna had ridden enough over the years to be a fairly competent rider (beginner/intermediate) but certainly not what you would call advanced. In my estimation, by age 20, Dawn had probably been a much more accomplished rider than Donna. When I am unsure about a person's skill level, my default horse is Cisco. To remind you, Cisco is a gem — nearly

bombproof, no separation anxiety, and very quiet, bordering on lazy. Donna rode Cisco and was mildly bored. She then rode Sport, and they got along very well. I also have a very flashy blue roan gelding named Diesel, who is a ranch favorite because of his striking appearance. Not long after Donna had frequently been riding at the ranch, she requested to ride "that gorgeous horse," Diesel. So, began the love affair of Donna and Diesel.

Diesel is moderately spirited and somewhat excitable. On the temperament scale (1-10), I would rate him at an average of "6." For the first few minutes after mounting, he can be closer

to an "8." Usually, within a few minutes, he has calmed to a "4" and a few minutes later, perhaps even a "2." Once his initial anxiety has waned, he is nearly the perfect trail horse. Donna, like me and many other trail riders, prefers a more spirited trail horse. Diesel is the poster-horse for the phrase, "Spirited Trail Horse."

Over the next few months, Donna visited Diesel almost daily. She started learning his habits and tendencies. As it turns out, Diesel and Donna are very well suited. Three years later, they have logged hundreds of trail miles. She has asked to buy him a dozen times. I continue to refuse the sale as he is one of my favorites, and I truly admire his trail willingness. With each refusal, she threatens to horse-nap him and sequester him away somewhere in Colorado. Colorado readers, please be on the lookout for a woman with short blonde hair named Donna and a beautiful blue roan Tennessee Walking Horse answering to the name Diesel. Note: They may be using aliases!

The point of both these stories is to stress the importance of finding the right horse. If you own or plan to buy a horse, it is imperative that you and your horse are compatible. This book will help you find the right horse. If you already own a horse, you will now have the tools and methods to train your horse to be more compatible with you, or, to trade in your horse for a better-suited partner. There is no more important message in this entire book than the compatibility of you and your horse.

Full disclosure: Donna did have a very unfortunate, freak horse accident (not on Diesel) and no longer rides. This was not due to lack of preparation but simple, bad luck. Lesson: Even with years of proper handling/training/experience, accidents still happen. By following the lessons of this book, hopefully, you will be better able to prevent or minimize such accidents.

Additional Reading

I recommend a fantastic book written in 2005 by Rhonda Hart Poe, *Trail Riding: Train, Prepare, Pack-up & Hit the Trail*. This book thoroughly addresses all direct and indirect issues that rider and horse will face when trail riding. When I say "thoroughly," I mean, down to the last fine detail.

This book, *T.R.A.I.L.S.*, and its associated training system begin with basic trail training lessons and expands upon them in a manner that should be both challenging and fun. It specifically addresses those virtues necessary to make your trail riding experience outstanding. By identifying where you and your horse's strengths and weaknesses exist, you will be better able to improve in those areas. This book also addresses the issue of identifying the best-suited trail horse for each rider's style and use. Between these two books, there should be no trail riding stone unturned!

Preface

Learning to ride with confidence and control can take years to master. Only through improved horsemanship can this be achieved. Effective horse training begins with solid ground training techniques and progresses through your development as a rider. **Horses immediately sense who rides well and who doesn't.** Without the correct riding skills needed to convince the horse that you are in charge, they will see through your bluff. This sense is why so many horses revert to old behavior upon their return from the trainer. This sense is also why almost all well-known clinicians have on-camera success to the applause of their admiring disciples, only to have most followers fail when the horse and rider return home. It has a lot less to do with the horse than with the rider. What does it prove if a famous horse trainer, who has been riding since they were two years old, can get your horse to do something that you can't? It proves that they are a more competent, confident rider than you and that your horse will listen to them. It is a meaningless exhibition for the average owner.

Even though we consider our relationship with our horse to be a "partnership," this book will facilitate you becoming the majority shareholder in the partnership (**alpha leader**). Ultimately, how well your horse performs for you in whatever discipline you choose is up to **YOU**! This book will give you the methods, assessments, and instruction to improve your horsemanship, your horse's performance, and your overall riding pleasure.

Respect is the most important learned trait. I imprinted all my newborn foals as soon as they have exited the birth canal. I recommend the book, *Imprinting the Newborn Foal,* by Dr. Robert Miller. As much as I enjoyed this book and used its methods, all horse studies on the subject conclude that we should not disrupt the mare-foal bond during the first hours after birth. Later in the book, we will discuss a modified technique for bonding with the foal. **From birth through weaning and for the rest of their lives, our trail horses cannot be allowed to win one battle.** It helps to start young, but no matter what the age, horse owners need to live by this creed.

There can be days and times when we will call it a "draw," but the horse can **NEVER WIN**. If you only have limited time to work with your horse, make sure you can finish every lesson to at least a draw. Do not attempt to cover too much on any given day unless you have ample time to devote to training. Respect is the most important concept of the training portion of this book. In one form or another, every behavior relates back to your horse, respecting both your direction and your space. "Respect" is the reason that an experienced trainer can have success with your horse while you may not. Within the first 30 seconds of a trainer interacting with a horse, he has gained that horse's respect. Gaining your horse's respect is done through being the Alpha to your horse. This is the entire premise of the T.R.A.I.L.S. system.

Instead of approaching horse ownership from a cause and effect perspective, like most clinicians, I want you to approach it from a more scientific perspective. I know this doesn't sound like fun, but do not be afraid! As you progress through the book, you will clearly understand how the two can coexist in a fun, constructive way and how much more sense it makes to approach horse ownership and training in this manner. Let me explain both schools of thought.

Cause and Effect

In this school of thought, we observe the wrong horse behavior and attempt to correct it. I would call this "troubleshooting." Again, because most of us don't want, or have time, to reinforce previously learned behavior, the horse tests us when under saddle. Correcting bad behavior on the trail is difficult, if not impossible. Therefore, bad behavior does not get corrected soon enough or often enough. We enable the horse to repeat bad behavior until it prevents us from enjoying the ride, then we pay for help to correct it. Enter the clinician with "the fix."

Most clinicians would rather you buy the wrong horse and allow them to mentor you to transform it into the right one. This approach is fraught with error, as most hobbyists do not have time to accomplish this outcome. It is my opinion that most horses for sale are between 10 and 50% broke (safely trail-ready). Most horses have almost zero training in safely taking a rider around a pasture, let alone on a trail. They usually have only one overwhelming instinct —**self-preservation!**

I think having a mentor is a great advantage. Having a great horse from the start is a much greater advantage. Having both is blissful. For every rider who has reached a high level in any clinician's system, there are hundreds, if not thousands, who drop out early in the process. Whether it's lack of time, lack of money, or lack of confidence, it is likely they are not enjoying their riding experience as much as they had hoped nor has their horse even come close to realizing its potential. The DVDs, books, shows, and clinics may give you a pearl of wisdom or two, but are unlikely to get you where you want to be. My goal is for you to be is safely going down the trail, happily and frequently.

Science

The T.R.A.I.L.S. system will give you a logical, scientific way to evaluate any horse's ability frequently. The goal is to use this system to help obtain the right horse (if you don't already have one), then work and monitor the progress at predetermined intervals.

The T.R.A.I.L.S. scoring system is self-explanatory. The scoring sheet will prompt you for a score in each category. You should be able to pick up the scoring sheet, review it for one minute and begin the scoring assessment.

The T.R.A.I.L.S. system has 25 categories of evaluation. The "Ground Manners" section has thirteen scoring categories of evaluation, and each is scored on a sliding scale (0-2 to 0-5) dependent upon the importance of that category to the overall safety of the horse/human interaction. The "Under Saddle" section has twelve categories of evaluation, and is also scored on a sliding scale (0-5 or 0-6) dependent upon the importance of that category to the safety and enjoyment of trail riding. Whenever you are indecisive about a score, always pick the lower of the two scores for consistency. The total possible score is 100. The scoring system is weighted in favor of the horse's tendencies under saddle as compared to its ground manners, because the act of riding is the more important issue of the two. While ground manners are essential, our goal is to safely travel down a trail on a respectful, willing horse. A low score in any category will show you where your horse needs work prior to the next scoring interval. This book can be used as a reference to the scoring system or can be read in its entirety to further your horse training abilities.

T.R.A.I.L.S
Trail Riding Assessment and Instructional Learning System

The motivation for this book was brought about by the author's observations that most horse owners end up with the wrong horse companion. The solution to this problem has created a multi-million-dollar fix industry that takes your money to teach you to inadequately re-train your horse. While I appreciate the talent and wisdom of most of these clinicians, I am astounded by the number of people willing to spend a small fortune on course after course, book after book, or DVD after DVD to convert one kind of horse in another type of horse. The bottom line is this: "Why not purchase a horse that more closely suits your riding style, personality, and time constraints from the start?" The hope of most horse owners when buying a horse is to spend time riding, not constantly trying to correct poor horse behavior. There is more than enough of a challenge, just trying to keep a good horse, "good."

While there are dozens of examples of poor horse behavior (most addressed later), I will cite one example to make a point: refusal to "trailer." Here, I write from personal experience and direct observation. How many hours have been wasted, and how many trips have been postponed or canceled because a horse would not get on a trailer? Yes, this behavior can be corrected. Yes, the horse has every right not to want to climb into a trailer. Yes, we can spend weeks, months, and years trying to coddle, encourage and bribe them to get on a trailer, but at the end of the day, I think you bought this book because you want to ride horses, not enter into daily negotiations with them. This example and many more beg the question: "Is it worth the time and energy, or is it worth the risk of injury to you or your horse if you buy the wrong horse?"

In most cases, by age three, a horse has already decided whether it will load or not. Even if you get an adult horse to load most of the time, one refusal can start the battle over again. Not only is this frustrating, but it can be very dangerous, depending on the location where they refuse to load. It's also worth mentioning to those of you who purchase and trade numerous trailers to find one that your horse might enter. Much of what we know and do with the wrong horse would be considered insane in any other part of daily life.

This book is divided into sections about choosing the right horse for you and then maximizing your horse ownership enjoyment. Even a great horse with excellent manners needs constant reinforcement and redirection. Eventually, we would all like to enter the refinement phase of horse ownership, which can take years. The hobby of horse ownership requires a great deal of time. Some people enjoy the challenge of obtaining problem horses and training or "re-schooling" them. I applaud you. There are many project horses out there deserving of a second chance. Unless this is a passion or a business, most of us would be wise to avoid this mistake. The overwhelming majority of horses for sale are not adequately trained, and those that are trained are designed for a specific discipline, and very rarely is the discipline trail riding. The market is saturated with undertrained horses because they fail or retire from their competitive careers. The Thoroughbred industry is the perfect example. There are 80,000 foals born every year. On average, 1% of those foals go on to become true racehorses. One percent of 80,000 equals 800. Continuing the algorithm, this leaves 79,200 two- and three-year-old Thoroughbreds out of a job, annually.

What happens to these animals when they fail in competition? Their owners sell them to the public with accompanying accolades such as "great pedigree," "two years of training," "reduced price," and the list goes on. What have these horses been trained to do? They have seen the inside of a barn, a warm-up track, and a racetrack. They lived in a stall at all other times and fed on a very high protein diet, so when they do get unleashed on a track, they run like a strung-out methamphetamine addict driving a stolen Ferrari with a swarm of DEA agents in pursuit. Ponder that visual and imagine yourself purchasing that horse for personal enjoyment on a trail ride. It seems absurd, but I can assure you that exact situation is happening at multiple locations around the world as you are reading this sentence; it is not unique to the Thoroughbred industry. Nearly every other breed and competitive discipline have the same issues. Very few of these horses get training for the average rider. The law of percentages and the business of the horse industry preclude the "full" training of any horse that is bred and raised for competition. These horses are specialists, if you will. Some can and will make great horse companions, but most will rarely be given enough time and energy to realize that potential. The newer competitive trail riding discipline is the exception to this statement. Because emotion clouds our vision, most people buy a horse on impulse. I have done this more than once. Why inherit problems if you don't need to?

As my horse sense developed, I noticed that many horses and riders were poorly suited partners. Most people choose their horse partners for all the wrong reasons. Most are based on emotional decisions rather than suitability, compatibility, or practicality. Some common mistakes include breed, aesthetics, age, size, athleticism, and price preferences. Patience and an open mind are the biggest virtues one can exercise while searching for a horse. I cannot stress this enough! Let's address these characteristics one by one.

Breed

Many people favor one breed. Favoritism may stem from family influence, geography, price, availability, riding companions, or history. Whatever the reason, this may limit one's choices.

Non-gaited horses cover one mile in 12–20 minutes. By comparison, most humans walk faster than this pace. The next gear up is the trot. Trotting will require the rider to post while riding. Posting is "to rise up, out of the saddle, and then gently sit back down in rhythm with the horse's motion while it is trotting. Posting the trot is generally more comfortable for both rider and horse." Trotting may be uncomfortable on the trail as the rider will need to continuously post to make it comfortable. The next gear up is the canter. Cantering can be comfortable but rarely can either horse or rider canter for more than a minute or two. A casual trail ride on a non-gaited horse should cover about 4 miles per hour. Just being out in nature is all many trail riders' desire, so the pace is unimportant.

Gaited horses have three speeds, not including the canter, all should be comfortable. Most gaited horses can cover four to six miles per hour. By definition, a gaited breed does not have a suspensory moment between footfalls. With at least one foot on the ground at any given time, there is no trampoline effect that causes the rider to bounce or need to compensate (posting) to prevent bouncing. With many of the gaited breeds, the rider must learn the proper cues. These horses almost always need proper cues from the rider for them to gait comfortably. When some gaited horses are allowed to do the gait they choose, it can be rougher than any non-gaited horse. The cues are not difficult to learn, but each horse may respond differently to the cues. Usually, intermittent rein pressure, half halts or tipping their nose slightly to one side keeps them gaiting nicely. An up and down rhythmic bobbing of the head is a strong indication that the horse is in a preferred gait.

It is difficult, but not impossible to mix gaited and non-gaited horses on trail rides. The pace of the two breeds is significantly different. Unless you have a strong preference towards one type, buy a horse that is the same as the people with whom you will ride.

Non-Gaited Breeds

Thoroughbred, Quarter Horse, Draft Horse, Mustang, Ponies, Mules, Paint Horse, Morgan (some are capable of gaiting), Morab, Miniature Horse, Mangalarga Marchador. These horses have four distinct types of forward movement:

Walk — (all horses) a slow gait of all four-legged animals covering 2–3 mph. Three of four legs are on the ground at any given time.

Trot — diagonal legs move in pairs, 8-12 mph. At a slow trot, one hoof is on the ground at all times. At a faster pace, all four hooves are momentarily off the ground at once.

Canter — typically, the canter is a 3-beat movement, 10-17 mph. This gait has a period of suspension after each stride. This gait starts with the hind leg then leads to two hooves striking the ground together (opposite hind and diagonal front) with the other front hoof landing last. The sequence changes depending upon which "lead" (front leg first) the horse is on.

Lope or gallop — a 4-beat movement, 20-30 mph. The lope or gallop is a faster canter where all four hooves strike independently.

Gaited Breeds

Listed by most common U.S. trail riding breeds:

<u>**Tennessee Walking Horse**</u>
Dog walk — (same as all horses), 2-3 mph
Flat walk — 4-6 mph
Running walk — 5-8 mph

<u>**Missouri Foxtrotter**</u>
Dog walk — (same as all horses), 2–3 mph
Fox Trot — 4–12 mph
Flat-Footed Walk — perhaps faster

<u>**Icelandic**</u>
Dog walk — (same as all horses), 2–3 mph
Walk
Trot
Tolt — this is the gait for which these horses are known. 4–20 mph
Flying Pace — up to 30 mph (usually a show gait)

<u>**Paso Fino**</u>
Classic Fino — show gait
Paso Corto — trail gait. 4–8 mph
Paso Largo — up to 30 mph

Esthetics

As we all know, every person has a different definition of *pretty*. Most people already know the color of the horse they want to buy long before they even start the process of searching. Most horses of color (gray, palomino, buckskin, etc.) usually carry a higher price tag. If a potential horse owner has a color preference and is unwilling to have an open mind about others, patience is imperative. Somewhere, there is a horse of the color you want with many of the other qualities you need to thrive together. Be patient or have an open mind to other colors.

Age

Because horses live a longer life than most pets, we have the opportunity to purchase them after they have gone through their rebellious stage. For the average rider, I would suggest eight years (plus or minus two years) depending on the energy level. For the beginner or below average rider, I believe twelve is the minimum age. These are extremely arbitrary as it depends on so many other factors. Of course, a very quiet five-year-old is better than a spirited ten-year-old, but is much more difficult to find. If you just want to go on a slow, simple trail ride, find an older horse that is dead broke and as sound as you can find.

Size

Many people think they want a certain size horse. For a variety of reasons, a short to moderate-size horse is most ideal. There are many reasons that anyone under about 5'8" should consider a horse 15h or smaller. The main reason for this is mounting without a mounting block. There are devices to help people mount without a mounting block, but it is very difficult for older riders on the trail. Studies have shown that horses of smaller stature can carry a rider or a load further than horses of similar age and larger stature.

Athleticism

People consider some breeds to be more athletic than others. Thoroughbreds and cutting horses tend to be the most athletic. Both breeds can be too athletic for the average rider. Translation: You have a much better chance of ending up on your butt with these breeds. While all horses can buck and rear, some are not really built or bred for it. I consider bucking and rearing to be the most dangerous horse misbehaviors for an amateur rider. I have started (initial training of an unbroke horse) five of my own and purchased fifteen other Tennessee Walking Horses. Not once in my 20 years has one bucked or reared with me. I have had more than a few unintended dismounts, but not for these two reasons. While I am readily aware that they are perfectly capable of both bad behaviors, I just haven't witnessed it. I have had other breed owners tell me that they agree that some breeds are far less likely to buck and rear.

Price

By far and away, price tends to be the cause of most people ending up with the wrong horse. For many of the same reasons, buyers and sellers decide on a horse's sale price based on many flawed criteria. Do not allow emotion to guide your choice. Even if you keep your horses on your property, it's still an expensive hobby. Without injury or sickness, expect your yearly overhead cost per horse to be a minimum of $1500 (usually higher). If you board your horse elsewhere, you are looking at a minimum of several thousand dollars per year. My point is, we spend a small fortune on our horses, and I think it is fully justifiable to consider increasing your budget to obtain a horse with much more training. The cost of ownership far outweighs the initial purchase price. If you think you are ready to buy a horse, but only have a small amount of money saved, consider waiting an additional six months to one year. Start a horse budget of $400 per month (the amount you would be paying for boarding). After six months, your $2500 purchase budget is now $4900. Now, you have increased your chances of finding a horse more suited for you. I believe a budget of $4500 should help increase your chances of finding the right one. Of course, there are some great horses you can purchase for a lot less. If you find one, you just saved yourself a bunch of money. However, with a larger budget, you will be less likely to settle for the wrong one.

Boldness

"Boldness" is a relatively new characteristic discovered in a study by Briard and Petit in 2015. A bold horse is much more likely to be in the front of the herd. A *bold* horse does not have anxiety about being on the forward fringes of the herd, where it is more vulnerable to attack. Exact correlations have yet to be made between boldness and how it relates to trail riding. However, in my experience, I believe I have observed a positive correlation between boldness and good trail horse performance. Boldness will be mentioned several times in the coming chapters.

In closing this section, I would strongly encourage you to make your horse-buying journey a thorough one. Be patient, educate yourself, and try your hardest not to buy on impulse.

Enough about the horse, let's discuss the rider.

The Rider

The average trail rider starts one of two ways: Either a person rides as a youth and reenters the horse world later in life, or the person decides later in life to start riding. Rarely do time and finances permit young people to stay in the horse world through their twenties. As people become interested in horsemanship in their thirties and forties, they imagine the glamorous, romantic dream that so many of us have about horse ownership. Unfortunately, by this age, our bodies and abilities have significantly declined. Most people this age have done very little in the way of fitness, coordination, strength, and flexibility training. Many people have gained weight and are top-heavy. This shift greatly impacts our seat in the saddle and our ability to maintain balance. Our minds remember all that we could do in our teens and twenties, but the reality is that we are far less capable later in life. I have seen this demonstrated time and time again. I have lost count of the number of people overheard saying, "I have ridden all of my life" or that when they were young, they could ride "anything." Within minutes of mounting, it is obvious that, if this were true, it is not anymore. In some cases, the horse was liberated from rider within seconds of mounting. Please be realistic about your abilities before buying a horse. There is no better way

to prepare yourself for the search for a horse than to take some lessons. Lessons *can* be deceptive because many lesson horses are dead broke.

Nonetheless, you can still get some feel for your current abilities from a few lessons. The reality is that if you are not moderately athletic or physically fit, your ability to significantly improve your riding level is limited. I know this is not what anyone wants to hear, but it *is* the reality that we all face. It is a far greater likelihood that a well broke horse will rise to your riding level than you rising to the level of a not-so-broke horse. Another common scenario is purchasing a horse that seemed like a deadhead. He may have been undernourished, not wormed for years, and a little thin. We take the horse home; the vet de-worms it and tells us to put some weight on him by feeding more grain. The next thing you know, the horse is nothing like the one you purchased. This increase in protein and calories, along with a dramatic reduction in parasites, has turned Mr. Nice Guy into Mr. Fresh Guy. Within a few weeks, our new horse has already outpaced our abilities.

The first two sections of this book will address a method of choosing the right horse. The remaining chapters will give you and your horse a method of interacting, which should provide plenty of challenges to improve your horsemanship. This investment in your bond with the horse should yield exceptional dividends for years to come.

Part Two

"A man on a horse is spiritually,
as well as physically,
bigger than a man on foot."
– John Steinbeck

1
Safety

Safety, safety, safety!!

There are many intentions of this book, but none more important than personal safety. The author and contributors to this book are well aware of the high-profit motives of many trainers and training programs. We intend to provide the reader with basic to advanced horsemanship methods and practices where *you* can train your horse safely and effectively. Most importantly, we will stress *your* personal safety. Unlike so many other methods, this book and its complete training and assessment system will give you the tools necessary to have the best possible chance of a safe and enjoyable trail riding experience. It opposes the "problem solving" current philosophies that many trainers advocate where only one problem is solved at a time through an expensive clinic or DVD series. The central theme of the entire book,

training methods, and assessment system are to prepare you and your horse for maximum safety while having predictable riding enjoyment with each outing.

From *The Welfare of Horses*, Chapter 1, Horse Behaviour: Evolution, Domestication, and Fertilisation by D. Goodwin. (British) Abstract:

The evolution of the horse began some 65 million years ago. The horse's survival has depended on adapative [sic] behaviour patterns that enabled it to exploit a diverse range of habitats, to successfully rear its young and to avoid predation. Domestication took place relatively recently in evolutionary time and the adaptability of equine behaviour has allowed it to exploit a variety of domestic environments. Though there

Proper care and containment are necessary for horses to participate positively in the human-horse relationship.

are benefits associated with the domestic environment, including provision of food, shelter and protection from predators, there are also costs. These include restriction of movement, social interaction, reproductive success and maternal behaviour. Many aspects of domestication conflict with the adaptive behaviour of the horse and may affect its welfare through the frustration of highly motivated behaviour patterns. Horse behaviour appears little changed by domestication, as evidenced by the reproductive success of feral horse populations around the world.

The takeaway from the above paragraph for me is, domestication over the past 6,000 years has changed horse behavior very little, if any, since the beginning of the species some 65 million years ago. So, it is certainly in our best interest to attempt to find and train those horses that are best suited for us.

There are a myriad of factors related to the human-horse relationship. Needless to say, we want a positive human-horse relationship, but many factors are out of our control. For example, we cannot change the past human-horse relationship(s) for the horse, nor can we change the past human-horse relationship(s) for ourselves. Therefore, let's attempt to control those human-horse relationship variables that we can in our current relationship. Horses cannot help but bring baggage into a new relationship.

Humans can attempt not to bring baggage into a new relationship but are often unsuccessful. Studies have shown the following to help build positive human-horse relationships (Hausberger, 2008; Hinde, 1979; Keeling, 1999; Casey,

2002; Hama, 1996; Jezierski, 1999; Pasille, 1996; Munksgaard, 1997; Reinhart, 1991):

1. Reducing or discontinuing negative stimuli (physical discipline).
2. Increasing positive stimuli (appropriately timed food rewards).
3. Increased awareness and recognition of horse behavior cues.
4. Improved human management of horse care (horse welfare).
5. Increase the frequency of human-horse contact.
6. Riders need to be more physically fit.
7. Riders need to be better riders (balance, cues, awareness, etc.)
8. Tack needs to be appropriate and comfortable.

Horses may seem to have affection for humans, but this is only a by-product of handling and conditioning. A horse that runs to you to accept treats or affection is usually only responding to the "treat" conditioning. It may seem fond of you, but the reality is that it almost always wants to be with other horses as opposed to being with a human.

The majority of pet owners are guilty of believing that our pets think and act in a fashion similar to humans (anthropomorphism). Believing that your horse would pick your companionship over that of the herd is a misguided idea when you stop to consider it, isn't it? The behavioral process that is happening when our horse seems to show us affection is that the horse is choosing cookies, carrots, apples, butterscotch, grain, etc., over the few

blades of grass, dry hay or nothing edible, currently available in its pasture. Studies have shown that grooming is **NOT** a positive experience for horses (McGreevy and McLean, 2005; Waran and Casey, 2005). Think about that. What does a horse do immediately after grooming? They roll!

Anthropomorphism (noun) (def.) – the attribution of human motivation, characteristics, or behavior to inanimate objects, animals, or natural phenomena.

This notion (anthropomorphism) is one of the biggest reasons we do not connect with or understand horse behavior. Horse's brains are small and primal. They are geared almost exclusively towards survival (eating and physical self-preservation). Therefore, the less we attempt to see them for more than self-preservationists, the better we will understand and interact with them, and the safer we will be around or on top of them.

Horseback riding is one of the most dangerous recreational sports (Ueeck et al., 2004) with more accidents per hour happening than, for example, during motorcycling (Chitnavis et al., 1994). In the USA, "it has been estimated that horseback riding accounts for 2,300 hospital admissions each year, with an overall injury rate of 0.6 per 100 hours of riding" (Christy et al., 1994).

I cannot stress the topic of personal safety enough. All of us in the horse-world have many stories about near or real catastrophes related to being on or around powerful, unpredictable prey animals. The notion of riding 800- to 1,500-pound animals sounds like a very romantic hobby and harkens us back to a nostalgic time in history when horses were the main mode of transportation. But, consider that our grandparents, great-grandparents, and great-great-grandparents learned to ride horses as children. They were much better riders than any of us, and the horses were used daily as plow animals, transportation, and even pulled buggies to church on Sunday. Most horses of yesterday were so broke that they were more docile than family pets of today. Because of their daily use and the intense expectations placed on them by owners, they were very predictable. Most horses of today are far less predictable because they are used much differently, far less frequently, and our expectations of them are minimal. Many hobby horses go weeks or even months without being touched, let alone trained or reinforced. It is little wonder that they don't always perform up to our expectations when we make time to ride them. Even weekly use is a far cry from how often horses were used before motorized vehicles.

In this chapter, we will begin the discussion of the terms "Respect" and "Alpha Leader." For many readers, it will be assumed that both or either of these terms mean a heavy-handed approach to training. **I want to dispel this assumption from the beginning. In no way will I suggest any mistreatment or abuse of a horse.** Rather, because we have the superior brain and forethought, I am recommending that you humanely be the "Alpha Leader" between you and your horse, which will earn you the "respect" that is required to enjoy this hobby most safely. This entire book speaks to this concept.

Why do I include the issue of "respect" in the chapter on safety? Because a respectful horse is a safer horse!

It is important to remind all riders that horses function in a world based on respect. Quickly established in every herd is an order (pecking order) or hierarchy that sort from most dominant (alpha) to least dominant (beta, gamma, delta, epsilon, zeta, and so on). This process happens very quickly in a herd and is what **all horses understand and expect** in the course of their daily lives. We must be above our horses in the pecking order if we hope to gain their respect. **Note: Not equal to them, ABOVE THEM. Achieving this position does not take abusive acts, but simply a steadfast mindset that our horses must follow our rules, respect our space and authority, 100% of the time.**

Let's define and explain the concepts of "Alpha Leader" and "Submission":

Alpha Leader (def.) — the individual in the community with the highest rank. Male or female individuals or both can be alphas. Other animals in the same social group may exhibit deference (lower position in the social hierarchy) or other symbolic signs of respect particular to their species towards the alpha or alphas. Alphas may achieve their status by means of superior physical or mental prowess and/or through social efforts and building alliances within the group. Synonyms: herd leader, dominant leader, alpha, alphas.

Submission (def.) — the action or fact of accepting, deferring or yielding to a superior force or to the will or authority of another person or animal. Synonyms: yielding, acceptance, consent, deference, compliance, capitulations, "submission to authority."

Because horses live in a world of social hierarchy, they are accustomed to being told by herd mates where they rank within the group (see pictures below). They are more comfortable knowing where they rank than not knowing. Most horses only have brief encounters with humans compared to the vast majority of their lives spent in the herd. Because their world is based on the hierarchy system, they yearn to know their place. When it is not clear whether they are above or below a human, they are left to figure it out on their own. Until shown differently, all horses, especially young ones, will try to assume the position of the alpha. This is just their instinctual tendency.

The great news is that they really don't care whether they are above us or below us, they just need to know. The even better news is that they don't get their feelings hurt by submitting to us. Many trainers agree that the horse feels relief when they submit to us because the act of submission is the beginning of them trusting us to make decisions for them. We do this by teaching them to respect us at many levels. The process of teaching respect is the main premise of this book and is shared by nearly all horse trainers. **Put succinctly, the human must become the "alpha leader," and the horse must "submit" to us.**

One of the cardinal signs of horse submission is licking of the lips. You will see this during your ground training, especially during longeing. Animal science behavior experts believe the action of licking may indicate a switch between the sympathetic and parasympathetic systems where a perceived threat is suddenly recognized to be a non-threat. So, in the sense of licking their lips, this may, in fact, be a form of submission. At the very least, from an anecdotal perspective, the frequency and consistency of this reaction are far too common for us to dismiss it as anything other than signaling a new dynamic for that human and that horse on that day.

Because safety is our primary objective, you will be tasked with teaching your horse respect, first and foremost. This will be a difficult task for many of you who believe you can befriend a horse first and expect respect to follow. When a young horse learns respect early, that respect can become almost permanent. The "almost" part of that sentence means that some regular reinforcement is always necessary but, for those well-trained horses, it may only take a small amount.

However, new owners can quickly ruin well-trained horses by not reinforcing earlier training. **The issue of respect cannot be over-emphasized.** The concept is no different from raising good or bad children. Some children want to follow the rules and strive to please their parents. These children need much less parenting. Unruly children require constant, persistent, and consistent parenting even into adulthood. Horses are no different. Some will learn quickly and require much less ongoing reinforcement (understand that "ongoing"

Beware of lingering in a paddock with multiple horses.

We are all friends.

Without notice, this mare decides to remind the haltered horse of the pecking order.

The situation can become dangerous, quickly.

The situation degrades even faster when additional horses are added. Both mares decided to reinforce the pecking order at the same time.

by definition means "going on" or "forever")! Others will be a challenge for their entire life. Unlike bad children who only cost you time, money and heartache, a bad horse can cause you injury or death. This is why choosing the right horse is of paramount importance. Or, if you already own a horse, you may need to change the dynamic between you and the horse.

There are two main ways to command respect from a horse. One method is on their back through exceptional horsemanship. Most riders are not competent enough to command respect from a horse through exceptional riding. Therefore, method two, "ground training," is the preferred means of earning the respect of a horse. This book utilizes ground training challenges, initially, then progresses through mounted training and challenges to increase you and your horse's confidence towards obstacles and perceived trail threats.

Why do you think it is that horses are timid with timid riders and more confident with confident riders? This is no coincidence. There are a few explanations for this phenomenon but the one I agree with is that a compliant, submissive horse does not feel the need to make as many decisions to ensure its safety or survival. This is a philosophically complex explanation which I hope to explain adequately. Let's pretend that you have *not* established yourself as the "alpha" in your relationship with your horse (at least it is not clear to the horse). So, whether it's in handling or riding because you have not established yourself as the leader, the horse feels compelled to make decisions. You have not instilled confidence or trust in the horse. Another way to say it is that by not being the "alpha" you have not earned the respect of the horse. It is imperative from the first encounter that you clearly convey in all actions and requests, that you are the "alpha." You decide where they walk, where they stand, how they interact with other people and horses in your presence, etc.

When you ride, you make all the decisions on what trail, which side of the tree to pass around, which place to make the water crossing, etc. **ALL DECISIONS!** These are all definitive messages to the horse that you are in charge, and they have no responsibility for decision making. This is the accepted dynamic as our brains are much larger and more developed, and horses want and need to be told what to do. When left to their own devices, horses almost always make the wrong decisions regarding rider safety. **Horses are instinctually programmed with one goal: SELF PRESERVATION**. So, if they realize we are making all the decisions for them, they are much more relaxed and far less reactive. Horses do not get their feelings hurt and are happier when told what to do. ALL PROFESSIONAL TRAINERS AGREE ON THIS! I make no apologies if this sounds harsh or controlling because we are discussing YOUR personal safety and, ultimately, your riding enjoyment.

This may be a simplified human, emotional explanation for a very primitive animal-to-animal dynamic, but it makes sense to me. I hope it does to you, too, because being the "alpha" to your horse is the only effective means to a great outcome.

I am not suggesting that horse trainers do not play a role in this process. If you buy or already have a horse that you are not confident in training yourself or if your time is limited, by all means, employ a trainer. However, at some point, you will need to take over the ongoing, day-to-day training and reinforcement of your horse. Most people cannot afford ongoing horse training fees ranging from $300-1000 per month. How many times per year can you afford to attend a clinic or demonstration for basic problem-solving? If you hire a professional or amateur trainer, you should participate as much as possible in the process. After the horse returns from training, it is solely up to you to maintain discipline and respect. It should be every horse owner's goal to continue the progress of the horse themselves.

By following the prescribed methods in this book, most of you should successfully earn the respect of your horse and be able to enjoy horseback riding safely for many years to come. This assessment and training system will give you tools (techniques) and numeric goals (qualitative evaluation) to keep improving horse, rider, and the overall horse owning experience.

Worth mentioning is the "one-rein-stop." The one-rein-stop is a technique to stop a badly behaving or run-away horse. Consider this the "Emergency Brake" for horses. This technique will be discussed in Book Three, Chapter 18, Reining. In short, it is the aggressive pulling to one side to stop a horse from bad behavior. It should only be used in extreme situations like when a frightened horse attempts to run away with a rider. A horse that is more compliant with neck flexion (Book Three, Chapter 15, Neck Flexion) will also be easier to stop with this technique.

Another very important safety issue is avoiding the "kick zone". Suffice it to say, no matter how much experience you have with any horse, **NEVER ENTER THE KICK ZONE!** Even perfect horses make

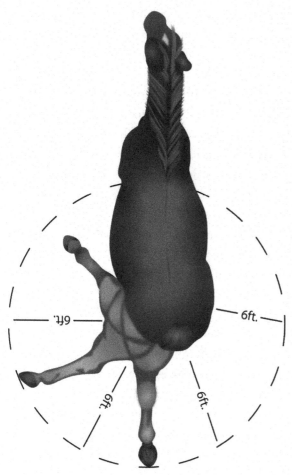

Always respect the kick zone by never entering it.

mistakes in interpretation of threats. Error on the cautious side by never being in the kick zone.

There is certainly more to safety than an obedient, mindful horse. As with any hobby, accidents will happen. Horseback riding accidents can be much more severe than in most other hobbies. Remember, we are engaged in a hobby with large, powerful animals with very small brains that have survived in a predatory world through explosive,

reflexive flight instincts. Murphy from "Murphy's Law" states, "anything that can go wrong will go wrong!" Some speculate that Murphy may have owned horses. Basic safety procedures that demand discussion are found throughout the book, but the first section is not too soon to begin. It behooves you to stay on top of the horse. Falls from horses account for 80% of the injuries sustained to riders.

Here is a list and some discussion regarding basic safety and preparation.

1. Do not buy or keep a horse that is too much horse for you.

2. Do not buy highly reactive horses.

3. Do not keep highly reactive horses.

4. Never make excuses for highly reactive horses.

5. Command the respect of your horse.

6. Become a better rider.

7. Wear a helmet.

    An alarming study (Winkler et al., 2016) on traumatic brain injuries (TBIs) places horseback riding related falls far above football (45.2% versus 20.2%, respectively) as the most common cause:

    From 2003 to 2012, in total, 4788 adult

sports-related TBIs were documented in the NTDB, which represented 18,310 incidents nationally. Equestrian sports were the greatest contributors to sports-related TBI (45.2%). Mild TBI represented nearly 86% of injuries overall. Mean (± SEM) length of stays (LOSs) in the hospital or intensive care unit (ICU) were 4.25 ± 0.09 days and 1.60 ± 0.06 days, respectively. The mortality rate was 3.0% across all patients, but was statistically higher in TBI from roller sports (4.1%) and aquatic sports (7.7%). Age, hypotension on admission to the emergency department (ED), and the severity of head and extracranial injuries were statistically significant predictors of prolonged hospital and ICU LOSs, medical complications, failure to discharge to home, and death. Traumatic brain injury during aquatic sports was similarly associated with prolonged ICU and hospital LOSs, medical complications, and failure to be discharged to home.

8. Gradually ease your horse into new situations. Horses are suspicious and react negatively to most changes.

9. Choose the proper saddle for your riding level and horse's personality. A Western saddle is a lot easier to stay in if your horse spooks or becomes unruly. Everyone remembers the feeling of having "nothing to hang on to" when you first tried an English or alternative saddle. For most experienced riders who rely on balance rather than grip,

the type of saddle is of less importance than at the novice level.

10. Choose the proper bit for your riding level and horse's personality. Bits are used for control. The selection process will be discussed in the chapter on bridling. For now, know that the bit you choose, combined with the finesse through your fingers, will determine the level of cooperation or resistance of the horse.

11. Do not place your entire foot in the stirrup. The balls of your feet should rest in the middle of the stirrup.

12. Purchase boots that are narrower than your stirrups or stirrups that are wider than your boots. Dragging horse accidents are some of the worst.

13. Always remain prepared for a spook while in the saddle. This may not seem possible, but as you become a better rider, you will have a natural tendency to be more prepared for abrupt horse reactions without even consciously anticipating it. In the meantime, learn to keep a little pressure on the horse with your thighs and calves. This alone will keep you from coming off most of the time.

14. Never walk behind a horse. Even horses considered to be "perfect" have bad days or incorrect perceptions. Ultimately, a horse is

programmed to survive. Survival depends on a horse protecting itself from real and perceived threats. Like humans, horses lose visual acuity, have blind spots, floaters, see mirages, have incorrect interpretations, etc. Therefore, it is best to NEVER walk behind ANY horse. If you must, walk as closely to the hindquarters as possible while keeping constant physical contact with the horse by placing a hand on the rump.

15. Avoid distracted riding. Cell phone use is very popular while on a horse. Whether its picture taking, Internet surfing, emailing, texting, or talking, it is a dangerous act because your attention is diverted. It can wait.

16. Ride with people respectful of your skill level. On occasion, the better riders will do things that may be potentially dangerous for the other riders in the group. Galloping, jumping, and difficult water crossings are a few advanced riding activities that should **not** be attempted if even one person in the group is anxious about them. Horses, by nature, will try to keep up with the herd. Therefore, beginner and intermediate riders will become unwilling passengers when their horse attempts to keep up with or catch up with the herd. **All trail rides should be conducted with the degree of difficulty is in line with the ability of the least competent rider.** Some riders are so timid or lack confidence in their ability that riding with them is simply no fun. Rarely will people on either side of the timid/confidence scale be able to communicate this effectively to the other. So, if you are terrified continuously to ride with your group, I suggest you find a different group.

17. Dismount in perceived dangerous situations. I am always appalled that motorists and pedestrians expect our horses to be more desensitized than they are. I can't count the number of times that motorists, bikers or hikers appear to have no concern for the reaction of approaching horses. Their ignorance of potential dangers will not change, so expect to have frequent challenges where you ride. Shod horses walking on concrete are dangerous enough without careless motorists screaming past. Some horses are rarely around bicyclists or hikers with backpacks. Most horses follow other horses or humans better than they lead. The herd usually reacts in unison with the lead horse. This is a natural mechanism of herd survival. So, instead of jeopardizing the safety of the group, it is occasionally better to dismount and lead the group on foot.

18. Use common sense.

There are dozens of finer points of safety that you should research and understand. Please take the time to familiarize yourself with horse safety and accident prevention. Horseback riding can be exhilarating and enjoyable but always endeavor to make it as safe as possible.

HELMET FACTS

Here's Why You Need Your STM/SEI
Approved Helmet for Every Ride...

Courtesy of University of Connecticut's College of Agriculture, Health, and Natural Resources

An injured brain does not heal like a broken bone. Even seemingly insignificant head injuries can have serious long-term effects.

- Horseback riding carries a higher injury rate per hour of exposure than downhill ski racing, football, hang-gliding and motorcycle racing.

- Medical Examiner reports show that 60% or more of horse-related deaths are caused by head injuries. Helmets can reduce this possibility by 70-80%.

- Each year approximately 70,000 people are treated in emergency rooms because of equestrian related activities.

- The American Medical Equestrian Association calculates that ASTM/SEI approved helmets have reduced all riding-related head injuries by 30% and severe head injuries by 50%.

- Repeated trauma to the head, even when minimal, can cause cumulative damage to the brain. Each new accident expands the original damage, and the brain cannot recover 100% from injury.

- Riders under the age of 21 formerly had the highest head injury rate. Expanded use of ASTM/SEI helmets among this age group has shifted the highest head injury rate to those people ages 22-35.

- Non-ASTM/SEI certified helmets offer no protection whatsoever and are strictly for cosmetic purposes.

- Head injuries are responsible for more than 60% of horse-related deaths.

- Head injuries are the most common reason for horse-related hospital admissions.

- Liability insurance must be provided by manufacturers on their products as part of the SEI certification process.

2
Understanding Separation Anxiety and Herd Mentality

This chapter is, perhaps, the most important chapter of this book. Read and reread it until it makes perfect sense to you. The messages herein will help you understand why it is so important to prepare your trail horse, in advance through training and testing.

The single biggest obstacle to overcome with any horse training method is the horse's intense, genetic predisposition (desire) to be with other horses. This desire is known as "Herd Mentality," "Herd Behavior," or "Safety in Numbers." Many synonyms exist to describe a horse with a strong behavioral need to be with other horses: "herd bound," "herd sour," "barn sour," or "buddy sour." I believe that most of our training issues are linked directly to this innate instinct.

I rather enjoyed reading the assertion made by biologist W.D. Hamilton in "Geometry for the Selfish Herd" that "each individual group member reduces the danger to itself by moving as close as possible to the center of the fleeing group. Thus, the herd appears as a unit in moving together, but its function emerges from the uncoordinated behavior of self-serving individuals."

Drawing on what we know, the larger the herd, the higher the chances of any one individual surviving an attack. Because a larger herd has additional sentries monitoring for danger, the herd is safer because there are more eyes, ears, and noses to sense danger. Much like a home alarm system, a house with only a front door alarm is much more vulnerable to intrusion than a house with alarms on all doors and windows. Add motion sensors, and the house is even safer. Scientists have also discovered that the more reactions animals have to "false positives" or "false alarms," the higher the

Horse begins looking back at barn/barn mates within 25 feet.

Horse turns to look back at barn/barn mates at 100 feet.

survival rates (Conradt, 2013). Reaction to a false threat means that an evasive action taken to avoid any potential danger, no matter how mild, is more beneficial to survival than not. Stated another way, if an animal reacts to *all* threats, real or not, it increases the odds of reacting appropriately to the real threats.

Conversely, an animal that does not react to false threats (false negative) often enough will eventually make an error in judgment on a real threat and, therefore, remove itself from the gene pool by being eaten or gravely injured. Back to the home alarm example: if your alarm system calls the police to tell them there is an invader every 20 minutes (false alarm) and they come to investigate, your chances of ever having a home invasion are almost zero.

Our domesticated horses have almost zero real threats in modern-day containment, yet they still have many reactions to false threats. Desensitization is the only method to decrease false threats. Why do I review these scientific origins? Answer: To make the point that we have a lot of genetic and instinctual hurdles to overcome when asking our horse to leave the herd even for a short distance or for a brief time. Know that for most horses there is a very strong preoccupation to return to the herd. Decreasing this urge will make our horses more respectful, cooperative, and safer.

The "preoccupation to return to the herd" is dangerous, whether we are grooming, leading, or riding. The greater the distance between a single horse and its herd, the more anxious and dangerous it becomes. "Boldness" is a relatively new characteristic discovered in a study by Briard and Petit in 2015. **The characteristic of boldness is very favorable in a trail horse.** A bold horse is much more likely to be in the front of the herd. This does not necessarily make it a herd leader but is simply a horse that does not have anxiety about being on the forward fringes of the herd, where it is more vulnerable to attack. I have owned and trained trail horses and can say, without reservation, that a bold horse is a better horse. We will discuss this concept in later chapters.

Until horses start talking, we can only speculate on why they react the way they do. Perhaps someone should have asked Mr. Ed some more serious questions before he passed?

Horses are individuals but share so many common characteristics that we can discuss them as a "group" if we understand that the range of any particular behavior is fairly broad and that generalizations are just that, generalizations! A book cannot be written for the training method best suited for each horse. Therefore, we will endeavor to find enough common ground in the broad category of "Horse Training" to benefit the majority of horse owners.

The phrase "Temperament" is used to quickly define the relative calmness, or lack thereof, of each individual. Temperament can be changed through training and desensitization.

In general, we are dealing with three main determinants of a horse's temperament: genetic predisposition, environmental conditions, and learned behavior. These concepts will be discussed, in detail, in the following chapter.

3

Temperament

The word "temperament" is used to quickly define the relative calmness, or lack thereof, of each horse. Temperament is rated on a numeric scale from 1–10, with one being the calmest. It is a subjective rating, meaning that the score is determined by a person's opinion. Remember, the person making that decision may have a bias or a hidden motive. Any horse rated over a 4 is considered to have a "spirited" temperament. When attempting to sell a horse, most owners lower the temperament score. By subjectively lowering the temperament score, the number of inquiries from potential buyers will increase.

Below are the factors that influence a horse's Temperament:

Genetic Predisposition is the genetic tendency to be like your parents. If one or both parents have traits that make a horse highly excitable, the chances are good that the offspring will also share those traits. Certain horses were bred for high energy. If your riding style is not comfortable with ambitious forward motion or spirited trail willingness, you will want to consider breeds that are calmer and more docile. We advise steering clear of the "hot" breeds unless you are an intermediate to experienced rider, or you are young enough and athletic enough to improve your riding skills significantly. This decision alone will significantly reduce the number of causative factors for trail excitability. See the "Temperament Scale" figure.

Environmental Factors are out of your control, but you can decide not to ride when conditions are not ideal. These factors include wind, barometric pressure, rain, wet trails, heat, cold, and smells, just to mention a few. There is a large risk for excuse-making here. Once you start to cancel your rides because of "environmental conditions," there is often an increasing tendency to do so. Many riders make too many excuses for not riding because of environmental factors. For example, people say, "my horse is really spooky in the wind." So, on a 35-mph windy day, you may want to consider whether it is safe to ride. The following week, the winds are 25 mph, and you decide not to ride. Next week, 15 mph, and you are still convincing yourself that it is too windy to ride. Pretty soon, it is *always* too windy to ride. The same is true for all the other environmental factors. My advice is to do your best to persevere through reasonable environmental factors. Once you start making excuses not to ride, it can be the beginning of the end of your riding hobby.

If you decide not to ride on a day that you deem environmentally unfavorable, that may be a great day to use that time to desensitize your horse from the ground. Whether it be tying a tarp to the round pen allowing it to flap and pop while your horse is in there, walking your horse on a lead away from the barn, taking it to the windiest part of the pasture or paddock, or simply grooming in the wind. Don't lose the opportunity to use the adverse conditions to make your horse better.

Learned Behaviors are simply behaviors that an individual must learn instead of behaviors that happen automatically. Instinct and reflex are examples of behaviors that do not have to be learned — horses are born knowing how to stand, eat, walk, and run. Anything that they have to practice to improve is "learned behavior" – accepting saddles and bridles, entering trailers, accepting riders, respect of humans, etc.

For survival reasons, horses like consistency. All prey animals are hypersensitive to change. Recognizing and reacting to change is what keeps prey animals alive. They like to be around their herd mates, and they grow very accustomed to a routine. Most horses are on a pretty regimented schedule for feed, turnout, and pasture mates. Most days are nearly identical in a horse's life. They are brought in and turned out in the same order, every day of the year. Any change in the schedule gives them anxiety. You can control their reaction to change by exposing them to frequent changes in their routine (referred to as "desensitization").

Since the domestication of the equine species, humans have bred for and refined for specific characteristics to assist in and ease the burden of human endeavors. The most basic categories are transportation and agriculture. Within each of the broad categories, subdivisions have been refined.

Gaited horses were bred for a more comfortable and rapid form of transportation. Draft horses were bred for increased agricultural production. The broad category of equine recreation placed additional need on the species to diversify further. With our need for speed, breeds like the Thoroughbred, Arabian, Quarter Horse were engineered through careful reproduction. Economic and competitive factors cause breeders to continue to refine the breeds for specific demand. Horse breeds that are used for speed or endurance are bred to be "hot," meaning they have high energy and can be highly excitable. Depending on the

discipline, "hot" can be a very good thing. "Hot" can also be a desired characteristic for good riders. For the average trail rider, "hot" is not good.

Included in this section on Learned Behavior are **Care and Containment**. Studies have shown that horse's behavior can be influenced by its immediate physical environment and care. This should not surprise anyone as we have all seen the devastating effects of abuse on all creatures. Bad welfare or increased emotional state can certainly lead to undesirable reactions of horses when ridden (Hausberger, M., et al., 2008). From Hausberger, M., et al. (2008), here is a review of the human-horse relationship:

> Domestic horse personality and the rela-tion between horses and humans might also be affected by the general manage-ment. Physical suffering may induce undesirable reactions to humans (Pritchett et al., 2003; Jaeggin et al., 2005), leading sometimes to aggression (Casey, 2002). Confinement (box, stall) has been shown to be one factor involved in the develop-ment of stereotypes or change of behavior when horses are turned out even when they work regularly (Chaya et al., 2006), but also in the reactions at work (Rivera et al., 2002). Also, social deprivation at a young age is found to affect the relation-ship: horses may seek more contact with humans, but this is associated with un-wanted behaviours such as biting or kick-ing the trainer (Sondergaard and Ladewig, 2004).

If you have a horse or intend to purchase one, it is in the best interest of both parties to ensure that the horse receives good/great care and containment. This intention has financial implications, so, it is highly advised that you accurately calculate the cost of proper care and containment, vet bills, emergencies plus 25% to be prepared for unanticipated expenses.

Gender Differences have not been observed in multiple studies (Hausberger et al., 2004b, Visser et al., 2001 and 2002, Henry et al., 2005, Lansade 2005) on horse temperament thereby dispelling the myth that mares are more temperamental than geldings or stallions. However, due to mare behavior when in season, their reaction to other horses could be rightfully considered a negative trait for the human evaluation of a potential human-horse relationship.

Standard disclaimer: Like people, there is a wide distribution of temperament within each breed. As seen in the Bell-Shaped Curve of Statistics (diagram below), 68% of the subjects will fall within one standard deviation from the mean, 24% within two standard deviations, and 6% within three standard deviations. Meaning, while exceptions will occur, the vast majority (68%) of subjects will define the group.

Most people who are experienced in the equine world will broadly define a horse's personality as "hot-blooded," "cold-blooded," or "warm-blooded." In general, each of these terms describes how a horse will react in certain situations, relate to their riders and trainers, and for what type of work they are best suited. This serves as the basis for the graph and lists below:

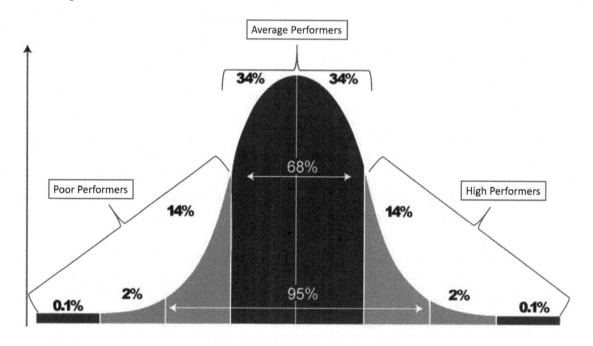

Hot Breeds

(Average temperament range 5–10)

Akhal-Teke
Andalusian
Anglo Arabian
Arabians
Appaloosa
Kiger Mustang
Malakan
Marwari
Morgan
Orlov Trotter
Thoroughbreds
Welch Pony
Zebra

Warm Breeds

(Average Temperament range 2–7)

American Paint Horse
American Warmblood
Andalusian
Appaloosa
Canadian Horse
Dutch Warmblood
Falabella
Friesian
Fjord
Halflinger
Hanoverian
Holsteiner
Irish Sport Horse
Irish Draught Horse
Lipizzaner
Mustang
Oldenburg

Pasofino
Quarter Horse
Shetland Pony
Trakehner
Tennessee Walking Horses
Welsh Pony

Cold Breeds

(Average Temperament range 1–5)

American Cream Draft
Ardennes
Australian Draught
Belgian Heavy Draft
Black Forest Chestnut
Coldblood Trotter
Clydesdale
Czech Coldblood
Dole
Dutch Draft
Freiberger
Friesian
Haflinger
Icelandic
Lithuanian Heavy Draft
Noriker
North Swedish Horse
Percheron
Poitevin
Rocky Mountain Horse
Shire
Schleswig
Suffolk Punch
Swedish Ardennes
Yakut

Temperament Scale

1	2	3	4	5	6	7	8	9	10

Included is a section from an alternative chapter (First 10 minutes of trail ride), here, that discusses the multitude of factors that can influence a trail ride on any given day. It's an appropriate discussion for this chapter on Temperament as, on any given day, a horse's behavior can vary greatly. Refer to Part Three, Chapter 26, **First 10 Minutes of Trail Ride** for the entire chapter and scoring rationale.

A well-broke, calm horse is invaluable to your trail riding experience and overall riding joy. Many horses are not willing or able to start a trial ride calmly. This chapter deals with the issue of the first ten minutes after you mount the horse for a trail ride. Whether it's at the trailhead as you begin a trail ride or on your own property, the first few minutes after mounting can be a very difficult time for you and your horse.

Initial trail calmness is dependent upon many factors:

1. **Temperament.** The relative genetic disposition of the horse. Many horses, such as Arabs, Tennessee Walking Horses, and Thoroughbreds are bred "hot." For the moderate to experienced riders, this is a positive attribute. Hot breeds will be much more excitable during the initial ten minutes on the trail.

2. **Weather.** Cold and cool weather will give your horse more energy than usual. This is particularly true in warm climates where the turning of seasons brings relief from moderate to oppressive heat.

3. **Turnout.** The frequency and duration of turnout will affect your horse's relative energy level. If you ride early in the morning and your horse is stalled during the night, it will likely have higher energy and excitability. Bad weather may keep your horse stalled for extended periods and will also result in an increase in energy.

4. **Wind.** Horse's survival instincts are piqued during moderate to high winds. Because their hearing is impaired, thereby making

them more vulnerable to predatory attacks, horses are on high alert during windy conditions.

5. **Feed.** Because most horses get a jolt of energy from high-calorie meals of sugar and protein (grain) and alfalfa, they can be more energetic after a meal. Much like a child on a sugar high, this can impact their energy level and excitability.

6. **New surroundings.** When trailering to a new area, the horse will be subject to different smells, sounds, animals, manmade objects, and vegetation. This will heighten their flight response, thereby increasing their excitability.

7. **Other horses.** Whether you meet up with friends or simply cross paths with other riders, your horse will be exposed to other horses. Many mares will be in season on the trail and, we know that many geldings still have enough testosterone to believe they are stallions. It only takes one horse in a group to spook to cause a herd reaction.

8. **Separation anxiety.** If you are taking your horse away from its pasture mates, it will have anxiety about leaving safety. All herd animals are "herd bound" for safety reasons. The survival of any one individual is profoundly increased when living in a herd. When removed from the herd, all herd animal's senses will be in a heightened state.

A solitary herd animal will be solely responsible for its own survival, thereby making it more reactive.

9. **Miscellaneous.** In one broad category, we can list many other stimuli that will increase the horse's excitability: bicycles, kids, dogs, vehicles, wildlife, domestic animals, sirens, trains, tarps, barrels, pavement, and the list goes on.

It is rare that only one of these factors exists singularly when you try to start a trail ride. Frequently, it is the majority of these factors that exists on every trail ride.

Another trick to make your horse more docile is to dramatically decrease grain and alfalfa consumption for the day of and the day before you trailer out. You may safely substitute grass or hay for grain as a method of reducing energy levels. Consult your veterinarian before you change your horse's diet.

Desensitize young horses to as many stimuli as possible.

4

Desensitization

Desensitization (def.) — *the diminished emotional responsiveness to a negative, aversive, or positive stimulus after repeated exposure to it.*

In one form or another, everything we do to make our horses better is a form of desensitization. It is completely unnatural for one species of animal, especially a prey animal, to accept another species of animal, especially a predator, to sit on its back. Imagine how much time it might take you to feel comfortable, allowing a tarantula to crawl up your arm. There is no way to prepare yourself for that challenge, but through repeated, successful attempts without being bitten, you would eventually tolerate it even though you may never enjoy it. There are hundreds of videos and books demonstrating ways to desensitize horses to stimuli. The only wrong way is an unsafe way. All safe methods are accepted and encouraged. The general idea of desensitization training is to create mild to moderate challenges (chaos) as often as possible so that the horse will continue to adapt (ignore) to external stimuli. Only through desen-sitization can we improve a horse's ability to cope with unforeseen challenges.

Desensitization cannot start too early. Frequent interaction with your horse is the key to improving your horse-human bond. Contrary to many trainer's opinions, the use of food rewards **has** been proven in numerous studies (de Pasille et al. 1996; Munksgaard et al. 1997) and, conversely, contact with humans without feeding mediation **has not** proven to improve animals' response to humans (Jaog et al. 1999; Hemsworth et al., 1996). The association of the human presence or handling with a positive reinforcer (food) is a clear positive association for animals, which may lower the negative impact of handling. **The summary is: bribe early and bribe often!**

There is an important caveat to this advice: the horses must have enough respect for you that they are not constantly sniffing, prodding, irritating, or distracting as it searches your personal space for treats (positive reinforcement = food). This can be tricky but not impossible. As we discussed in previous chapters, as long as you are the Alpha Leader to your horse and maintain constant respect, they will understand when positive reinforcement is expected. Like children who cry, "I'm hungry," and, with proper parenting, realize it's not going to get them food any sooner, horses begin to understand that treats are at the sole discretion of the owner.

A daily human example of desensitization is when parents, kids, or spouses "tune out" one another. I've been told that husbands are often accused of "tuning-out" their wives. After years of constant verbal input and output, one person becomes desensitized to the sound, level, and message being sent from the other. The receiver of the intended message is accused of "ignoring" the sender of the message when no response or an inadequate response is offered. The receiver has been "desensitized" through years of listening. Another example is the contrast between people with and without children. When people without young children visit the homes of those with young children, they are often shocked at the chaos. The people without children might say to the people with children, "How do you stand the chaos?" To which the common reply is, "What chaos?" The parents of the children have been "desensitized" to noise, movement, messes, etc. And, so it is with our horses, the more we can get them to ignore stimuli, challenges, and chaos, the better and safer they will be around humans and on the trail.

As much as I dislike chaos, it can be helpful when desensitizing a horse to many common trail challenges. My ranch has people coming and going frequently. On any given week, there are different dogs, vehicles, trailers, horses, and smells. Cows graze on the property line to the north. From a horse desensitization standpoint, I would welcome even more activity like a bike trail, shepherds herding sheep, a duck pond, cats fighting, goats free-grazing, lion taming, dump trucks dumping, two turtle doves and a partridge in a pear tree! I would need to move to the city for some peace and quiet, but you get my point.

Desensitization is easiest when it's a part of the horse's normal environment. This defines "desensitization," a gradual acceptance of stimuli until it is considered "normal." Our goal is to orchestrate as much desensitization time for our horses as possible. Any time your horse has a less than favorable reaction to any stimulus, the time to manage it is **right then**. For example, on a trail ride, you come upon an abandoned, rusted-out car in the middle of a forest, your horse stops, spooks, or snorts. Once the horse composes itself, point it towards the car and encourage the horse to keep moving towards it. Keep encouraging until they stop to smell it. Once the snorting and reluctance stop, you can continue the trail ride. There is rarely a convenient time to stop and address a problem on the trail, but there is no better time than immediately after it happens.

Because our commitment to desensitization often falls short of the goal, it is advised to dedicate time each month for nothing else. Carve out a day, a morning, or even an hour to desensitize your horse to as many objects, situations, and challenges as your imagination will allow. Making time for desensitization will pay huge dividends in the future.

There are two main forms of desensitization training:

1) **Specific** — focus on specific objects or situations to which we are directly exposing the horse (bags, saddles, tarps, farm animals, plastic, trailers, etc.). While we hope it helps them become more accepting of other objects and situations, we are only exposing them to that one specific challenge. Specific desensitization will not help decrease separation anxiety or herd mentality. I believe horse owners spend too much time on specific desensitization and not enough time on general desensitization. Let's face it, specific desensitization is usually performed near their barn and barn mates, minimizing the effect it has on separation anxiety.

2) **General** — broad-based desensitization decreases the horse's desire to return to the herd. Because many horse behavior problems stem from their strong desire to be with other herd animals, humans are just an annoyance. By orchestrating times when your horse is away from their barns and barn mates, we are taking a more global approach to desensitization.

It could be argued that any desensitization exercise has a broad benefit for improved safety, but I believe it warrants two categories so that an appropriate amount of time is spent on both. Consider "specific" desensitization as a treatment of a symptom: like when you take aspirin to relieve a flu-related fever. Then consider "general" desensitization to be like a flu shot that controls the frequency and severity of the illness. I believe an even balance of both specific and general desensitization is best. One could even combine the two by exposing them to specific challenges while they are well-detached from the herd. For example, after your horse is comfortable grazing away from the barn or herd, consider plastic bag noise desensitization. As progress is made, be creative about what specific desensitization can be accomplished in this manner. Specific desensitization should *not* be added to general desensitization until the horse is more comfortable away from the herd.

Below is a partial list of **Specific** desensitization methods and materials that should give you a great start and some ideas:

- **Horses fear plastic bags** — hang plastic bags in the stall allowing the wind and fans to keep them moving.
- **Horses fear tarps** — place a tarp over the shavings in half the stall. Once acclimated, allow the tarp to cover the entire stall. Place tarps in the round pen when longeing. Tie a tarp to the lead rope or longe line.
- **Horses fear bicycles** — ride your bike or have the kids ride their bikes back and forth past the stall.
- **Horses fear motorcycles** — have someone ride a motorcycle past the stall or pasture.
- **Horses fear trampolines** — put one next to the barn and jump on it often.
- **Horses fear balloons** — tack up balloons above them in the stall.

A bold example of general desensitization (away from the herd) combined with specific desensitization (mounting and quietness at a halt.)

- **Horses fear large objects coming towards them** — get a large exercise ball and kick it at them in the pasture or arena.

General Desensitization is more challenging to execute. The key to general desensitization is to remove your horse from its usual surroundings, barn mates, and routine as much as possible. Therefore, you will need to be even more creative in your attempts to utilize this important part of the training process.

If space and finances permit, you can pasture your horse well away from the herd. If possible, take them on trips alone. If your horse is stalled and pastured with other horses, they become emotionally dependent upon the herd. When removed from the herd, they experience separation anxiety. Controlling separation anxiety is very difficult because we are around our horses only a few hours per week, and they are with their herd all the remaining hours. One simple way of safely decreasing separation anxiety is to walk your horse on a lead rope out of sight from its pasture mates (See pictures below). Allowing the horse to graze while away from the herd will make it a positive experience and reward the horse for being away. In the beginning, the horse will call back to the herd and may even refuse to leave. It may take a few days or weeks to build the horse's confidence to leave the herd. Eventually, there will be little or no drama from the separation. If you have a horse trailer and can take the horse off the property alone, it will be a big step in decreasing separation anxiety. Extended periods away from the herd, and the routine, are very good for building courage and independence in your horse. Did you know that horses that perform for movies always live alone? The handler becomes their herd, thereby minimizing filming day issues.

General desensitization recommendations

With truck and horse trailer:

- Take frequent day trips with just your horse (or just one horse if you have more than one).
- Take frequent overnight camping trips with your horse.
- Find a place where you can arrange a short-term boarding situation to accommodate just your horse.
- Find a trainer that can keep your horse alone for a month or more.
- Find a friend or relative with unused horse accommodations and ask to keep it there for a month.
- Take frequent trail rides alone.

Without truck and horse trailer:

- Ask a friend with a truck and trailer if they would join you on the getaways mentioned above (negotiate fee).
- Ask a friend to trailer you and your horse to and from a trailhead (negotiate fee).
- Ask a friend to go camping with you and your horse (negotiate fee).
- Attempt to separate your horse from its pasture mates, even if it is just visual separation.
- Walk them as far away from their barn as possible.
- On small properties, walk the horse away from its barn and friends on the road or out into the neighborhood.
- Ride away from the barn alone.
- Reward horse with grazing or treats when anxiety subsides.

The preoccupation with their herd/barn will diminish. Because some horses have a very low tolerance for separation, the above recommendations could be dangerous. You may want to hire a professional to help you with these endeavors.

Many trainers and horse owners believe in the philosophy that the horse should be "worked" near the barn and herd, while being able to relax when away from those familiar surroundings. Round pen work can be done near the barn, and low-stress riding (walking, grazing, standing) away

Decrease separation anxiety by walking the horse away and out of sight of their herd/barn.

Reward frequently with relaxed grazing.

Increase distance over time.

The preoccupation with their herd/barn will diminish over time.

Through leading, new challenges can be encouraged.

Separate from the horse and encourage them to look at terrain and follow.

from the barn. More simply, apply pressure near the barn; allow relaxation away from the barn.

As mentioned earlier, researchers have identified an individual horse type, "bold." These are horses comfortable on the outside fringes of the herd. Finding a "bold" horse partner will make trail riding safer and more enjoyable. Most bold horses will require less desensitization training. This characteristic will add to difficulty in finding a great trail partner, but should be considered in your purchase. It may be possible (research has not yet been done) to improve boldness by separating the horse from its herd and presenting new challenges while separated. See, Alternative Tests chapter

This horse had been frequently walked as a yearling and has little fear of new challenges.

Plan your retreat or area of safety in advance. By not rushing through challenges, the horse learns patience and more careful footfalls.

Stop and hold the horses at random places to encourage patience.

Be creative and expose the horse to as many low stress situations as possible.

Continue the walks as often and as far from the barn as possible.

on Trail Willingness. This can be accomplished on or away from your boarding facility. For ground challenges, the horse must be very well halter broken.

All horse reactions can be decreased through desensitization. Desensitization clinics can be found online. These partial and full-day clinics expose horse and rider to multiple stimuli that may be encountered during a trail ride and to some that won't. As seen below, horses can quickly become accustomed to extreme stimulation. This "Desensitization Clinic" features multiple forms of negative stimuli, including firecrackers.

Desensitization clinic includes flags, barrels, ground objects, bags, tarps, and firecrackers.

Foal Desensitization

"Imprinting Training of the Newborn Foal" is a book written by a veterinarian, Robert M. Miller (1991). This book extols the method developed by Dr. Miller of handling a newborn foal to desensitize it to human contact immediately upon birth, while the human can safely and gently overpower the newborn to teach it submission. Dr. Miller states that there is a 30- to 45-minute lull (window of opportunity) after birth while the mare is exhausted and the foal is attempting to

stand (and suckle), during which time Dr. Miller recommends applying this technique. Dr. Miller states that many years later, he can recognize those horses that were imprinted at birth as their behavior was noticeably better than those that weren't. I have imprinted six of my nine foals. I cannot tell the difference between those six and the three that were not imprinted. I enjoyed the book and do believe there is useful information in it. However, all scientific studies conclude that this technique (imprinting at birth) does not correspond to the natural way of imprinting and that the foals show a high resistance and high level of stress to the procedure:

> In natural herd conditions, mares actively seek isolation 2–24 hours prior to foaling (Waring, 2003) and in the first few days after birth, mares prevent other horses from approaching their young (Estep et al, 1993; Van Dieren-donck et al., 2005), which might be a way to avoid the interferences at the crucial moment of bonding of the foal to its dam (Crow-ell-David and Weeks, 2005).

> Mares form a strong reciprocal and exclusive bond with their foals rapidly after giving birth, which is established through the first bouts of licking (in the first 30 minutes) and nursing (Houpt, 2002, Grogan and McDonnell, 2005). The rupture of the dam-foal bond, even on a short-term basis, induces extreme distress (McCall et al., 1985, Moons et al., 2005). Over-handling of the neonate (Grogan and McDonnell, 2005)

accompanied with or solely the mare's high level of fear or anxiety related to exposure to humans, in particular, may induce an impairment of maternal abilities (Rushen et al., 1999, Forde, 2002, Janczak et al., 2003). First suckling occurs mostly between 30 and 180-minutes post-partum (Rossdale, 1967). During the first week of life, the foal tends to remain within 5 meters of its dam (Crowell-David, 1986), while this distance progressively increases when the young develops social bonds with other group members, especially the young ones.

Handling at later stages, in the days or weeks following birth does not seem to have long-lasting effects either, even if they facilitate haltering, leading and reduce emotional reactivity in the human presence on a short-term basis (Mal and McCall, 1996; Jezierski et al., 1999; Lansade et al., 2005).

An alternative technique which may be in the best interest of all parties is to pay attention to the mare while the foal observes:

> In order to identify which approach of the foal is the best, Henry et al. (2005, 2006b) have performed a set of experiments, including different approaches at birth or in the following days.

> Four approaches were thus tested in the postpartum period and compared to a controlled situation (no additional handling):

1. Two of them consisted of actively handling the foals.
    a. Bringing the foal to the dam's teat (a common practice in breeding farms)
    b. A forced handling (stroking) of the foals during 1 minute in the five days after birth

2. The other two treatments involved indirect approaches in the postpartum period
    a. A mere daily exposure during 15 minutes to a passive human in the five days postpartum period
    b. A gentle handling of the mare (soft brushing and food rewards) in front of the foal, without any direct attention from the experimenter to the foal during the same period (testing a possible social facilitation).

When the effects of the four types of handling were compared at later ages, it appeared foals which had been brought to the teat or forcibly handled, tended to refuse a direct contact with humans afterwards. It can also be noticed that during the handling procedures, foals attempted to escape from restraint. A passive human presence induced lower flight reactions than in controls at the age of 2 weeks, but the effects were not long lasting. Finally, foals whose dams had been brushed and hand-fed approached very readily the experimenter at the age of 2 weeks and accepted easily a direct human contact as well as, for most of them, a saddle pad on the back at 1 month. They were even easily approached in the paddock and stroked by a familiar or non-familiar experimenter one year later without any further handling which was totally impossible with the control yearlings. The use of this natural tendency of the foal to learn from the dam seems therefore promising.

Dr. Miller's technique is anecdotal (studies have not confirmed the efficacy of the technique). Based on the data, my personal experience, and humble opinion, if you must spend time in the stall, spend it with the dam while the foal observes. Then, start Dr. Miller's techniques two weeks after birth.

If you can't wait to be with the foal, visiting the foal in the stall is supported by the above study by Henry, test group 2a: *"a mere daily exposure of 15 minutes to a passive human in the five days postpartum."* Here's how: I enter the stall making sure the mare is not surprised. Once she understands my intentions, I quietly enter. Do not attempt to pet, coax, or capture the foal. Instead, simply sit down at eye level against the most distant wall and stay as long as it takes for the foal to have some curiosity. In a low voice, I talk to the foal, so it knows there is something else in the stall other than its mother. With each passing day, the foal will come closer to you. Some foals will come to you on the first day.

Nonetheless, no matter how long it takes, you will sit there and allow the foal to approach you. Once it does approach, allow it to inspect you with-

Desensitization of foals can be done passively in the stall until curiosity builds and the foal initiates contact.

Eventually, all foals begin to investigate.

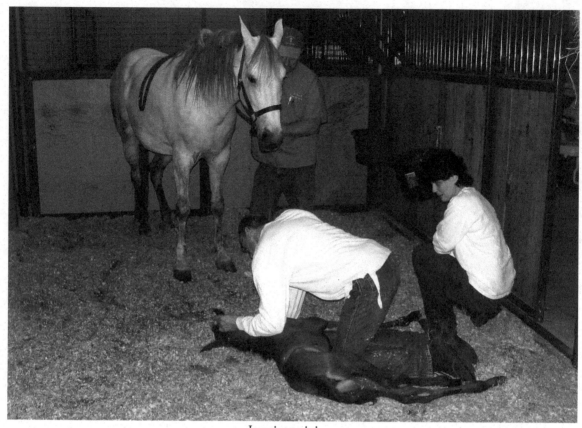
Imprint training.

out any attempt to touch it. As the foal becomes more comfortable, you will be able to slowly reach out and pet it. Over time it will trust you, and you will be able to handle it more aggressively. Do the same in the pasture or paddock. The goal is to get the foal so comfortable with human interaction that it will seek you out in the stall or the pasture. This will create a much better adult than those that run from humans when attempting to halter.

If you decide to "imprint," the technique is done slowly and carefully. As Dr. Miller recommends, in order to teach submission, a large part of imprinting involves restraining and controlling the foal. Again, when the foal only weighs 50-150 lbs., they are not difficult to control and restrain. For safety, the mare must be cooperative. This starts months before foaling with daily entry into the stall, moderate handling, and grooming. If the mare trusts the owner/caregiver/wet-nurse, she will allow you to handle the foal without much or any protest. For the first attempt at handling the foal, a second person should halter and control the mare. Once she has become accustomed to daily human contact with her and her foal, either in the stall or the pasture, you will likely not need any control of her.

The imprinting technique is well explained in Dr. Miller's book. In short, expose the foal to as many stimuli as you can safely accomplish. I lift my foals up like you would a large dog and gently lay them on their side. They will struggle a little bit at this age and weight. However, you should be able to safely manage the task. Once they are down, they will attempt to rise. Your will must be stronger than theirs. It is not difficult to keep them down with pressure on their bodies or by holding their legs. The risk of getting struck by a flailing hoof is high if you don't manage it properly. The minimum amount of force necessary to accomplish the goal is the correct amount. For smaller handlers, you may need the help of a stronger person. Remember, this is the first 24 hours. Once they submit to being handled in this manner, they will become more accustomed to it (desensitization). Once they are down and restrained, you can begin specific desensitization techniques.

You will need to prepare before you go into the stall. Safely within arm's reach, place clippers, plastic bags, a horseshoe, and a hammer, etc. Rumpling the plastic bag in their ear, turn the clippers on and run them all over their body and near their ears, tap on the bottom of their hooves, hold the horseshoe and bang on it with the hammer, etc. Anything you can imagine that they will be exposed to later in life

is a good lesson. Use your imagination. I believe the restraint and control leading to submission are the most important messages of all. I strongly recommend Dr. Miller's book to anyone planning to breed and raise horses.

Based on all the research, it seems clear that repeated, positive interaction with the foal starting two weeks after birth yields the most optimum results:

> To maintain the beneficial effects of early handling, it seems necessary to repeat handling on a regular basis. The study of Jezierski et al. (1999) showed that foals, which are handled 5 days per week from ages 2 weeks or 10 months to the age of 24 months scored better on the manageability tests (catching, leading, picking up feet, being approached by an unfamiliar person) at 12, 18 and 24 months than non-handled foals.

Like any unfamiliar procedure, it is always best to educate yourself before attempting something new. Dr. Miller's book, *Imprint Training of the Newborn Foal,* is one resource to educate yourself in handling newborn foals. *Blessed are the Broad Mares* by M. Phyllis Lose is another great read for expectant owners. Both books are full of valuable horse handling information.

5

Pressure, Release, Reward, Repeat (PR³)

The basic philosophy for horse training used throughout this book involves these four words. It will be stated, restated, and repeated in nearly every chapter. Learn it, study it, memorize it!

Pressure (def.) — the burden of physical or mental distress.

Release (def.) — to relieve from something that confines, burdens, or oppresses.

Reward (def.) —a thing given in recognition of service, effort, or achievement.

Repeat (def.) — do something again, either once or several times.

This concept is not new. Trainers of animals and educators of people have been using this technique for thousands of years. We will describe the technique in detail in this chapter and reference it often.

The premise here is that the trainer should get into the habit of using this concept: **Pressure, Release, Reward, Repeat (PR³)** for consistency. No matter how small the challenge or how small the positive response, we will use this formula.

Prior to initiating any challenge/pressure, always **Announce** your intentions. Think of this as using turn signals while driving. It is not absolutely necessary but highly recommended. In driver's training, the term is "signal your intentions." For simplicity, we will not add the "A" to our PR³; but, whether it be ground manners or under saddle, you will always "announce" your intentions with a subtle or obvious warning that a request is coming. We never want to surprise a horse unless they are fully trained, and you are 99% confident that the surprise will be tolerated or ignored by the horse being challenged. The two different techniques are as follows:

1. **Ground Manners:** Horses have a heightened awareness/reactivity when they are tied, separated from their herd or, anything outside their normal routine. Therefore, start all ground-work challenges from a distance. In later chapters, each challenge will be described in detail. For now, know that introducing a challenge from a safe distance followed by observation of reaction is recommended. For example, you would not walk up to an untrained horse and switch the clippers on against his or her ear.

2. **Under Saddle:** The very best warning or announcement of an imminent request, from the saddle, is a verbal cue followed immediately by a weight shift. As training continues, the verbal cue can be omitted.

The word **"Pressure,"** used in this context, refers to the challenge or stimulus presented to the subject. Pressure can be in multiple forms and appeal to all the senses (sight, sound, touch, smell, and spatial).

Pressure should be introduced slowly and calmly. There will be plenty of times when unexpected challenges will be thrust upon the horse in the course of its interactions with humans and nature. By slowly introducing intended training challenges, you can begin the process of decreasing the horse's reactions gradually. The goal is NOT to scare the horse! Take your time and build trust. Starting with baby steps will yield a better, less-reactive horse.

The word **"Release,"** used in this context, refers to the removal of the pressure when the subject demonstrates any acceptance, desensitization, or indifference to the challenge or stimulus.

The word **"Reward,"** used in this context, refers to the positive affirmation of the desired response in the subject. Reward comes in several forms:

1. The simple "release" of "pressure" is a reward. Many trainers consider this the only necessary "reward." The big advantage of this reward is that the horse is not preoccupied with or constantly harassing the trainer for food rewards.

2. Praise reward. Verbal praise or gentle stroking. Verbal praise spoken in a positive tone is often used to reward the horse for a positive response to pressure. Petting or stroking the horse is another form of praise reward.

3. Food rewards. This is the only scientifically proven reward method.

Most often, reward comes in the form of all three. Upon observation of a positive response, the pressure is removed, kind words are spoken, the horse is stroked, and a food reward is given. **This cascading reward method is clearly the most beneficial.**

Studies have shown that "Release" and "Reward" must be **well-timed** to produce the best results. A well-timed Release (not asking for too much too soon) and lots of Reward/praise for the correct action, in the beginning, expedites the learning process and keeps a potentially 'scary situation' less intimidating and more rewarding for the horse.

A poorly timed Release is damaging to the learning process. Never Release/Reward the horse when the horse disengages (moves back, sideways, or attempts to avoid stimulus). Horses ONLY learn from the Release, so if you Release while the horse is trying to get away, you've just Rewarded that reaction.

Our goal is to encourage curiosity, willingness, and even courage. To be even more succinct, we want to encourage or foster "Boldness." The "Boldness" characteristic was coined by Briard and Petit in 2015. Certain horses are born with this attribute, but I believe we can improve boldness in horses not born with it by fostering a training environment based on positive experiences where the horse is a willing participant.

NEVER scold a frightened horse. Negative reinforcement does have a place in horse training, but not with every horse and only when all positive techniques have failed. I have several horses that are so unruly when tied or under saddle that a swat on the neck is the only way to get them to calm down. I always give them 10-20 minutes to work out their issues on their own. Once I realize they are not going to cooperate, I will take off a glove and swat them on the neck. This technique, combined with a louder than usual, "STOP IT," is usually all it takes for them to settle down. Like children, each horse requires a different approach and level of discipline. Remember, our goal is to evaluate and reward, or to correct the behavior, not to explain the behavior through a human interpretation of the emotion. Far too often, people believe the horse has an "intention." Mostly, horses only react to stimuli or perform a requested act from habit. They rarely, if ever, have intention.

The word **"Repeat"** is used to refer to the action of repetitive learning. Repeating the challenge often during the initial training is crucial to learning. Reinforcing previously learned behavior is also crucial to long term success, as studies have shown that horses have a low retention rate if not reinforced.

And, the final thought for each training session is, "Quit while you're ahead!" Finish on even the slightest bit of cooperation, relaxation, or positive note. If you push too hard, too fast, you'll end up going backwards on the training scale. No matter the level of acceptance of the horse, quit when the horse is on a relaxed note, and he is engaged and willing. Never finish a training session when the horse is uncooperative, afraid, or anxious.

Example: Desensitization training with hair clippers.

Technique:

1) Turn on the clippers 5 feet from horse. The horse reacts to the sound. Keep the clippers running until the horse looks away, its head drops ever so slightly or simply does not shy away. This could be the end of the training day. Your reaction to that mild success is:
    a. Turn off clippers (Release).
    b. Put clippers down (Release).
    c. Verbally praise horse (Reward).

d. Walk towards horse slowly, continue verbal praise, stroke horse, food reward (Reward).

e. Return horse to stall or pasture (Reward).

2) Repeat process.

3) Repeat and continue. Starting 5 feet from the horse, turn on clippers. Remain at that position until there is no reaction. Move towards horse until there is a reaction. Maintain position until there is no reaction. Release pressure. Reward. Move closer until there is a reaction, maintain position until there is no reaction. Release pressure. Reward.

a. Turn off clippers (Release).

b. Put clippers down (Release).

c. Verbally praise horse (Reward).

d. Walk towards horse slowly, continue verbal praise, stroke horse, food reward (Reward).

e. Return horse to stall or pasture (Reward).

4) Repeat process.

5) Repeat and continue. Starting 5 feet from the horse, turn on clippers. Remain at that position until there is no reaction. Move towards horse until there is a reaction. Maintain position until there is no reaction. Release pressure. Reward. Move closer until there is a reaction, maintain

position until there is no reaction. Release pressure. Reward. Allow the horse to smell non-running clippers. Reward. Turn clippers on, horse reacts. Maintain this position until the horse does not react.

a. Turn off clippers (Release).

b. Put clippers down (Release).

c. Verbally praise horse (Reward).

d. Continue verbal praise, stroke horse, food reward (Reward).

e. Return horse to stall or pasture (Reward).

6) Repeat.

7) Continue. Turn clippers on and touch the horse on the shoulder with the non-blade side of clippers. Hold until there is no reaction.

a. Turn off clippers (Release).

b. Put clippers down (Release).

c. Verbally praise horse (Reward).

d. Walk towards horse slowly, continue verbal praise, stroke horse, food reward (Reward).

e. Return horse to stall or pasture (Reward).

The main point to understand is that you can stop on a positive note at any time. This challenge can go on as long as you have time or until the horse has no hair left. Continue on to the legs, the mane, and the ears but only stop when you can consider a non-reaction. With clippers, in particular, you should always stop on a high note.

Meaning, if you push too far and the horse reacts or resists on any one part of the body (usually the ears), you may be reinforcing the wrong reaction. For example, you have spent one hour desensitizing the horse to the sound, the touch, and even actual clipping of the neck and muzzle. When you go to do the ears, the horse simply will not allow it. You have just trained the horse to not to allow you to clip its ears. This can be said for ending any challenge on a refusal. It teaches the horse that it must allow everything up to the refusal but nothing after. So, in conclusion, you must commit to taking each step to completion on any given day, or you will jeopardize your overall success.

Part Three

"We will never have to tell our horse
that we are sad, happy, confident, angry, or relaxed.
He already knows — long before we do"
– *Marjike de Jong*

1

The Perfect Horse

There is no "perfect" horse. There are, however, some great horses that I would like to help you find or develop.

Understanding horse behavior and applying training methods are not all that intuitive for most people. Robert Redford played the lead character in the 1998 movie, The *Horse Whisperer*. The film is based on the book *The Horse Whisperer*, written in 1995 by Nicholas Evans. Writer Evans states that the lead character, the horse trainer played by Redford, is modeled after horse whisperers Tom Dorrance, Ray Hunt, and, in particular, their younger disciple Buck Brannaman. The average moviegoer would likely come away from the movie thinking that this particular horse trainer was born knowing how to communicate with horses and could easily fix any horse problem in a matter of minutes.

Like talented professionals at the top of any profession, there is always the advantage of genetic predisposition (people born with certain traits or abilities beyond the average). However, the other side of being truly great at something, rarely discussed, is the amount of work it takes to reach the top. This is called the "Learning Curve," and everyone goes through it. Some just go through it faster and stay at it with more tenacity. Buck Brannaman had two mentors that are revered as the pioneers of "starting" horses rather than "breaking" horses. "Starting" horses is a more gentle and safe method that balances control of the horse's natural instincts and gradual desensitization to train them to accept things they wouldn't otherwise accept. Buck's recognition as a stellar horse trainer is the culmination of his personal trial and error, countless hours of observation, years of experience, and exceptional mentors; I am a huge fan. The point here is that it takes time to master anything. Malcolm Gladwell states, in several of his very popular books, that it takes approximately 10,000 hours to master something. These 10,000 hours include study and preparation, as well as the actual activity. It is unlikely that many of us will ever come close to even 1,000 hours of horse training activities, let alone 10,000. Therefore, we must be as efficient as we can in the time we have with these animals.

More often, people ruin horses because they enable and often inadvertently nurture bad horse behavior. In this first section, we will discuss the right horse for you. This is primarily based on a realistic assessment of your riding skills. Most people err in evaluating their riding skills. As with most self-assessment critiques, we, as humans, give ourselves too much credit. Psychologically, it helps us with self-esteem but does little to help us find the right horse. Everyone can become a better rider with practice, improved fitness, and coaching. However, if an error in judgment causes us to buy a horse that is too spirited for us, one that we can't grow into, then the whole endeavor will likely result in failure and disappointment.

Sellers often exaggerate a horse's good qualities and omit or downplay a horse's bad qualities. Much like buying a used car, the buyer and the seller have two very different perspectives. We must have a method or plan to ferret out the real details of each horse we inquire about or strongly consider as a candidate for purchase.

The following chapters will give you a logical way to complete your journey. Each section will present a sequence of questions and assessments to help you accomplish your goal. DO NOT RUSH THE PROCESS, DO NOT BUY ON IMPULSE and NEVER BUY OUT OF GUILT.

Part Three, Chapter 5, **TRAILS interview Method for Pre-purchase** will show you a logical interview process once you've located a potential candidate. If you set up enough time with the owner, you should be able to come away from the onsite interview with enough information to make an educated decision.

2

Choosing the Right Horse

As stated earlier, we need to look at this endeavor as a process or a journey. We need to proceed logically with caution and patience. First, answer the following questions:

1. What type of riding do you intend to do with your new horse?

2. How long since you last rode a horse?

3. On a scale of 1-10 (1-poor and 10-very skilled) rank your horsemanship?

4. With whom will you ride?

5. What type of horse(s) do your riding buddies have?

6. How has your fitness level changed since you last rode?

7. Have you gained more than 20% of your body weight since you last rode?

8. Have you had any limiting injury or surgery since you last rode?

9. What is your horse purchase budget?

10. Have you already decided on the horse you intend to buy?

11. If no to #10, do you have a preference on color, size or breed?

12. What is your time frame for your purchase?

13. Will you board or keep the horse on your property?

14. Have you budgeted for monthly expenses, expected and unexpected?

Many of these answers should influence our decision to buy a horse.

I find that most people overestimate their riding ability. If it's been years since you last rode, I strongly suggest that you take a few lessons. I also recommend a lesson facility or trainer that will allow you to ride several different horses that will test your skill level. **I cannot overstate how much your riding skills can diminish since your last riding experience.** You should interview trainers to find those able to help you assess your skill level. Again, unless you can spend a lot of time riding or taking lessons, it is difficult to significantly improve your riding ability after age 35.

Therefore, most people need help in assessing their riding ability. Overrating our abilities is more the rule than the exception. Most people remember being better riders than they were (past) and believe they are better riders than they are (present). Let's face it, this is true of most of our measured talents. How many average high school athletes remember themselves much better than they were? We all suffer from the "Glory Day" syndrome to some extent. However, in the horse purchase endeavor, it is much more important than dialogue at a high school reunion. Your well-being is at stake here! The horse selection process does involve some degree of honest self-assessment. The more honest you are with your assessment, the more likely you are to find the right horse.

Why do I begin a chapter that should be one of joy and hope with so many negative observations? To attempt to convince my readers that choosing the best available horse for you is of paramount importance to your joy, safety, and longevity in this hobby.

The horse-rider relationship encompasses many facets that, at different levels, can influence the performance of the combination and the welfare of both horse and rider. The number of different horse characteristics is likely as large as the number of rider's personalities, and hence, it is very reasonable that only a proportion of possible combinations of personalities result in optimal matches between horse and rider. Researchers have concluded that the relationship that exists between horse and its rider was also an important factor when determining the risk of injury while riding (*Hausberger et al., 2008*) and (*Keeling et al., 1999*). Approximately one-quarter of all horse-related accidents are due to the horse being frightened, and miscommunication between horse and rider. If you're a fan of any team sport, you will understand that, most often, it is the team chemistry as much or more than the individual stars that affects the outcome. We have all seen those teams loaded with talent that do not win the championship. Whether it be the teammate-to-teammate dynamic (1980 USA Olympic Hockey Team) or the coach-to-team dynamic (Bill Belichick and the Patriots) or both (Jim Valvano and the N.C. State Wolfpack defeat heavily favored Houston Cougars in the 1983 NCAA basketball championship) who create the magical synergy or lack thereof that has the most influential effect. Why would it be any different for the human-horse dynamic?

Unless you are a fantastic rider, all research and anecdotal conclusions have proven that the compatibility of horse and rider (horse-rider relationship) is the key factor in determining the relative safety, ease, and overall enjoyment of horse related activities. A great rider may have thousands of potentially favorable partnerships with horses. A novice or poor rider may have less than a dozen potentially beneficial partnerships when attempting to purchase a horse. As you will see demonstrated below, the number of potentially great possible partnerships, even nationwide, is extremely low.

There are three phases to the search.

Phase One is that phase where we are simply imagining what it is that we want. This Phase involves daydreaming, wishing, and hoping that what we want exists exactly as we picture it, at a price we would consider very reasonable.

Phase Two is that part of the search where we begin educating ourselves on the item we are trying to acquire. This is the part of the search where we begin to actively investigate how close Phase One is to reality. Some people will buy books, others will interview friends, and others will visit local barns or the Internet to educate themselves on the particulars of the topic of interest.

Phase Three is where we head out to pick up some hooves and pet a few noses. If we intend to be successful, this phase takes perseverance, tenacity, patience, and resolve or, pure luck. If we look at this Phase Three, "the search,"

as equally gratifying to "the find," it can be as much fun as horse ownership. With the right attitude, we place ourselves in the best psychological state to begin our mission to find the absolute best horse available at the price we can afford.

Starting Your Search

Let's get started. Most people start their search with online horse sales websites. I like these sites because one can garner some useful information about each horse and rule many out. All websites require that the seller answer questions to assist in the search.

One important factor is the horse's temperament (relative calmness of the horse). The accepted Temperament Scale is a numeric scale 1–10, with one being very quiet and ten being very spirited. Often, sellers do not tell the truth in this category. However, we can use temperament to rule many horses out. Temperament is a subjective finding. I believe in this category, we should have a margin of error of +/- 2 points to compensate for seller misrepresentation. If a seller is honest enough to rate a horse above a "4," I think it is safe to say the horse is moderately spirited, or more. Therefore, if you are an average rider, let's agree to rule out any horse whose owner claims the horse's temperament is "4" or higher. If you are a moderately accomplished rider, let's include horses up to "5". This will narrow your search considerably. For many years I tried to purchase a dead-broke gelding as a lesson horse. These horses are nearly impossible to find. I am not suggesting a deadhead horse for everyone, I am just making the point that really quiet horses are rare. So, as a starting point, for most adult riders, let's limit ourselves to a horse that the owner claims is 1–3 on the temperament scale. The experienced rider range is 1–5. Of course, there may be exceptions, but these ranges will yield a good number of candidates and keep most people safe.

Now, by narrowing the search further by area, age, color, and breed, it is likely there are very few horses from which to choose. One online site boasts 43,000 horses for sale. It's amazing how few horses are good candidates for purchase when we disqualify them for just a few simple reasons.

As a demonstration, let's search www.equine.com for the search parameters:

1. Quarter Horse, gelding, age range 7-10, temperament 1-3, trail experience, black, any price, within 100 miles of Lincoln, NE. Search results: **Two horses in the entire state of Nebraska., $18,000 and $11,750 asking sales prices.**

2. Tennessee Walking Horse, age range 6-11 years, temperament 1-5, trail experience, within 125 miles of Sacramento, CA. Search results: 0

3. Missouri Foxtrotter gelding, age range 8-12, temperament 1-3, trail experience, brown, within 100 miles of Philadelphia, PA. Search results: 0

Let's open-up the search to a broader region by assuming you would be willing to travel 500 miles for the perfect trail horse, any breed at any price. On the same website I entered:

4. New England region, trail horse at any price:
   Purebred Only:
   Purebred Only (252)

   Primary Breed:
   Quarter Horse (69)
   Thoroughbred (55)
   Morgan (25)
   Paint (Solid) (19)
   Paint (Tobiano) (16)
   More Choices...

   Secondary Breed:
   Quarter Horse (15)
   Thoroughbred (13)
   Pinto (10)
   Thoroughbred Cross (6)
   More Choices...

   Discipline:
   Trail Horse
   More Choices...

   Price:
   $15.00 To $1,000.00 (59)
   $1,000.00 to $2,000.00 (71)
   $2,000.00 To $3,000.00 (57)
   $3,000.00 To $4,000.00 (58)

$4,000.00 To $5,000.00 (63)
$5,000.00 To $6,000.00 (41)
$6,000.00 To $7,000.00 (22)
$7,000.00 To $8,000.00 (25)
$8,000.00 To $9,000.00 (6)
$9,000.00 To $10,000.00 (12)
$10,000.00 To $20,000.00 (30)
$20,000.00+ (7)
More Choices...

Sex:
Gelding (208)
Mare (139)
Stallion (2)
More Choices...

Height (Hands):
15.2 (55)
15.3 (43)
15.1 (36)
15.0 (28)
16.0 (28)
More Choices...

Age:
6 Months To 2 Years (6)
2 Years To 4 Years (16)
4 Years To 6 Years (43)
6 Years To 8 Years (59)
8 Years To 10 Years (51)
10 Years To 15 Years (120)
15 Years To 20 Years (40)
20+ Years (14)
More Choices...

Base Color:
Bay (106)
Chestnut (60)
Black (34)
Grey (30)
Pinto (23)
More Choices...

Attributes:
Open Show Winner (9)
HYPP N/N (7)
Jackpot Money Earner (4)
Breed Assn Show Champ (4)
Sire/Dam of Register of Merit (4)
More Choices...

Type of Ad:
Horses For Sale (340)
Horses For Lease (9)

5. **Southwest Region, trail horse at any price:**

Purebred Only:
Purebred Only (209)

Primary Breed:
Quarter Horse (132)
Paint (Overo) (19)
Paint (Tobiano) (19)
Arabian (13)
Paint (Solid) (11)
More Choices...

Secondary Breed:
Quarter Horse (16)
Palomino (5)
Paint (Solid) (3)
Paint (Tobiano) (3)
More Choices...

Discipline:
Trail Horse
More Choices...

Price:
$15.00 To $1,000.00 (30)
$1,000.00 To $2,000.00 (54)
$2,000.00 To $3,000.00 (65)
$3,000.00 To $4,000.00 (52)
$4,000.00 To $5,000.00 (37)
$5,000.00 To $6,000.00 (19)
$6,000.00 To $7,000.00 (17)
$7,000.00 To $8,000.00 (13)
$8,000.00 To $9,000.00 (8)
$9,000.00 To $10,000.00 (14)
$10,000.00 To $20,000.00 (20)
$20,000.00+ (3)
More Choices...

Sex:
Gelding (132)
Mare (125)
Stallion (10)
More Choices...

Height (Hands):
15.0 (46)
15.1 (34)
14.3 (29)

15.2 (27)
14.2 (22)
More Choices...

Age:
6 Months To 2 Years (10)
2 Years To 4 Years (28)
4 Years To 6 Years (27)
6 Years To 8 Years (50)
8 Years To 10 Years (51)
10 Years To 15 Years (69)
15 Years To 20 Years (26)
20+ Years (5)
More Choices...

Base Color:
Sorrel (62)
Bay (50)
Palomino (27)
Black (22)
Chestnut (22)
More Choices...

Attributes:
HYPP N/N (12)
Open Show Winner (11)
Incentive Fund Enrolled (10)
APHA Breeders Trust (7)
Money Earner (6)
More Choices...

Type of Ad:
Horses For Sale (267)

Now, for demonstration purposes, let's search the entire USA for a trail horse or any breed, at any price:

6. **USA, Trail horse, any breed, any price**
Purebred Only:
Purebred Only (2070)

Primary Breed:
Quarter Horse (904)
Thoroughbred (214)
Tennessee Walker (157)
Paint (Tobiano) (145)
Arabian (138)
More Choices...

Secondary Breed:
Quarter Horse (117)
Thoroughbred (54)
Pinto (43)
Arabian (28)
More Choices...

Discipline:
Trail Horse
More Choices...

Price:
$15.00 To $1,000.00 (549)
$1,000.00 To $2,000.00 (643)
$2,000.00 To $3,000.00 (569)
$3,000.00 To $4,000.00 (449)
$4,000.00 To $5,000.00 (353)
$5,000.00 To $6,000.00 (220)
$6,000.00 To $7,000.00 (121)
$7,000.00 To $8,000.00 (103)
$8,000.00 To $9,000.00 (65)
$9,000.00 To $10,000.00 (78)
$10,000.00 To $20,000.00 (207)
$20,000.00+ (49)
More Choices...

Sex:
Gelding (1398)
Mare (1281)
Stallion (87)
More Choices...

Height (Hands):
15.0 (384)
15.2 (327)
15.1 (286)
14.3 (235)
More Choices...

Age:
6 Months To 2 Years (109)
2 Years To 4 Years (211)
4 Years To 6 Years (345)
6 Years To 8 Years (453)
8 Years To 10 Years (428)
10 Years To 15 Years (815)
15 Years To 20 Years (298)
20+ Years (83)
More Choices...

Base Color:
Bay (678)
Chestnut (379)
Sorrel (350)

Black (316)
Grey (199)
More Choices...

Attributes:
Open Show Winner (87)
HYPP N/N (70)
Incentive Fund Enrolled (70)
Money Earner (49)
Breed Assn Point Earner (44)
More Choices...

Type of Ad:
Horses For Sale (2728)
Horses For Lease (38)

It may not be crystal clear when you read the above search results, but what it shows is that, as you start to refine your search, the number of qualified horses dwindles very dramatically (**2,728 of 43,000 qualify).** If you want a gelding, you have just reduced your options by close to half (**1,400**). If you have a limited budget, you have just reduced your options by another one-half (**700**). If you want a specific color, you have just reduced your options by more than half (**300**). If you want a specific breed, this will reduce your

options by up to 90 percent (**30**). Do not forget that many advertisers have not properly rated their sale horses for trail riding. "Trail Riding" is a horse dumping category for many horses that failed at another discipline(s). Many owners feel that selling a horse for trail riding is the best way to unload the horse. Many of these horses have never even been on the trail. Others have been out on the trail but are certainly many hours, weeks, months, or years from being safe on the trail; and many will never make great trail horses, period! Removing those horses that do not have trail experience reduces your options by another large fraction. So, we started our search with 43,000 horses. Our initial, minimal criteria narrowed it to 2,728 horses.

By refining for breed, price, and gender, we discovered less than 50 horses nationwide that could meet our needs. If we factor out those sellers who misrepresented their horse, the number could be less than 25. If we demand a "bold" horse or trail leader, we may have just reduced our magic number of matches to less than 10. Wow! I hope I have adequately made my point about the difficulty of finding the right horse! Now, consider the luck it would take for an average rider to find the right horse, by chance, without much effort.

3

Interview Process

Many preliminary questions should be answered before or after you visit the horse for the first time. I recommend asking these questions via email before visiting the horse for the first time. This will save time and, more importantly, rule out many horses, thereby preventing the real possibility of making an emotional purchase.

It is often difficult to obtain honest information from horse sellers. Once you locate a potential horse and, before you waste time going to see it, ask the owner some basic questions about the horse and make notes of the answers. Then, ask specific questions about the horse beyond what the owner claims. Consider yourself a private investigator and attempt to ask questions in a way that may give you more accurate answers. The reputation of a "horse trader" did not get started without cause.

You will need to choose which of the following questions are the most important to you. If you ask all the questions listed, at the first inquiry, you will likely irritate the seller so much that you will not get any answers. So, it is better to start with a few questions and see how thoroughly they are answered. These questions can be followed up with a second inquiry that may be a little more probing and includes items to some of those answers from the first email. You can use the same method with a phone call. Here are some specific questions that need to be answered:

General Questions:

How many special supplements or medicines does the horse require?

Is the horse a hard or easy keeper?

How much feed per day does the horse get (how many scoops or pounds)?

How many hours per day is the horse stalled?

What type of fencing is the horse accustomed to?
Does the horse have any conformational issues?
Does the horse have any skin problems/allergies?
Does the horse have any hoof injuries/problems?
Does the horse have any leg or joint injuries/problems?
Has the horse experienced colic? "If yes, to what degree?
Has the horse ever had colic surgery?
Any other health problems?
Can the horse pasture with other horses, safely?

Ground Manners:
How well does the horse lead?
How long does it take to load the horse in a trailer?
On what type(s) of trailer will the horse load?
Has the horse set-back? If yes, how recently, and how often?
Does the horse strike-out or kick?
How well does the horse stand for clipping?
  More specifically:
  Muzzle?
  Bridlepath?
  Ears?
  Legs?
How well does the horse stand for the farrier?
  Front hooves?
  Back hooves?

How well does the horse stand for the vet? More specifically:
  Palpation?
  Shots?
  Tubing?

Under Saddle:
Has the horse bucked, reared, spooked, or bolted?
Will the horse lead a trail ride?
Will the horse leave the group?
Does the horse kick?
How many hours of trail riding has the horse had?
How many different places has the horse been taken to trail ride?
Is the horse kept barefoot, or does it require shoes?
Does the horse require special shoeing or shoes?
How often has the horse been lame?

One question that should be asked if you believe a particular horse is a good candidate for you is: "Would you (seller) be willing to take the horse back after a defined period of time under certain conditions if the horse is not a good fit for me"(trial period)? Typically, this requires a well-defined agreement, but I believe the answer to this question will give you great insight into the buyer's integrity. A reasonable return policy might be:

1. The horse is photographed from all angles before the sale. Any injuries (bites, cuts, lacerations, imperfections) are photographed (and noted), in general, and up close. Hooves are photographed from above and below.

2. The horse is video recorded while standing, walking, and trotting.

3. A written description of anything unusual is completed.

4. A general agreement is written about what condition(s) could lead to a return.

5. A vet check.

To keep the risks to a minimum, a vet check is mandatory. It will cost one or both parties some money, but both the seller and the buyer need to have the horse "vet checked" if there is a return policy in place. This will minimize the chance the buyer will injure the horse and attempt to return it. Because vet checks can be pricey ($200–500), this will only be possible for a horse at a higher price point. Radiographs and drug tests will add to the cost. My best estimate is that horses selling for more than $2,500 could be considered for this arrangement. Most of the time, it will take a fairly benevolent seller to offer a return policy on any horse under that price. In the event of a return caused by an injury claim, both vets would have to agree that the problem was pre-existing before the sale of the horse. In a very lenient return policy, the horse can be returned for anything other than an injury caused by the buyer. You can see how controversial this becomes. I believe in return policies for the sake of the horse. However, if you ask for one or offer one, it should be thoroughly defined, bordering on a legal document.

There are many liabilities to offering a return policy. I offer horse buyers a chance to return the horse if it does not work out for them during the first 30 days. Hopefully, a horse does not end up in a bad environment, but, if so, I would hope that most sellers would want their horse returned rather than have them in a bad situation. Most horse sellers are not that attached to the horse being sold. Therefore, a "return policy" is highly unlikely for most sales. Knowing this makes our investigation that much more important. For a variety of reasons, return policies can be risky. I would not expect many sellers to agree to this, but it is not an unreasonable request. The worst thing that can happen is the seller says, "No." You can then decide whether to pursue the purchase. In lieu of a return policy, strictly follow the other buying recommendations in this book.

One way to negate the need for a return contract is to arrange to ride the horse on multiple visits. If your riding abilities do not allow you to ride every horse you look at, you may need to ask a friend or a trainer for help. It is imperative that someone ride the horse at least once and preferably more than once before the purchase. Because horse traders have been known to administer anti-inflammatory drugs or sedatives to facilitate a sale, unscheduled visits are advisable. This will certainly help weed out those sellers who have misrepresented themselves. Again, for horses under $1,500, you may not be able to make any demands or requests. It is not unreasonable to ask to ride less expensive horses more than once, but the seller may quickly tire of such requests. If they are not agreeable and you have any level of doubt about a horse, move on.

Some trainers believe that a horse owner can over-desensitize a horse, meaning the horse does not have any enthusiasm or even the slightest flight response. For working-class horses that are called upon to rodeo, ranch, or compete, this may be valid. For most of us trail riders, the more dead-broke they are, the better.

In summary, a buyer has the responsibility to research and investigate each potential candidate. There are no shortcuts to finding the right horse. Only blind luck can allow you to find the best horse partner with little effort. In the next chapter, we will discuss the evaluation points that you can use to judge compatibility and suitability between you and each candidate.

Here is a checklist for your questions:

General Questions	Yes	No	Other	Notes
How many special supplements or medicines does the horse require?				
Is the horse a hard or easy keeper?				
How much feed per day does the horse get (how many scoops or pounds)?				
What type of fencing is the horse accustomed to?				
Has the horse experienced colic? If yes, to what degree?				
Has the horse ever had colic surgery?				
Does the horse have any conformational or health issues?				
Skin or skin allergies?				
Leg or joint stiffness?				
Leg or joint injuries?				
Hoof problems?				
Hoof injuries?				
Can the horse pasture with other horses, safely?				
How many hours per day is the horse stalled?				
Ground Manners:				

General Questions	Yes	No	Other	Notes
How well does the horse lead?				
How long does it take to load the horse in a trailer?				
On what type(s) of trailer will the horse load?				
Has the horse set-back? If yes, how recently and how often?				
Does the horse strike-out or kick?				
How well does the horse stand for clipping? More specifically:				
Muzzle?				
Bridlepath?				
Ears?				
Legs?				
How well does the horse stand for the farrier?				
Front hooves?				
Back Hooves?				
How well does the horse stand for the vet? More specifically:				
Palpation?				
Shots?				
Tubing?				
Under Saddle:				
Has the horse bucked, reared, spooked or bolted?				

General Questions	Yes	No	Other	Notes
Will the horse lead a trail ride?				
Will the horse leave the group?				
Does the horse kick?				
How many hours of trail riding has the horse had?				
How many different places has the horse been taken to trail ride?				
Is the horse kept barefoot, or does it require shoes?				
Does the horse require special shoeing or shoes?				
How often has the horse been lame?				

A printable version is available online to subscribers at: www.trails.horse

4

Preparing for the Interview

By the time you decide to interview a horse in person, you should have narrowed down your search to a few horses within a reasonable drive. By now, you have asked the seller to provide you with enough information that you have ruled this horse "in" as a potential partner. Below are my recommendations for the most productive interview:

1. Print at least one copy of the "In-Person Interview Scoring Sheet" from this book or website.

2. Ask the owner to leave the horse in the stall or the pasture so that you may observe the way the horse is caught and haltered on any given day.

3. If you have horse grooming supplies and tack, take them. If not, see #4 below.

4. Ask the owner if he or she is willing to share the grooming supplies, saddle, and bridle that day.

5. Ask if the owner has a trailer and is willing to demonstrate the horse's ability/willingness to load.

6. Bring several grocery store plastic bags. Once you've evaluated the horse for its tolerance of the plastic bag while tied, it can serve as the "tarp" after being placed on a round pen panel, fence or near the grooming area for direct evaluation of tolerance when the horse is being led or when it is longeing.

7. A small tarp if you would rather use this instead of a plastic bag.

8. If the owner does not have a mounting block, you can substitute a bucket.

9. A pen or pencil to grade the horse.

10. Appropriate riding apparel or a trainer. It is very important that you ride or observe the horse being ridden at this interview. If all else fails, ask the owner to ride while you score the horse.

Instead of asking the owner for a list of all the horse/barn accessories, we can assume they have most of the items necessary to complete most of the tests, or you can assemble a makeshift test kit, described below. Your amount of preparation and the number of items you decide to bring will depend on the cooperation of the owner and how thorough you are, personally. Many first-time horse buyers do not have any horse paraphernalia, so a quick trip to the garage or the hardware store may be necessary.

At a minimum, you can take:

- Plastic bags
- Two ten-foot pieces of rope (halter, lead rope, lunge line)
- A bucket (carrier for items and can serve as a mounting block)
- A flathead screwdriver (this can serve as a hoof pick)
- A small blanket or tarp (these can also serve as a makeshift saddle)

If the owner has very little tack or horse paraphernalia, you will need to improvise. Study the scoring sheet and use your imagination. With a bit of creativity, you should be able to score the horse on at least ten categories. With a little more imagination, you should be able to complete at least five more. For example, many of the "Under Saddle" categories can be loosely judged by using the two pieces of rope to evaluate categories like neck flexion, backing-up, and leading away from the barn. Persevere to gather as much data as possible. This will help you in two ways: 1) It will allow you to better remember each horse, and 2) it will help keep you from making an emotional purchase.

Remember, by following even a small percentage of these recommendations, you will be better prepared to evaluate the crucial factors when deciding to pursue or decline any one horse. Like most social encounters in life, when we are not prepared for the interview, we tend to forget the real purpose of the visit. It is highly unlikely that a long-term friendship will develop out of your encounter with the owner, even if you purchase the horse. So, be friendly, but be prepared and stick to business.

5

T.R.A.I.L.S. Interview Method for Pre-purchase

The T.R.A.I.L.S. scoring system is self-explanatory. The scoring sheet is self-explanatory and will prompt you for a score in each category. You should be able to pick up the scoring sheet, review it for 1 minute and begin the scoring assessment. Whether using the scoring method for a purchase or for training, the logic is the same; you will score the horse as objectively as possible in each category.

The T.R.A.I.L.S. system has 25 categories of evaluation. The "Ground Manners" section has thirteen scoring categories of evaluation, and each is scored on a sliding scale (0–2 to 0–5) dependent upon the importance of that category to the overall safety of the horse/human interaction. The "Under Saddle" section has twelve categories of evaluation and is also scored on a sliding scale (0–5 or 0–6) dependent upon the importance of that category to the safety and enjoyment of trail

riding. The total possible score is 100. The scoring system is weighted in favor of the horse's performance under saddle as compared to its ground manners because the act of riding is the more important issue of the two basic categories.

Moreover, most ground manners can be improved rapidly through repetition. In Part 4, 25 of the chapters discuss each of the testing points. You will read a brief description of the test, why it is important to trail riding, and how to improve your horse's performance. There is enough separation between scoring definitions that you will be able to assign a number to the horse's performance for that task. There will be gray zones where the horse's performance lands between two options. **Always choose the lower of the two scores for consistency.** Below, you will find a modified version of the T.R.A.I.L.S. test for pre-purchase interviews. You will need to review the scoring chapters in Part 4 for a better understanding of the scoring methodology.

By adding the individual category scores for a total score, the system will give you a qualitative method of remembering each horse. And, it will provide you with a method of scoring horses against each other to help you make the final decision for purchase.

If you are still a little confused, don't fret as the categories and scoring system are very simple to learn. At a glance, you will understand how the system works. You should be able to use the scoring system below without any more education.

A perfect score is 100, but any score above 85 is considered exceptional. At the time of printing, no horse has scored 100. You will benefit from each of the following chapters if you decide to read them before starting your search. Once you have purchased your horse, the later chapters will also provide methods for correcting behavior issues while improving the T.R.A.I.L.S. score.

You will not be able to score the horse in all categories until you purchase it. However, by using the below scoring sheet and scoring it in as many categories as is convenient, you should walk away

from the interview with enough knowledge to make your decision clearer while keeping multiple horses separate in your memory.

The In-Person Interview Scoring Sheet

When you go to interview a horse, you can evaluate/grade it in many of the following categories. By using the modified T.R.A.I.L.S. scoring sheet on the next page, you can logically and statistically evaluate any new horse for potential purchase. It is not necessary to evaluate each of these categories unless you have the time and/or the seller is willing to give you sufficient time with the horse. If you cannot ride the horse, you can evaluate 10 categories. If you, a friend, or a trainer can ride the horse, you can score it in between 15-20 categories depending upon the situation. The plus sign (+) is placed in front of those categories that can be evaluated at a riding interview. Either way, this number will be more than adequate to glean enough knowledge to judge the horse qualitatively. The scoring table below will help you grade the horse at your first or second visit:

Test:	Score	Notes
GROUND MANNERS		
Haltering ease and time of haltering (0-2)		
Leading (0-2)		
Ties (0-2)		
Hooves/Farrier (0-2)		
Clips (0-2)		
Reaction to Plastic Bags (0-2)		
Trailering (0-4)		
Tarp Tolerance (0-2)		
Saddling (0-2)		
Bridling (0-2)		
Mounting Aids (0-4)		
Readiness to ride (0-4)		
UNDER SADDLE		
+ Mounting (0-5)		
+ Neck Flexion (0-5)		
+ Backing up (0-5)		

Test:	Score	Notes
+ Side Passing (0-5)		
+ Reining/ Steering (0-5)		
+ Riding/ Leading away from barn, alone (0-5)		
+ Responsiveness (quickness to respond to request) (0-5)		
+ Quietness at a halt (0-5)		
+ Opening/ Closing a gate (0-6)		
+ Drag a log (0-5)		
+ Crossing Water (0-5)		
+ Plastic bag tolerance (under saddle) (0-5)		
+ Cantering (0-5)		
GENERAL OBSERVATIONS		
+ General ease of riding (Owner) (0-5)		
+ General ease of riding (Buyer) (0-5)		
+ Overall experience (0-5)		
Total Points	/ 100	

It is unlikely you will be able to score the horse in all categories. Therefore, the formula below will give you the percent score, no matter the number of categories scored. For those of us that find maths a little daunting, the calculation is quite simple. Divide the total number of points possible by the horse's score and multiply by 100. Using the formula below, the number of categories scored will not matter. However, the fewer categories scored, the less meaningful the data. The below formula will give you the percentage score for each horse **no matter how many categories are judged**:

$$\text{Horse's total score} \div \text{Total Possible Score} \times 100 = \text{Percent Score}$$

Ex: $9 \div 20 \times 100 = 45\%$ **(poor candidate)**

$13 \div 20 \times 100 = 65\%$ **(has potential)**

$16 \div 20 \times 100 = 80\%$ **(strong candidate)**

Below is a blank formula for arriving at a score:

$$\text{Horse's total score} \div \text{Total Possible Score} \times 100$$
$$= \text{Percent Score}$$

$$(\quad) \div (\quad) \times 100 =$$

If you are confused about the math, just total the score. When you compare horses, make sure they are scored in the same exact categories. By merely comparing scores you will have an "apples to apples" method to compare horses.

Some categories are more important than others. Each person should decide which catego-ries are most important to them. For example, a horse that leads poorly should improve quickly with proper handling. Or, one that does not stand quietly when tied or at a halt on the trail, should improve with time. Unless you have a strong will, unlimited patience, are willing to pay a trainer, or have access to drugs (for the horse), categories like clipping, tying, shoeing, trailering, and spookiness can be deal-breakers. Horses that won't be caught in a pasture, set-back, buck, or rear and/or won't load on a trailer are absolute deal breakers for me.

If you observe multiple areas of weakness, move on to the next horse. A horse scoring under 50% at the initial test is considered a weak candidate. A score between 50 and 75% has potential. Above 75% is a strong candidate.

Highest on my list of important characteristics under saddle is "trail willingness" and "lead horse willingness," also described as "bold" horses. These attributes suggest a horse that is less herd bound, less reactive and, likely safer. The very best way to evaluate this characteristic is to lead or, prefera-bly, ride the horse away from their barn and herd mates alone. Their reaction to this challenge is very telling towards their boldness.

Almost all horses are reluctant (to say the least) to leave their familiar surroundings and herd. Therefore, consider a simpler, modified scale of evaluation to be:

Willing
Reluctant
Dangerous
Won't.

"Willing" or "reluctant" are acceptable results when considering a horse to have "trail willingness" or "lead horse willingness." As I've stated before, some natural trail leaders do not like to follow. This may be irritating, but I can assure you that a bold, willing horse is a better purchase than a herd-bound, unwilling partner.

"Dangerous" or "Won't" are certainly red flags for purchase. Horses that will not leave the barn or their barn mates at the interview may never be willing.

You can make your own list. Remember, most horses will still be for sale next week. If you think you have found a good candidate but are not sure, look at a few others as expeditiously as possible, then come back and re-evaluate.

6

Interpreting the Interview Data

Even though the data produces a net score for each horse, some considerations warrant discussion. Young horses and calm horses may not score well on the T.R.A.I.L.S. evaluation, but are certainly worth consideration. If their weaknesses are not dangerous, they may be great finds for less money. It is important to determine when, through lack of training, a horse simply does not know what is being asked, and therefore scores poorly. For example, low scores in many categories will result in a low total score (below 50%). Sluggish behavior may score low in some categories, but might mean a very calm, cautious horse for a person who likes a slow, peaceful trail ride. Many great horses have been made after the age of five. A calm horse with a good brain can be a phenomenal trail horse with the proper time and training. The decision to pursue a low scoring horse takes some further investigation. If you decide to purchase a low scoring horse, be prepared to spend time and/or money to improve its performance. One of my favorite horses would have been a low scoring horse had this system been around when he was purchased. Many years later, he is the highest-scoring horse on my ranch and a babysitter for beginners. I got lucky.

Conversely, many advanced riders should avoid the well-trained horses that do not have much spirit. These horses may score well with the T.R.A.I.L.S. evaluation, but be too sluggish and lazy to satisfy your need for trail speed or the occasional play day. Some high scoring horses will not make great trail ride leaders but, rather, calm and cool followers. This is fine, and some riders prefer these characteristics, but consider this in your list of preferences as you begin your search for your trail partner. Many times, it cannot be determined which horses will make good leaders and which ones will not. If you purchase a horse that is not brave enough to lead a trail ride, you may be disappointed. Many horses that are initially reluctant to lead can be taught to lead through trail riding alone, professional training, or by taking turns leading on trail rides. When you are at the interview, you can attempt to ride or ask the owner to ride the horse away from the barn and evaluate the reaction. If not a riding interview, you could simply lead the horse away from the barn and observe its level of comfort/discomfort. This is not a definitive method to determine the relative braveness of a horse, but it can give insight to its level of herd-boundness. Most horses that are moderate to severely herd bound do not make good leaders. Once you become familiar with the scoring system, you can look through the list to decide which categories are most important or least important to you based on your personality,

riding competence, and with whom you will ride.

Another serious consideration: Do you have the time, energy, will, and coordination to improve your riding skills significantly? Honest self-evaluation (introspection) is always difficult. There are some signs that will help you determine what possibilities for riding improvement exist. Age, athleticism, fitness, BMI (body mass index), number of riding opportunities per week, and time since you last rode, all are factors influencing how much chance you have for improvement. I think everyone knows where this is going so I will not belabor the point. If you see yourself growing into a horse that is currently too spirited or hot for you, then, by all means, that horse is in the running for you. However, for the older trail enthusiast, it is outstanding advice to buy the horse that is right for you today.

7

Introduction to the T.R.A.I.L.S. Scoring System

Below are the scoring outline and definitions for the system. In subsequent chapters, each number will be further described. The definitions are self-explanatory. In each chapter, suggestions will be made on how to improve your horse's performance in each of the categories. Photographs will help demonstrate these techniques. Our website will further assist you in improving and refining your training techniques. Visit us at:

www.trails.horse

On the website, you will have access to documents which, when printed, will make the scoring system portable for your convenience. Please use discretion when using these documents as they are copyrighted. Copies are intended for use by the owner of this book and subscribers of the website only.

I have learned a couple of simple truths about horses over the years:

1. Horses never feel regret for their actions.
2. A highly respectful horse is a better outcome than one that is disrespectful.

More often, especially with female owners, the level of discipline is far too low or non-existent. Horse society is based on bluffs. If a horse successfully bluffs a pasture mate into submission, they will almost always stay above them in the pecking order (see Part One). Most herds work this order out in a few hours from introduction. You MUST be the leader with your horse. This starts with every little battle. You MUST win each encounter.

Funny example: The farrier comes out to trim your horse's hooves. You are kind enough to hold your horse while the farrier does his work. The farrier begins lifting the back hoof and the horse kicks. You give the horse a treat to distract him from the farrier's advances. You have just rewarded the horse for attempting to kick the farrier.

We do not need to be excessively physical with our horses to have a good outcome. We need to be firm and consistent. The proper amount of correction/discipline is the least amount that will work. For each horse, that level will be different. You should be able to quickly find that level of discipline that is right for your horse.

SCORING SHEET

GROUND MANNERS/ HANDLING

1) **Haltering (Stall or Pasture) – relative ease of haltering. Use treats to improve the score.**

   0- Cannot be haltered
   1- Reluctant to be haltered (more than one minute)
   2- Mildly reluctant (less than one minute)
   3- Easily haltered

2) **Leading**

   0- Dangerous when led (spins, circles, drags, etc.)
   1- Crowds, pushes, pulls, attempts to graze when led
   2- Respectful when led but tries to graze
   3- Stays slightly behind the handler, non-reactive, never tries to graze

3) **Ties**

   0- Low tolerance of tying, dangerous to horse and people
   1- Restless when tied
   2- Quiet when tied

4) **Hooves/farrier**

   0- Will not lift feet and/or kicks at the handler
   1- Good with front, reluctant with back
   2- Good with both front and back, but leans on the handler
   3- Easily lifts all four feet and holds

5) **Clips**

   0- Becomes dangerous at the sound of clippers, cannot be clipped
   1- Accepts muzzle and bridle path but is reluctant with ears
   2- Stands quietly for all clipping

6) Reaction to Plastic Bags

0 - Horse is highly reactive to the sound and movement of a plastic bag from 15 ft away
1 - Horse is moderately reactive to the sound/movement of a plastic bag from 5 ft away
2 – Horse does not react to the bag even when it touches the shoulder

7) Trailering

0- Will not load, becomes dangerous with pressure (needs sedation)
1- Requires 20 minutes or more to load (periodically dangerous)
2- Requires 5 to 20 minutes to load (not dangerous)
3- 1 to 5 minutes (needs slight encouragement)
4- Loads in less than one minute (mildly reluctant)
5- Readily loads

8) Tarp Tolerance

0- Terrified of non-moving tarp (pulls away, spooks at first sight, attempts flight)
1- Unafraid of tarp, but will not step on/over
2- Mild awareness of non-moving tarp (moves near, on/over tarp but mildly reactive)
3- Indifferent to non-moving tarp (moves over tarp as if invisible)

9) Walking over Ground Objects/Debris/Holes in-ground/Challenges

0- Will not walk over objects (refuses, walks around)
1- Walks/runs over objects with head up
2- Walks over objects carefully with head up
3- Walks over objects while looking down and choosing footfall

10) Saddling

0- Won't accept pad or saddle, becomes dangerous if challenged
1- Accepts saddle but nervous
2- No visible reaction to saddling

11) Bridling

0- Will not be bridled
1- Accepts bridle but is slightly uncooperative, tosses or drops head
2- Bridles easily

12) Mounting Aids

0- Will not approach mounting aid
1- Will walk past mounting aid, but will not stop next to it
2- Impatiently stands near aid then moves away
3- Stands next to aid until rider mounts block, then moves away
4- Stands quietly at the correct distance, holds until released

13) Readiness to ride/ Longeing

0- Uncooperative after 30 minutes of longeing
1- Requires 10-29 minutes longeing prior to riding
2- Requires 5-10 minutes longeing prior to riding
3- Requires 1-4 minutes of longeing prior to riding
4- No longeing necessary, ready to ride immediately after saddling

UNDER SADDLE

14) Mounting

0- Cannot be mounted
1- Can be mounted but highly resistant, crow hops or bucks after mounting
2- Requires two people (one holding, one mounting)
3- Will not stand still for mounting, walks off, anxious
4- Will stand for mounting, but walks off immediately
5- Stands for mounting, holds afterwards, waits for release

15) Neck Flexion

0- No flexing in any direction
1- Braces against rider's request to flex
2- Requires two people (one holding, one mounting)
3- Flexes while turning circles
4- Flexes well to both sides without moving, but rider must hold with pressure
5- Flexes well to both sides, holds head passively until released

16) Backing up

0- Will not back
1- Will back up one step with much pressure
2- Backs with moderate pressure but throws head
3- Backs well but requires significant rein pressure, may throw head
4- Backs well but only straight backward
5- Backs well in patterns as directed by rein and leg pressure

17) Side passing

0- Will not side pass
1- Baby step to one side with much encouragement
2- Baby steps to each side with much encouragement
3- Side passes well to one side, poor to other with mild encouragement
4- Side passes well to both sides with continuous leg/heel pressure
5- Side passes to both sides with light or no pressure (verbal commands)

18) Reining/Steering

0- Very difficult (barely able to be ridden)
1- Difficult (slow reaction to turning or stopping)
2- Will direct (bridal) rein but takes time to respond
3- Direct reins well and/or early neck reining
4- Almost automatic response to neck reining, weight and leg cues
5- No visible need for any reining, all leg and weight cues

19) Alone on Trail

0- Will not allow mounting without horses nearby, extremely uncooperative
1- Will not trail ride alone (dangerous, spinning, refusing, running back)
2- Extremely anxious, frequently spooks, ignores rider, refuses
3- Reluctant alone, spooky, stops, frequently refuses, slowly recovers
4- Goes alone, mildly spooky, occasional refusals but recovers
5- Goes alone, mostly willing, infrequent refusals, won't hold the gait
6- Calm, no issues, attentive to rider, holds gait

20) Trail Responsiveness/ Trail Pace

0- Will not move any faster than a slow walk
1- Sluggish, lazy, may have an attitude when asked
2- Sluggish, needs kicking, spurs, crop
3- Willing but lacks enthusiasm
4- Requires minimal encouragement, maintains speed
5- Responds immediately when asked, maintains speed

21) Quietness at halt

0- Will not stand still, at all
1- May stand but moves often
2- Stands when tired but is restless otherwise
3- Stands still but requires tension on reins
4- Usually stands for tack/ clothing adjustments, photographs
5- Stands quietly at all times on loose or no rein

22) Opening and closing gates

0- Afraid of the gate, will not approach
1- Approaches gate but will not stop next to it
2- Will approach gate and stop, but moves when the rider leans
3- Will stand for the untying of the gate, but unable to close
4- Completes task but poorly
5- Completes task but more than one minute
6- Completes task in less than one minute

23) Crossing Water

0- Will not approach the water
1- Very anxiously approaches water with much encouragement
2- Will approach water, but will not cross under saddle
3- Approaches, enters with front feet only, will not cross
4- Will cross with pressure, may not lead
5- No hesitation through any water challenge as a leader

24) Plastic Bag Tolerance Under Saddle

0- Highly reactive when bag removed from gullet (spooks and moves)
1- Moderately reactive when bag removed from gullet (spooks in place)
2- Mildly reactive when bag removed from gullet (ear turns back)
3- No reaction until bag placed on lower neck
4- No reaction until the bag is placed on the ear(s)
5- No reaction to bag in any position or increased sound

25) Cantering

0- Refuses to canter
1- Dangerous canter/ gallop
2- Canters but uncontrolled, not comfortable
3- Willing to canter but unbalanced, doesn't know leads
4- Solid, balanced canter but does not know leads
5- Solid departure/transition, well-balanced, knows leads

26) Alternative Tests
See master scoring sheet online or review Part Four, Chapters 26-1 to 26-5, **Alternative Tests**.

8

Preparing the Scoring Course

The beauty of the T.R.A.I.L.S. system is that most of the tests we administer to the horse are tasks we already do on any day that we groom and/or ride:

1) Catch the horse
   a. Halter
   b. Lead
   c. Tie

2) Groom the horse
   a. Hooves
   b. Clip
   c. Reaction to plastic bags

3) Transport
   a. Trailering

4) Preparing the horse for riding
   a. Tarp Tolerance
   b. Walking over ground objects
   c. Saddling
   d. Bridling
   e. Mounting Aids
   f. Readiness to ride

5) Riding
   a. Mounting
   b. Neck Flexion
   c. Backing up
   d. Side passing
   e. Reining/Steering
   f. Boldness (will horse leave grooming area alone?)
   g. Trail Responsiveness/ Pace
   h. Quietness at a halt
   i. Opening/Closing a gate
   j. Crossing Water
   k. Plastic Bag tolerance under saddle
   l. Cantering

The exceptions might be that we do not clip, test tolerance of plastic bags or tarps, and/or trailer on every ride. Otherwise, it's a normal day of riding. We recommend testing your horse in all categories at intervals of 30, 60, or 90 days to assess weaknesses and discover areas for improvement. So, preparing for those testing days may take a little more time than usual, but that time will pay huge dividends in the long term.

Below are the scoring items that will require special preparation/attention on testing day:

1. Clippers – have clippers ready in grooming area

2. Plastic bags – have plastic bag(s) in one of your pockets

3. Trailer – have a trailer hooked up to a truck. If you have a large, heavy horse trailer, it may not need to be connected to a truck for stability.

4. Tarp – have a folded tarp lying in the round pen, arena, or on the ground. This test is based on a non-moving tarp. On windy days you should secure it with rocks to avoid movement.

5. Mounting Aids in place.

6. Gate – most ranches have gates that can be used for this test. Many do not. If this test is not possible, you may substitute another test found in the back of your book, in Chapter 26, Alternative Tests.

7. Water crossing – you may need to create one if you don't have a water feature where you test. Find a low spot on the road or driveway and fill it using a garden hose. This test does not require much water. A medium to large size puddle is adequate to challenge the horse.

Total preparation time may take 30 minutes. With each passing test, you will become faster with preparation. You will need to commit the scoring system, or at least parts of it to memory as you will not be scoring the horse while riding. If you prepare for a normal day of riding plus the above seven stations, you should easily be able to record the score upon completion of the ride. When you think you have completed that day's tests, tie the horse while still saddled and document its score. If you've forgotten a station, mount up and perform that test.

Part Four

"The horse, with beauty unsurpassed,
strength immeasurable and grace
unlike any other, still remains
humble enough to carry a man upon his back."
– Amber Senti

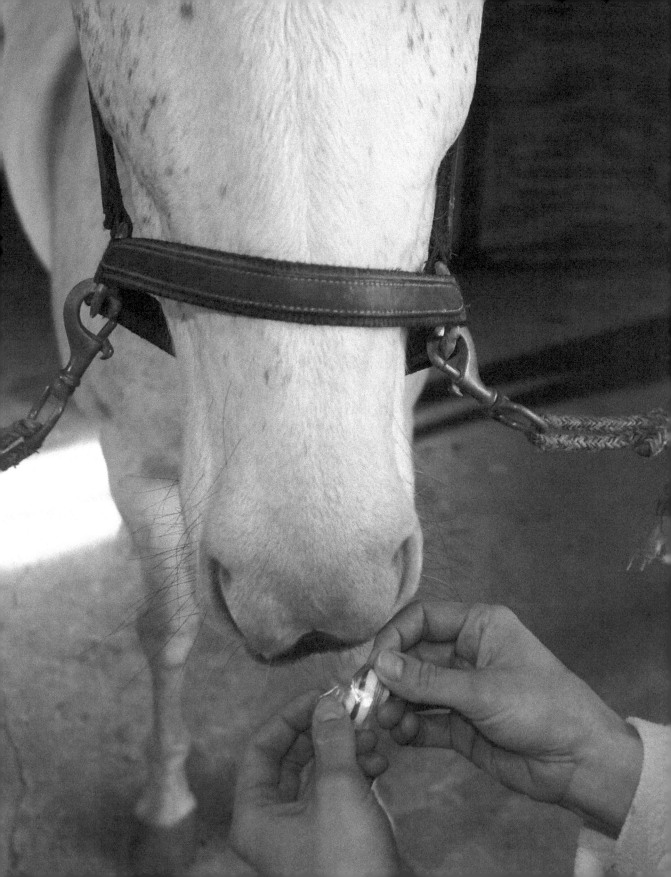

Cellophane wrapped candy treat

1

Ground Manners — Haltering

1) Haltering (Stall or Pasture) – relative ease of haltering. Use treats to improve the score.

    0 – Cannot be haltered
    1– Reluctant to be haltered (more than one minute)
    2 – Mildly reluctant (less than one minute)
    3 – Easily haltered

This category judges how easily a horse is haltered. One of the most frustrating issues is: owning a horse that runs away when you want to catch it. I have owned several horses that, on occasion, will not be caught. This, like trailering, can be a deal-breaker during the pre-purchase. No matter the size of the stall or pasture, a horse that doesn't want to be haltered, is a danger to that person trying to halter it.

If you are willing to spend time bribing these horses, they can sometimes be converted. This form of bribing is with treats in the stall and pasture. I recommend peppermint, butterscotch, or any other candy with a plastic wrapper that crackles when opened. Many horses quickly begin associating the sound with a treat and can be quickly trained to come for the reward. If you are hesitant to feed your horse candy, place a handful of grain in a bucket, and shake. The treat itself does not have to make a sound, but for this technique to work, a sound must be associated with some food or taste reward. You can create a vocal sound that you want the horse to associate with a treat, or you could buy a whistle and dedicate that sound to the treat of your choice. Not all horses like candy treats so you may need to experiment. It does not take much time to find a treat that your horse will crave.

You will need to bribe the horse on a frequent basis, starting **without** carrying a halter or lead rope. Once you get the horse to the point where they will come to you for a treat without hesitation, start tak-

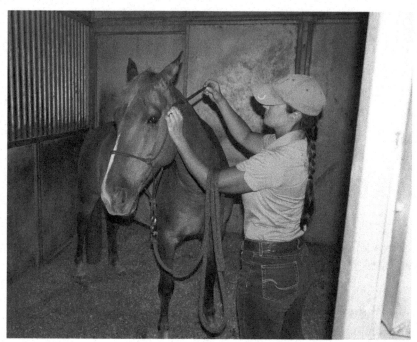

Horse assisting with haltering.

In-stall halter training for resistant horses.

ing the halter and lead rope, but **do not** halter. Continue desensitizing them to the halter over the next few weeks, but don't rush the process. Once they continue to come for treats without a lot of drama, you can start to lead them through the pasture. You can determine how quickly your horse will be ready to come, be haltered, and be led to the destination of your choosing. For some horses, this may take a few days, and for others, it may take a few weeks. However, some horses have such a distrust of humans, or are so averse to being worked, they can never be converted. I have two horses that I have owned for their entire lives, and both require unacceptable circumstances under which they can be haltered. Some horses simply cannot be retrained to be easily haltered. These two of mine are such exceptional trail horses that I accept that they are difficult to catch. If this is the only big issue with your horse, you may accept it, as well.

During the pre-purchase discussion, ask the owner if the horse is easily caught. Request that the horse not be caught until you arrive. You can then observe how quickly the horse is caught, or you can ask to catch it yourself. Many savvy sellers will never show how difficult it is to catch a horse they are attempting to sell. This is a category where a surprise visit or an early arrival to the owner's property is in order. It may sound dishonest to arrive unannounced, but the purchase of a horse is a very large commitment, and you want to make sure you are making the best possible choice.

If you discover that the horse you are interested in is not caught easily, I would look further. This behavior will decrease your training and riding time and, likely, become too frustrating to tolerate. When bad weather rolls in unexpectedly, you do not want a horse that is difficult to catch. Not only is it a danger to the horse, but many will question your sanity when you are outside, in a lightning storm, running around an open pasture trying to catch a horse running 30 mph!

For those of you with multiple horses, a difficult-to-catch horse can sour all its pasture mates. This can be catastrophic if your new horse makes all your horses difficult to catch. Should this happen, you will certainly regret this purchase.

To get the horse to improve on this category, you will need to have patience. The goal here is to make the horse associate treats with pleasant human interaction, not with being ridden. Once you have convinced the horse that the two are not always associated, you should be able to improve your score to a "3" very quickly. Our goal is for the horse to lower its head to be haltered without protest. Most horses learn the pattern of haltering and move their head in concert with the sequence of haltering.

Again, many older horses that are difficult to catch are equally difficult to train to be caught. If you are traveling to see a potential horse for purchase, this is something you need to know. For me, an older horse that runs from handlers for more than a few seconds is a deal-breaker.

Summary:

1. Many horses must be conditioned (bribed) to be caught.

2. The use of treats is a very effective means of training a horse to come when summoned.

3. Be patient but persistent when teaching haltering.

4. For hard to halter horses, begin the process of reconditioning in the stall.

Pre-purchase tips:

- Ask the owner to wait to catch the horse until you arrive.

- Observe the difficulty of catching and haltering the horse.

- Make an unscheduled visit(s) to the barn to catch the horse.

- Do not purchase difficult to catch/halter horses.

Un-haltering (Release of Horse)

Just as important as haltering is the un-haltering process. When it's time to release a horse in the stall or the pasture, there is a proper method. The incidence of handler injury may be higher with the un-haltering process than the haltering one. Many horses do not get properly trained to be released at the end of a handling session. We want to teach the horse patience and control. In the pasture, horses want to run from containment, blow off pent-up energy, or join other horses already free. In the stall, they want freedom from containment or are anxious to get to their grain. In all scenarios, they want to pull away from the handler, sometimes violently, as soon as the halter buckle or rope halter knot is partially released.

This is a terrible habit, and we must train against it. There are several safety issues:

1. If a finger or thumb should happen to get stuck in the buckle, loop, or clip while they are pulling away, there is a good chance of injury. There are reports of people losing digits over this bad habit.

2. If the lead rope is not managed, you can become knocked to the ground by it, abraded by it, or dragged in it.

3. When horses have a lot of pent-up energy, they occasionally kick-out when released. If a poorly trained horse pulls from the handler, spins to run, then kicks-out, you could be the recipient of said kick.

Whether it's safety or simply proper training, suffice it to say that we want our horses to respectfully and obediently stand quietly to be released. Once released, we want them to casually retreat. Below is the technique:

1. Walk the horse through the gate to their stall or pasture.

2. Turn the horse around to face the gate. Secure gate.

3. Walk horse away from the gate (stall a few feet, pasture 10-20 feet).

4. Manage lead rope so that it is loosely held in one hand (not wound around hand or arm) or lying on the ground between you and the

Halter release technique – unbuckle and hold

Horse stands quietly for halter release.

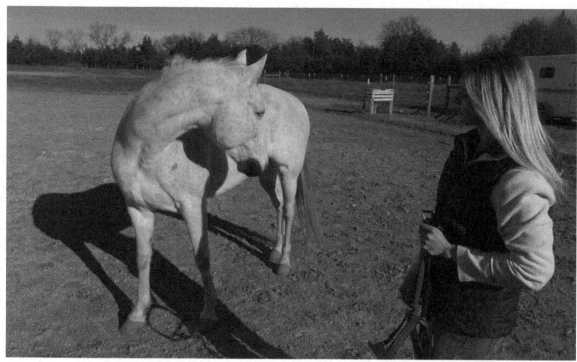

This well-trained horse still hasn't moved long after being released.

horse. In the event, the horse pulls away and runs, you will not be injured by the lead rope.

5. While saying "Whoa" or "wait," start the slow process of unbuckling or untying the halter.

6. Once the buckle or the knot is untied, do not release the halter.

7. Hold both loose ends, one in each hand. The horse does not need to anticipate the full release.

8. Vary the amount of time to release each day, so there is little to no anticipation of the release.

9. Bribing the horse with its favorite treat, after the release, will encourage them not to run away upon release.

10. After a few months of training, your horse should be patient for release with little to no additional training. (The entire sequence of release and the video are on the website).

Halter Breaking

Introducing a green or young horse to a halter can be a pretty harrowing experience. As the equine species developed, it survived because its flight instincts developed as fast, or faster than the predators around it. In order for them to survive, the species' senses and reactions had to keep improving. Part of surviving meant not being caught or contained. So, the initial haltering and control that we administer to a horse goes against all its instincts for survival. Most of the time, if a horse has been well-acclimated to humans, it will allow you to place the halter around it without much protest. It is the initial sensation of pressure that causes the reaction, which is usually severe. Young horses will pull, attempt to run, roll, rear, paw, or flop. Again, once their flight/survival instinct is engaged, they are willing to physically injure themselves to keep from being eaten. Who wouldn't?

There are two different phases to halter breaking:

1. Desensitization to halter and light pressure.

2. The actual act of "halter breaking."

Some handlers do not bother with Phase 1 as it must be accomplished over several days, minimum. In high-volume horse operations, there is rarely enough time to coddle young horses. And, in my own experience, Phase 1 is only justified if you have plenty of time as it does not seem to yield a significant decrease in the severity of the reaction at Phase 2.

Desensitization Phase

There are several different ways to halter break horses. Below, you will find the most common. As always, the primary theme here is safety first. This is one category where horse safety is very important, too. Not that "horse safety" is not always important, but because they are so athletic, coordinated, and stout (survivalists), horses escape most accidents uninjured. Two big exceptions are haltering and trailering. With both challenges, the horse is at the mercy of the handler and cannot really affect a good outcome for itself if human error is involved. Both endeavors involve containment. In other words, the handler removes the "flight" option, the horse's most predictably successful survival mechanism. Therefore, when we choose to place a horse in a potentially dangerous situation, we should be responsible enough to educate ourselves (in advance) on technique and safety to minimize the chances for a bad outcome.

The intensity of the reaction to haltering can be dangerous to horse and handler. Very young horses can be permanently injured should you decide to overpower them. Like all other animals, the musculoskeletal and neurological systems are still developing. Some handlers tie a non-halter broke horse to an immovable object and allow the horse to "figure out" that resistance is futile. I have done this and am very lucky that none of my young horses were injured (see the section on tying). I suggest beginning very slowly. After basic desensitization to humans in the stall, you can start by simply placing a small halter on a young horse without any attempt to lead it. It should be placed and removed multiple times during each session.

After a few days, you should leave it on the foal for extended periods. It is best to use a breakaway material (string, Velcro connections, thin leather) in the event it gets caught on a fence, latch,

Catch Halter

gate, etc. Young horses are very inquisitive, and they get into everything. It is best that the halter or makeshift halter fits snuggly around the head, thereby minimizing accidental snags. Foals are so flexible that there are many reports of their legs getting stuck in loose halters when they attempt to itch their heads with a hind leg. There is a form of halter known as a "catch halter"; it is usually made of leather and has a short lead of leather that hangs from the center about 6-8 inches. This type of halter facilitates catching a young horse by simply grabbing the short lead extension, thereby avoiding the haltering process. Within a few days of birth, a young foal is faster and stronger than

most humans, so we need to outsmart them from the start.

After a few days of halter wear, the young horse can be caught, and you may begin applying pressure. If you had the opportunity to imprint the foal at birth (or, better yet, the modified imprinting technique described in Part One Chapter 6), they should be much more cooperative. Either way, at some point, it must be halter broken. Hopefully, the mother is halter broken, and she can assist you. Put a halter and lead rope on mom. Start by leading mom around the paddock or pasture while the baby follows. This does not do a lot to halter break the baby, but it will introduce the foal to following a walking human.

Halter Breaking Phase

No matter how many ways you attempt to desensitize a young or unbroken horse to halter pressure, it will likely have an intense aversion to the initial pressure when asked to move with a handler. Each horse will have a different level of response to the initial pressure. The severity of the reaction to halter pressure is individual to the breed and temperament. At some point, expect a tug-o-war. Once you decide you and your horse are ready for the actual act of "halter breaking," it is best that they never break free from halter, rope, or handler. If a horse breaks free, even once, they realize it is always a possibility. They will be much more difficult to halter break, thereafter. Therefore, make sure you, another handler or your technique has a high chance of succeeding the first time. There are several ways to accomplish the task:

Halter and lead dam to begin desensitization to halter breaking.

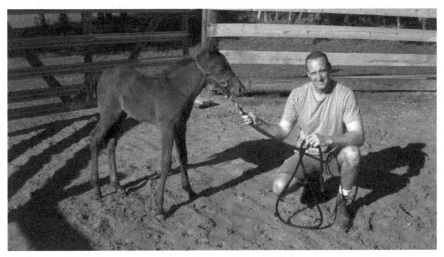

Desensitize foal to halter and lead rope.

This is the least desirable method of halter breaking. See other methods.

1. **Human held lead rope (One Person Technique).** Because it gives a handler more control of the situation, I like to halter break foals before they can completely overpower the handler. Take mom and foal to a safe paddock, pasture, or arena. It would be ideal if the foal was already accustomed to the halter and even the lead rope. If not, you might consider placing a halter on the foal while still in the stall. No matter what, the day of halter breaking takes preparation. Whether it is in the stall, in the pasture or some other area, a nylon halter needs to be placed on the foal. Most of my foals were so interested in humans they would come to us immediately upon our arrival in the paddock. This makes the entire process much easier. Let us assume that a nylon halter and lead rope are attached to the foal. Now, your will, strength, and leverage must be greater than the foal's. By moving away from and towards the foal, you can regulate the pressure they sense on the halter. It is advisable to progress slowly. If you can tie mom in a safe place and keep baby near her, you will have a better chance for slow training. This prevents mom from walking away, which creates more drama for the foal. If the foal is fairly calm with halter and lead rope, you can apply the slightest pressure

Use diagonal pressure to encourage movement.

until visible reaction, then release. Continue applying more pressure to increase their tolerance. Do not try to make them move their feet. I have found that mild static pressure is fairly well tolerated by most foals. It is when you try to move their feet that they adamantly refuse. Once they tolerate maximum pressure without moving their feet, it is time to try to get some slight movement. This is when the tug-of-war starts, you will need to modify the technique to encourage lateral movement, first. After some lateral movement is observed, loop the lead rope around the hindquarters to assist with forward movement.

Do not be too harsh on the angle as a non-aligned spine is more prone to injury. You can stand beside them and hook your arm under and behind the rump on that side. Some people use the tail as a handle for a mechanical advantage. This will push them off their base and make them take a step. If you are tall enough to keep a little pressure on the lead rope and push from behind with your arm, they will recognize that yielding to any pressure is better than not. With patience and persistence, they will learn to yield to the pressure and begin to follow you.

A combination of rope pressure from behind and lateral pressure can be used.

2. **Human Held Lead Rope (Two-Person Technique).** It is much easier to halter break with a second person pushing them along. Caution must be exercised to avoid being kicked. I am reluctant to overpower them at this young age and am fearful of injuring their neck, so, the two-person technique is my preference. Typically, with two people, this can often be accomplished in an hour. However, there should be no rush. If time permits, stop with small successes. The halter breaking process can happen over a few days or a week. Good stopping points are when they submit at any level of pressure. One person leading mom and another leading foal may also work faster. Depending on the age, size, and strength of the horse, it may demand the two-person technique.

3. **Mother Assisted Tying.** Tie mother and foal to an immovable object. Having mom around will calm the foal to the initial self-induced pressure when it first meets resistance. When mom does not react, the baby will generally react less severely. After

Proper leading of a newly halter broken colt.

the foal is calm, you can move mom away a few feet. At some point, the foal will react to the distance between itself and mom. Once this threshold is reached, stop moving mom away and allow the foal to settle; continue the exercise until all reaction stops.

4. **Self-taught halter breaking.** Place a halter and lead rope on a young horse and allow it to train itself. As the young horse steps on the rope, it will learn to give to and manage the pressure itself. Some people believe this to be dangerous, but reports of injury are rare. It is best to start this technique on a day when you can observe the situation continuously for an hour and periodically, thereafter. Most trainers do not remove the halter overnight, but I believe removal, when not supervised, is the safest way. After days of success, the halter can remain on the foal continuously until halter breaking is complete.

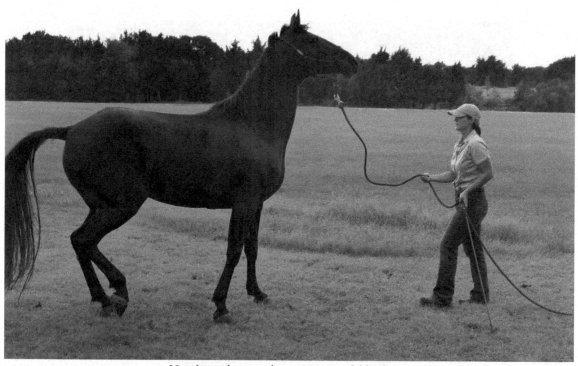

Unruly, pushy mare learning respectful leading.

In less than five minutes, respectful leading has been learned.

2
Ground Manners — Leading

2) Leading

0 – Dangerous when led (spins, circles, drags, etc.)

1– Crowds, pushes, pulls, attempts to graze when led

2 – Respectful when led

3 – Easily haltered

Many horses do not have respect for a handler. This can usually be corrected quickly. The firmer the handler, the faster the correction. Most horses learn respect from their pasture mates. Therefore, most are apt pupils for learning respect quickly. I have seen trainers retrain a disrespectful horse in a matter of minutes. The trainer on the opposite page took the black horse from crowding and pulling, to leading perfectly in less than five minutes.

Pulling like a bad dog on a leash, crowding the handler, or attempting to graze is unacceptable. By holding the lead rope near the halter, giving them a barrier of an elbow, or elbow bump, they will usually learn the minimum distance quickly. Imagine an 18-inch sphere around the handler. The horse should exist outside that 18-inch sphere. No part of the horse should be inside this sphere unless invited by the trainer. Pulling or snapping them back to 18 inches will reinforce the maximum distance. For more stubborn horses, you may need to be more physical. Some handlers smack the horse on the neck or head to keep them outside the human space. Making them circle (line longeing) will also teach them that unruly behavior will not be tolerated and only causes them to take more steps. With some stubborn horses, it may take an aggressive tug, yank, snap or pull to get their attention (see the first image).

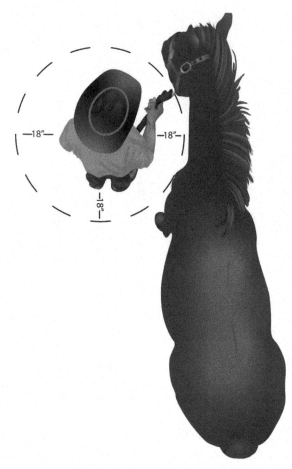

Teach the horse to honor the 18 inch "respect zone."
The horse can be in this zone only when invited.

The use of the end of the lead rope or a crop will also define boundaries. No matter how much your horse weighs, it hurts when they step on your foot. Respecting humans and our space when leading is the first form of respect a horse must learn in the entire process.

The proper position for a horse being led is at the handler's shoulder, head slightly down while walking at the same pace as the handler. Some

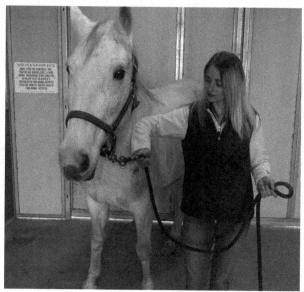

Elbow barrier technique for proper horse distance/respect.

handlers may have slight variations on this position, but, in general, this is accepted as the safest, easiest place to lead your horse.

Those of you who have been around horse trainers or have attended clinics have probably noticed how firm professional trainers are regarding the topic of "space respect." The horse's respect for human space is a priority. Most trainers will not tolerate even the slightest violation of their space. You should not, either. Make this a priority during your early groundwork with your horse. A respectful horse is a safer horse.

Most trainers agree that horses should not be allowed to graze when being led. If you just cannot discipline yourself to follow this rule, at least to try to use grazing as a reward after the horse has been worked. Alternatively, at the very, very least, YOU decide when the horse can graze while being

Pushing or pulling of the lead rope and encouragement with a crop.

led. A horse that decides to graze on its own is a disrespectful horse and goes against everything we are trying to teach and reinforce.

"Leading" behavior can often suggest a horse's tendencies under saddle. Leading can be used to assess a horse's tendencies related to herd bound-ness. If a horse becomes uncomfortable (whinnies, refuses, pulls back, etc.) when led away from its barn or herd, consider this behavior to be a good indication that the horse has herd-bound issues. Most horses do. This issue is discussed, in detail, in Part One, especially in the "Desensitization" chapter. It is their genetic predisposition (natural tendency) to be with other horses for survival. So, measure them regarding their level of reaction to being led away from their barn/herd. The more

agitated the horse when removed from their barn/ herd, the more critical you should be of other qualities that may offset this problem. Most horses can be cured of this problem in days, weeks, or months, if you are willing to put in the time or money to fix it. A severely herd bound horse re-quires a moderate to advanced rider who can ride it away from the barn, alone and on a frequent basis. Extreme herd boundness can be a significant problem for trail riders.

Poor leading can usually be corrected in less than a day. With some horses, it may take less than an hour. Be firm and consistent.

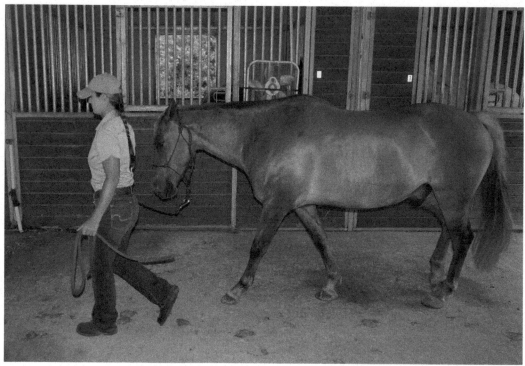

Proper and respectful horse behavior while being led.

Summary:

1. Be very firm and consistent when training the horse to respect your space.

2. The horse should not be within 18 inches of the human.

3. Corrections need to be more aggressive, with each horse failure to comply.

4. Constant reinforcement is necessary until the horse is 100% compliant.

Pre-purchase tips:

- Lead the horse near the barn and observe manners/respect of horse to handler.

- Ask the owner to lead the horse away from the barn/herd.

- Lead the horse away from the barn/herd.

- Observe the behavior of the horse being led from barn/herd.

- Do not buy a horse that has a panic attack when led from barn/herd.

3

Ground Manners — Ties

3) Ties

0 – Low tolerance of tying, dangerous to horse and people

1 – Restless when tied

2 – Quiet when tied

No matter your horse hobby or discipline, there is always the need to tie your horse to some object to ensure its safety, as well as the safety of people, property, and animals around it. Anytime a horse is outside its stall or pasture, it requires tying. Some horses are not safe when tied. Being safely tied for training purposes usually poses no threat to the horse but rather the people and property around it. Many horses are extremely impatient and misbehave when tied. Tying for training is a very effective way to teach patience (in this instance, patience = quiet acceptance) and to allow the animal the opportunity to think through perceived threats instead of reacting to them. Ultimately, proper tying behavior is a result of desensitization training.

When a horse's flight response is suppressed through being tied, some horses panic. Some of these panic attacks can be very dangerous to both the horse and nearby humans. The term "setting-back" is a violent form of attempted flight. For prey animals, survival instinct dictates that a potential injury is a better choice than death. In this case, the horse perceives being tied as a really bad situation and chooses, at all costs, to avoid it. There is no rational part to this process. The reaction is a basic survival instinct.

Usually, young horses are very restless when tied. As horses mature and have more experience with being tied, they tend to stand more quietly. Some breeds, like Thoroughbreds, tend to set-

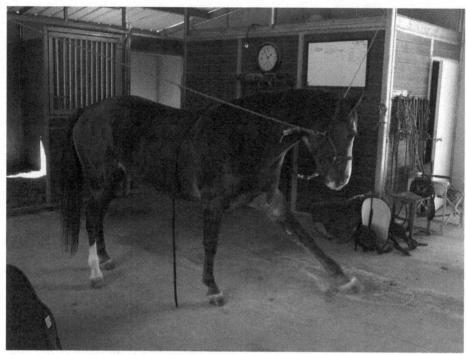

A restless, impatient horse demonstrates "pawing."

back. It is shocking to observe. Other breeds, like Tennessee Walking Horses, tend to paw at the ground or the air when impatient. While not very dangerous, this behavior can damage barns, trailers, and trees, not to mention be very frustrating for the owner.

All horse owners should learn to tie a "quick release" knot. The quick-release pattern or sequence is quite simple. It allows the handler to quickly untie a horse in the event there is an emergency.

Most professional and hobby horses have spent their entire lives being tied to some immovable object, and therefore, are not dangerous when tied. The use of a quick-release knot is not necessary 99.99% of the time. However, when a true

emergency does arise, it is more than convenient to have this knot ready to release. Usually, it is not the tied horse that causes the emergency, but rather another horse or human that creates enough drama to demand a quick release of a tied horse. Below are some extremely rare but not unimaginable scenarios when a quick release is of paramount importance:

- You are at a campground, and the neighbor's campfire suddenly gets out of control.

- You are at a horse show, and someone accidentally starts a barn fire.

Quick release knot.

- You are camping with horses, and a flash flood causes the nearby stream to become a raging river.

- You are in an event parking lot, and someone forgets to put their truck in park before they exit the vehicle. Said vehicle is barreling across the parking lot toward your truck and trailer.

- You or someone else has tied two horses too close together, and they begin kicking each other.

- Your young horse somehow gets its head

wrapped around a loop that was tied too long.

I realize these are highly unlikely scenarios, and most horse owners will never experience them. Unfortunately, Mother Nature creates havoc in our lives, and human stupidity is not at all uncommon. Please note that I do not mention setting back or extreme panic attacks as a reason to untie a quick-release knot. Why? In both situations, the risk of injury or death to the handler is too high to approach any horse having either of these reactions. I find the quick release knot to be most helpful when a handler ties horses too closely.

Most issues with tying are usually easily resolved through tying for extended periods. There are two schools of thought:

1. **Tie them up to a pole or tree as often as possible and babysit them.** The key is to tie them in a way that they cannot touch the trunk of the tree or the pole that supports the lead rope, and with their head high enough, they cannot graze. A tree limb or cantilever metal pole is ideal. Tie them from a 9-foot limb or pole. Use a lead rope or tie rope of 6-foot in length, thereby giving them a chance to rest their head, but no chance of eating grass. You can do this anytime you are around the barn doing other things. If you have more than one horse, you can alternate between tying and grooming. This is also a great time to clean and treat your tack. When the horse becomes restless, you will need to correct. Verbal

correction works for a while. When the person is within a few feet, it usually keeps the horse from becoming restless. Introduce more and more distance between you and the horse as it becomes more accustomed to being tied for extended periods.

2. Tie them and leave them. This is the "cowboy way." In many cases, horses are tied without supervision overnight. Most horse owners are concerned about the horse injuring themselves, which I believe makes this method less desirable than #1.

Pressure Releasing Aids. To assist in your endeavor to train for tying, these aids are the safest for the human and relatively safe for the horse.

Tie the horse to an immovable object with an intermediate pressure-relieving device. The idea for both techniques is the same, to give the horse a chance to recognize that it is not rigidly tied. This gives their brain the opportunity to control the flight response otherwise invoked. It seems to work for most horses. Below are the two methods:

a. Inner Tube. An older method uses a chain attached to the immovable object with a tire inner tube, or two, attached to the chain. A lead rope or another chain is attached to the halter. When the horse senses pressure as they pull back, it is not unyielding but, rather, gradually increases resistance due to the stretching of the tube. It reduces the perception that they are "caught," thereby reducing the severity of the reaction. It will not prevent all horses from exploding, but it certainly minimizes the reaction for many.

b. Specialty Clip. Variable resistance clips are available that have a design that allows the rope to slip through an area of the clip to create the same basic effect as the above inner tube method. An adjustable screw can be made tighter or looser depending upon the horse's size, strength, weight, and experience. When the horse senses pressure, as they pull against the pressure it is not unyielding restraint but, rather, gradual restraint for the length of the rope. The restraint is absolute when the knot at the end of the rope meets the clip. The premise is that the horse usually stops pulling when it recognizes that it has some freedom to move.

At some point, you will have to decide what level of quietness is acceptable to you. Some horses will paw or play with the lead rope for many hours, especially when there is more than ten feet separation between them and a person or another horse. You may elect to accept this as the best that can be done at a certain age. Eventually, with enough time, consistency, and maturity, most horses cease being restless.

Pawing or moving while tied is annoying for the owner but rarely dangerous. Conversely, setting back can happen in an instant and can be very dangerous for nearby humans. Any horse with a history of setting back is a potential threat to human welfare. Most owners will not disclose the occurrence to a buyer. You can always ask if there is a history of setting back and hope for an honest answer. For horses with this history, it is best to tie them on a longer lead rope (+\- 4 feet). This will give the horse more freedom to move and allow it to feel less trapped. Even though most horses pass through this phase, it can recur without warning and become dangerous to the people and horses around them. I would not recommend purchasing a horse with a history of setting-back.

For young and highly excitable horses, you may consider longeing them in a round pen or on a lead line to cause some fatigue before the tying exercise. Longeing can also be used as a consequence for not standing patiently when tied. Like children, some horses are just not capable of standing still for extended periods. The handler must decide at what age and for what length of time a horse should be tied.

Summary:

1. Tying is an effective way to teach patience.

2. Frequent extended periods of being tied will teach the horse patience.

3. Frequent safe tying and babysitting will teach patience.

4. With age and frequent tying, most horses will become patient.

Pre-purchase tips:

- Observe the horse while tied, consider introducing more distance between human(s) and horse for a more accurate reaction.

- Tie the horse away from its barn/herd at increasing distances. Observe behavior. Introduce more distance between human(s) and horse.

- Do not purchase any horse that sets-back or has a panic attack while tied.

Tying Scenarios

There are a variety of scenarios and techniques for tying a horse:

Tying to the Trailer – almost always, when moving horses by trailer, it is necessary to tie them to the trailer. All trailers come with hooks for tying. There is a boom extension (aftermarket product) that can be purchased and installed to your trailer. The fiberglass rod extends the tie point of the horse 48 inches away from the trailer. The entire system is expensive, upwards of $500. However, one hour of a horse pawing at your trailer will cause more than $500 of damage.

Tying to a Highline – a highline (also called a picket line) is a rope or wire connected to two trees or two posts above the level of the tallest horse's head. Usually, 7 feet is high enough so that the horse can move back and forth under the rope, allowing more room for movement and grazing. An alternative method is to tie lower, not allowing the horse to move under the rope. I do not like the lower method as some horses will walk under the highline rope with their head down for grazing or resting and raise-up into the rope and spook. The lower tying method is ideal when there is limited room for the entire highline method. The lower rope contains the horse(s) to a smaller area.

Note: On-trail and camping etiquette: It is a universally accepted courtesy to tie a highline to two trees in the least destructive manner. This means using nylon tying straps, towels, rubber mats, or some makeshift protection between the rope and the tree. Proper trail and camping etiquette are to leave no permanent trace of your stay.

Once the highline is in place, another rope or device (knot eliminators) is affixed to the highline at certain intervals so that multiple horses can be tied, if necessary. For horses that get along, you can tie a loose knot to the highline, so they have the freedom to move laterally, at will. For horses that do not get along, certain knots or metal knot eliminators can be tied to the highline so the horse can only move as far as the lead rope length allows. The lead rope is tied long enough to allow the horse to move, lie down, eat and drink if desired. For trail riders who like to ride and camp, having a horse that can be tied to a highline without incident may be a critical consideration. The last thing you want is to wake up and find your horse tangled from panicking; or worse, the horse escaped! There are complete highline kits available for purchase.

Tying to trees or other objects – The need to dismount is frequent (bathroom breaks, objects on trail, your hat blows off, you drop a glove or phone, assist other riders, adjust tack, etc.) Many times, this causes the need to tie your horse to an immovable, unbreakable object (tree, tree limb, log, metal pipe, fence, fence post, etc.) It's important to know how a horse will behave in a situation like this. Try to avoid using the reins and bridle for tying. If the horse spooks with the bridle engaged, it could cause severe injury to their mouth area.

Boom-tie trailer accessory

The most ideal tying scenarios are where the horse cannot touch a tree, truck, or trailer. If allowed to be too close to any of these objects, they will most certainly damage or destroy them. It is universally accepted etiquette to prevent a horse from damaging a tree. If you decide to allow it to damage your truck or trailer, that is up to you.

For a horse to be cooperative in any and all of the above situations, the technique must be learned and reinforced often enough that the horse considers it to be normal (desensitization). The last thing you want is to attempt any tying technique before you have the time to properly train the horse for it in advance. If you like to camp, take your horse camping with no intention of riding. Spend the entire trip setting-up camp, the highline, and simply staying around the campsite to babysit the horse and enjoy nature. If you decide to tie to the trailer or a boom extension instead of a highline, you will likely need to babysit even closer. If the horse learns to be calm faster than you expected, go riding!

Highline or picket line. *Photo courtesy of Robert Eversole "TrailMeister."*

Tying Technique

There is no better way to teach patience than to force your horse to stand tied for extended periods. Again, I will reiterate, your safety is the most important factor in horse ownership. If you believe tying a horse to teach patience is unfair to the horse, then, first, we must retrain **YOU** in the "rider safety" factor (see Part One, **Safety**).

Horses stand for the majority of their lives. Movement through grazing keeps them healthy and facilitates normal digestion. When horses sleep standing up, they are not moving. The point is, when you tie a horse safely, in a safe place, it is not much different than what they do for the majority of their lives, stand around. The difficult thing for most owners is to watch them in the first few hours when they are not patient. They may paw, pull back, and/or scream for pasture mates. It is uncomfortable to watch, but it is the most effective means of teaching your horse patience. It also helps with their problem of being herd-bound. Once they get comfortable being tied where they can see their herd mates, you should move them to an area where they cannot see the others. Much like a child leaving for preschool or kindergarten, horses have great trepidation about being alienated from their herd mates and familiar surroundings.

The tying exercise will also help your horse with its instinctual flight response. All prey animals have this response, and it is much like a reflex for humans. Evolution has caused those with the most extreme flight response to survive. When a horse is tied, the situation demands it to think through some of the challenges when it would otherwise run. This exercise will decrease trail spookiness, also.

The technique is pretty simple. A nylon halter is necessary so that it does not break. A sturdy nylon rope is also recommended. We have found the clip-to-rope connection at the end of rope to be the weak link. To prevent clip breakage, just use a rope without a clip. Tie the rope directly to the halter. Some owners use a sturdy chain with a sturdy clip. Tie the horse high enough that its head can rest, but there is no option to graze. Grass or ground surfaces are safest. You do not want the horse to be able to walk around the vertical support pole or hitching post. A cantilever (extended beam supported only on one end) is the best arrangement. For example, tie ten feet away from the tree trunk on a sturdy tree limb. A hot walker is a great option for tying (see above images). If tied too close to the vertical upright, the horse will either walk around it and shorten the rope for zero movements, or get its head pinned between the pole and the rope. This situation can elicit a panic moment and a flight response.

Note: We do not recommend tying a horse before it is 18 months old. You can certainly start sooner, but it will require constant supervision in the beginning. The reason not to tie young horses is that they can entangle themselves easier, and they do not have the emotional maturity to think through the exercise. And, because their skeletons, ligaments, and tendons are not fully developed, permanent injury can occur.

Method:

1. Find a suitable place for tying. Horse and handler safety is most important.

2. Use a nylon halter and rope without a clip. Alternatively, a sturdy chain and clip can replace the nylon rope.

3. Tie the horse so that grazing and entanglement are not possible.

4. Supervise horse for the first few sessions to ensure safety.

5. Move horse away from herd so they cannot see other horses.

6. Do not stop training until the horse stands quietly for extended periods (more than one hour).

4

Ground Manners — Hooves/farrier

4) Hooves/farrier

0 – Will not lift feet and/or kicks at handler

1– Good with front, reluctant with back

2 – Good with both front and back but leans on handler

3 – Easily lifts all four feet and holds

Improvement in this category takes patience. It is much better to begin with young horses than to try to get an adult horse to cooperate with their feet. With young horses, it is advisable to start picking up their feet in the first few days of their life. Once they do not react to having their feet controlled, you should start lightly tapping the bottom of the hoof with your hand to simulate the shoeing process. Continue this daily or as often as possible.

Picking mud, dirt, and rocks out of the hooves is a frequent desensitization exercise. Most riders make this a part of their normal riding preparation or do it during basic grooming. Like using turn signals while driving, it is best to "announce your intentions" when initiating the hoof picking task. Meaning, make contact with the horse at the shoulder where you plan to lift the hoof. This is especially important when doing the back hooves. You do not want to startle a horse when you're near the kick zone.

Below is the sequence that is universally accepted to announce your intention to manipulate a horse's hoof:

1. Start at the shoulder or hind quarter and slide your hand down the leg until you reach the hock.

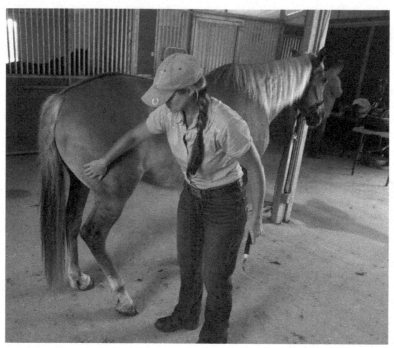

Step 1. Even though the horse can see you, announce your intentions by moving your hand from the middle of the back to the rump. This will become the cue that you intend to lift the hoof on that side.

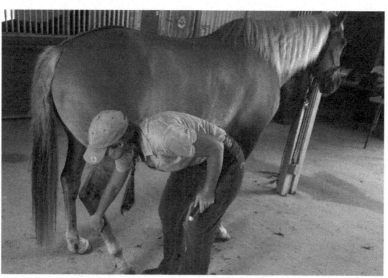

Step 2. Continue the contact down the leg until you reach the fetlock.

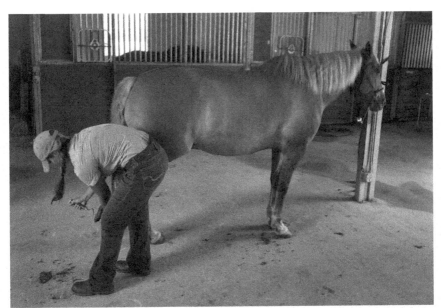

Step 3. Once at the fetlock you say aloud, "lift'"and pull upward on the fetlock hair. After a number of rehearsals, the horse will begin lifting that hoof for you.

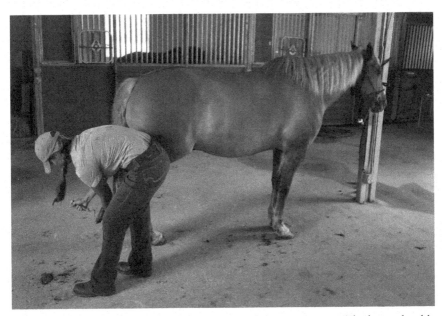

Step 4. Note, a calm horse, assisting in the hoof cleaning process. The horse should never be allowed to lean against you.

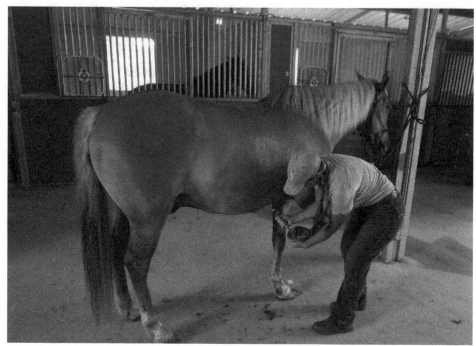

Step 5. Front hooves follow the same protocol.

2. Once at the hock, give the horse a few
    seconds to assist you by offering to lift the
    hoof.

3. If the horse does not comply, grip the fet-
    lock fur and pull upward on the leg.

4. Use your body weight to push the horse
    away from you, thereby causing them to
    transfer weight off the leg you're trying to
    lift.

5. If this is still not enough mechanical advan-
    tage, keep weight on the opposite leg with
    your body weight while using two hands to

lift the hoof you want to manipulate. This
will require some strength and coordination
and a moderately cooperative horse. Some
horses will resist enough or transfer weight
back to that leg quickly enough that there is
a good chance that you could get your foot
stepped upon. Be prepared for this possibility.

6. Repeat the process until the horse submits
    and allows you to hold that hoof up. Keep
    holding the hoof for 5 seconds. Repeat and
    add time to each repetition until the horse
    understands that it is YOUR decision
    when the hoof is released. Do not allow

them to lean against you. Rather, they must support themselves without leaning into the handler.

7. Repeat for all four hooves.

After a few dozen repetitions, the horse should start to lift its hoof before you lift it for them. It is advisable to hold the horse's hoof longer than it is necessary each time you manipulate the hoof. This will reinforce their training that they must comply and assist in the process.

Most adult horses have had farrier work throughout their lives. Of course, some horses behave better than others. The owner will need to spend as much time as possible picking up and holding the feet of their horse to desensitize them to the farrier work. Most horses that refuse or are reluctant to pick up their feet can be fixed through desensitization. Frequent requesting and holding of the feet in the "farrier position" is usually all it takes to make them cooperative enough for a drama-free farrier-visit.

This category is one where a highly uncooperative horse can and should be drugged. Sedation of a dangerous horse is the preferred method for farrier work. Properly administered dosages can take the edge off and allows the horse to have a non-dramatic experience. With each visit, the dosage can be reduced (graduated sedation reduction) until the horse does not react negatively to the farrier.

The average interval for hoof care ranges from five to eight weeks. For the desensitization to be the most effective, it should be practiced more fre-quently than the five to eight week interval. Most farriers have the ability to use drugs. One should be careful when giving drugs to colts and stallions. There is a dose limit of phenothiazine tranquilizers (Acepromazine, Reserpine, Fluphenazine, Proprioromazine) for colts and stallions. If the dose threshold is exceeded, it can paralyze the penile retractile muscle, and the horse will remain permanently dropped (paraphimosis). Consult with your vet before allowing anyone to administer tranquilizers to your colt or stallion.

Some vets offer farrier service during normal clinic hours. In this scenario, your vet may have a plan to desensitize the horse in a few visits. It can be expensive, but one method is to do one hoof per day with a day between each. This way, your vet can monitor the behavior and administer the proper amount of sedative to control the situation. This farrier/veterinary clinic arrangement will not exist in all areas. The less expensive and easier method is to handle your horse's feet as often as you can until there is no reaction.

Hoof manipulation and tolerance thereof is an easy assessment at the pre-purchase stage. If pre-purchase, ask the owner to lift all four hooves for an extended period. The buyer should also lift and hold all four hooves if the owner was safely successful at this endeavor. Reconditioning a horse to allow you to pick up its hooves easily takes time, energy, strength, balance, and endurance. An uncooperative horse will test a person who is not in good shape or who is impatient. Horses that show signs of poor farrier care or that are dangerously reluctant towards hoof manipulation should be disqualified for purchase. A violent reaction during hoof manipulation can result in severe human injury or death.

The goal of this section is for the horse to willingly lift the hoof upon request as the handler is reaching for it. The horse should calmly assist in holding the hoof for extended periods without leaning on or pulling hoof from the handler.

Summary:

1. Desensitize the horse to hoof manipulation as early and as often as possible.

2. Hold hooves longer than necessary while picking.

3. For difficult horses, consider a graduated sedation reduction program with farrier and/or vet.

4. Avoid purchasing horses that have great anxiety about hoof manipulation.

Pre-purchase tips:

- Have the owner pick up, manipulate, and hold all four hooves.

- Pick up, manipulate, and hold all hooves, yourself (if the owner safely accomplishes the same).

- Discuss the farrier schedule with the owner.

- If the horse does not have shoes, inquire as to reason; ask if the horse has ever been shod. If so, inquire about any special needs.

- Ask about any special hoof supplements, more frequent shoeing, founder, special technique, or shoes.

- A horse's hoof quality is very important. Poor hooves can be expensive and a deal-breaker.

- An older horse (over the age of five) that is moderately to severely uncooperative with their hooves should not be considered. Even with below-average hoof care, any horse over the age of five should be quite cooperative with hoof care/manipulation. Some farriers with short tempers can permanently ruin mildly uncooperative horses by administering the inappropriate amount of discipline when the horse is not completely cooperative.

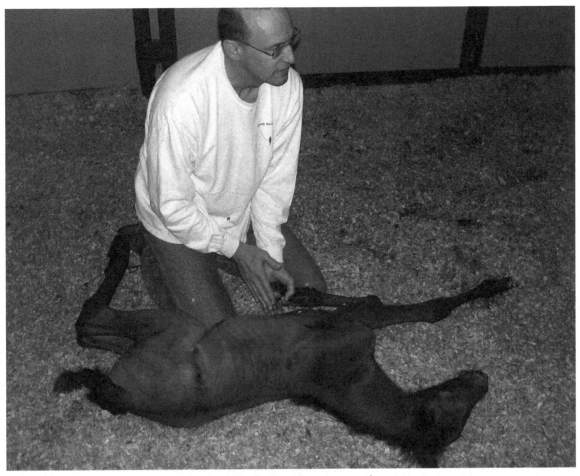

Early and frequent hoof manipulation cannot begin too soon.

5

Ground Manners — Clips

5) Clips

0 – Becomes dangerous at the sound of clippers, cannot be clipped

1 – Accepts muzzle and bridle path but is reluctant with ears

2 – Stands quietly for all clipping

Having our horses look well-kept through grooming is desirable for most horse owners. It is one of the many parts of horse ownership that gives us time to bond with our horses and decompress. It should be enjoyable, fun and even therapeutic. If the horse is uncooperative, it detracts from the overall enjoyment of the experience. Many people *only* groom during their barn visits. For many, grooming rivals all the other parts of the horse ownership experience, combined. One of my favorite quotes is, "There is something about the outside of a horse that is good for the inside of a man." This is never truer than when grooming a horse on a perfect day without time constraints!

Clipping tolerance is a learned behavior. Like many other horse endeavors, clipping requires repetition. Additionally, some parts of the horse will be more difficult to clip than others. It is highly advisable to start this process as early in a horse's life as possible.

Not only is it frustrating when a horse will not allow you to clip them, but it can also be dangerous. I have seen horses so frantically trying to avoid being clipped that they hurt themselves and their handlers. There are some very simple ways to teach a horse to tolerate clipping.

Slow introduction of the clippers is imperative. The sound of the clippers seems to frighten all horses, at first. Because they are much quieter, variable speed clippers or smaller trimming clippers are a great way to introduce the sound and the process, slowly. For safety, never start this process anywhere near the hindquarters. Below is the technique:

1. Stand away from but at the horse's shoulder. Allow the horse to become accustomed to the sound of the clippers. Do not touch the horse with clippers. Keep the clippers running until there is no reaction.

2. Move the clippers to the other side of the horse until there is no response. Continue with sound only until the horse relaxes.

3. Turn clippers off and touch the horse at the shoulder. Hold there until no reaction.

4. Repeat on the other shoulder.

5. Move backward along the spine and rib cage.

6. Move backward over hindquarters. Position yourself well in front of the hindquarters (kick zone).

7. Slowly move to the muzzle or bridle path.

8. Repeat on the other side.

9. Turn the clippers on but use the non-cutting side and repeat #s 3-8 above. Once the horse shows no reaction to all the above, move to #10.

10. With clippers on, turn them over to the cutting side. Repeat #s 3-8. This will be a completely different feel to the horse. Use the same pattern each time as you increase the pressure of the challenge with sound, touch, and the actual cutting process.

It is likely you will always use the same pattern but, to facilitate the most rapid desensitization, be as consistent as possible. After the horse fully accepts the clipping process, you should be able to start anywhere. If the horse reacts to clippers even after you have scored a "2", that simply means the horse needs additional desensitization to the clipping process.

Your horse must eventually accept the sound and the touch of the clippers no matter how long it takes, so be persistent. Small victories are very acceptable. If time and/or your patience are running short, stop when the horse shows the slightest sign of relaxation.

Once you get the horse to accept the simple clipping of the bridle path or muzzle, it is time to move on to the ears, which are always the most challenging. Rarely, will a horse allow you to trim its ears without protest. You should allow the horse to become familiar with the sound of the clippers near the ears but not cutting. First, hold the ear closed vertically. With the ear closed, most horses will tolerate trimming whatever hair sticks out of the closed ear. Second, once they accept this without protest, you can start slowly going inside the ear a little bit at a time.

There is a pressure point at the outside, base of the ear that serves as a very light twitch*. Firmly place the middle and ring finger at the base of the ear. By opposing the thumb inside the ear, moder-

Step 1. Introduce non-running clippers from a distance.

Step 2. Slowly close the distance as the horse investigates.

Step 3. Touch clippers to horse's shoulder.

Step 4. This look of indifference or boredom is the goal.

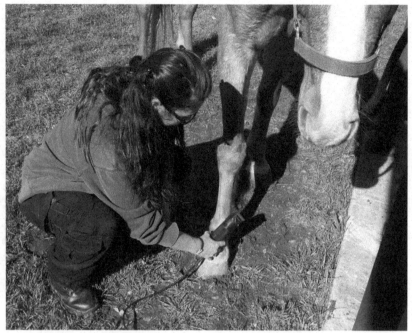

Step 5. Repeat process for legs and hooves.

Step 6. As horse relaxes, begin at the face and head.

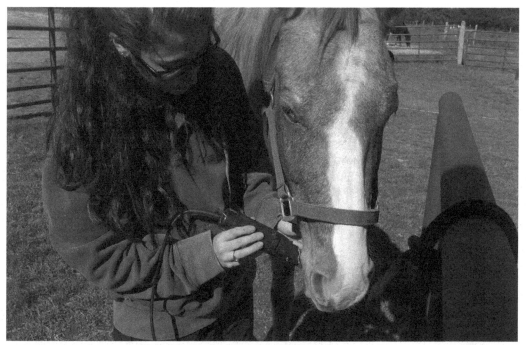

Step 7. Muzzle clipping is usually well-tolerated.

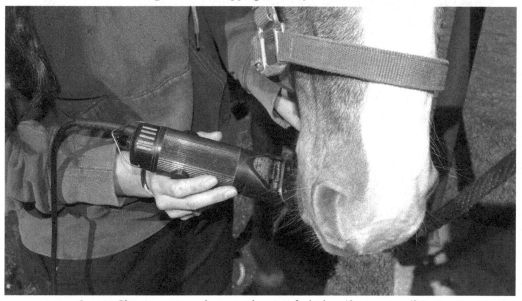

Step 8. Clipping against the natural grain of whiskers/fur is most efficient.

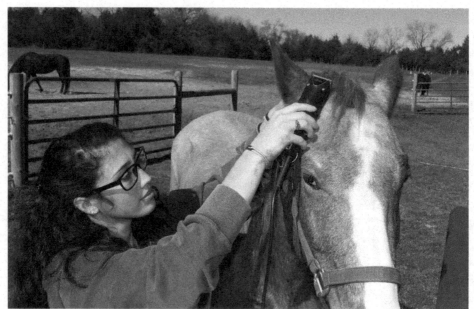

Step 9. Desensitize around but not in the ears.

Step 10. Lastly, desensitize inside ears.

Step 11. Pinch ear edges together to begin clipping the hair that sticks out.

Step 12. Close-up of technique

Step 13. Use downward strokes, against the grain.

Step 14. (Top-view) Repeat process with clippers running.

Step 15. This technique demonstrates the pressure points that can be used for inside ear clipping.

ate to heavy pressure can be applied to the pressure point while the inside of the ear is exposed for clipping. This technique has allowed many people to clip multiple horses in a relatively short period. It is possible to complete the entire desensitization process clipping, including ears, in one day if you choose. However, there is no good argument for trying to force your horse to accept all areas of clipping in one day. Proceed at whatever pace is comfortable and stop at any point on a positive note.

This is a rating category where significant improvement should be possible in less than a week. It can become a part of the ground manners and handling routine for the horse every day or every weekend for as long as it takes to score a "2" on the evaluation. See images below for examples:

* A twitch is a control/restraint device used to force an animal to remain still (comply) during certain veterinary procedures or during handling by owners when the likelihood of injury would otherwise be high. The most common place for a twitch is the upper lip. When done properly, it is not as inhumane as it appears. Remember, personal safety is the primary goal when handling any unpredictable animal. Note that unruly children in medical and dental facilities are placed on a papoose board for their safety and the safety of those around them. Unruly adults are restrained or sedated in a variety of ways in correctional institutions and nursing homes when the risk of injury to them or others is perceived to be high.

Summary:

1. Slowly introduce the sound of the clippers until the horse relaxes.

2. Slowly introduce the feel and sound of the clippers without cutting until the horse relaxes.

3. Start clipping the muzzle first where the horse can see and hear the clippers.

4. Finish with the ears.

5. Always end with some small victory.

Pre-purchase tips:

• Ask the owner to demonstrate the use of clippers in all areas.

• Clip or simulate clipping in all areas with the clippers running (if the owner demonstrates successfully).

• This challenge is usually fairly easy to correct if the horse's reaction is poor. Poor clipping is not a deal-breaker for a potential purchase.

6

Ground Manners — Plastic Bags

6) Reaction to Plastic Bags

0 – Horse is highly reactive to the sound and movement of a plastic bag from 15 ft away.

1– Horse is moderately reactive to the sound/movement of a plastic bag from 5 ft away.

2 – Horse does not react to the bag even when it touches the shoulder.

The sound and movement of small plastic shopping bags disturb the peace for most horses. Plastic bags clearly move in a way that is unusual to the movements of other objects in nature. Like all prey animals, horses are most comfortable in a world of consistency. They are most at ease with those sights and sounds that envelop their world. Any sight or sound out of the ordinary alerts them to potential dangers. Most horses rarely encounter a plastic bag rustling in the wind. Because of their relative lightness, plastic bags move and crackle even in the slightest breeze. Unless horses are pastured near a road with litter, some may rarely encounter these objects.

When a plastic bag is presented to them, it scrambles their senses. I believe that the movement of the bag is so foreign to them that their small brains cannot quickly or simply compute what it is. The sound of the bag is also foreign. It seems plausible that the crinkling or rustling sound must sound just like a predator in the underbrush moving to attack. Rather than attempt further speculation, suffice it to say that plastic bags are disturbing to horses.

Like tarp desensitization, plastic bag desensitization is important as these unexpected objects, when found in nature, are always a surprise for the horse. The calmer your horse can remain during a surprise plastic bag or tarp attack, the better it is for the rider. Therefore, prior desensitization training should certainly be part of our horse training regime.

As shocking as these objects can be to the unsuspecting horse, they usually become desensitized to them very quickly. By quickly, in less than 15 minutes, their score can improve to a score of "2". On testing day, you will always score the horse on its first reaction, not after working with the horse on the challenge. Remember: at the first, most subtle sign of any acceptance of any challenge you should reward the horse. Rewards can come in several forms: the release of pressure, verbal praise, contact praise, food reward. Many trainers use a combination of all these forms of reward for the best learning environment (See Part 1, PR³ Chapter).

The test and the technique (see pictures below):

1) Starting 15 feet from the horse, remove a plastic shopping bag from your pocket. Score the horse on its initial reaction when it sees and hears the bag.

Training: If the horse reacts with fear, remain in that position until there is no reaction. If the horse is terrified (frightened to the point of flight or danger), quickly compress the bag into your hand (make it disappear). Back up 5 feet and start over. If the horse continues to be terrified, retreat and repeat until the horse does not react. Identify the difference between fear and terror:

a. With a fear reaction, you will maintain your position and patiently allow the horse to realize that the plastic bag is no threat.

b. With a terror reaction, you will either back-off 5 feet or compress the bag into your closed hand to allow the terrified horse to regain its composure.

As desensitization progress is made, continue to slowly close the distance between you, the bag and the horse. Continue the process until you are safely at 10 feet without reaction. When there is no reaction, proceed to the next step.

2) Move to within 10 feet. Continue closing the distance. From 10 feet and closer, you will be repeating the process of 1) a. and b. above. Once you can safely touch the horse with the bag, proceed to the next step. The horse will likely flinch or shy away when the bag touches it the first time. It is best to use only a small portion of the bag at this point. The entire bag moving in the breeze is too much stimulation at this point of the session. Once you can safely touch the horse at the shoulder with a portion of the bag, proceed to the next step.

3) Using circular or small sweeping motions, begin moving the same reduced portion of the bag around the horse's shoulder. Enlarge the contact area as the horse calmly accepts the contact, motion, and sound. Proceed to the next step.

4) Continue this process by enlarging the area being contacted with the same motion. Make contact on the neck, mane, back, and belly. Avoid hindquarters until you have zero reaction to all other safer areas. Finish with hindquarters but always stay out of the kick zone. When there is no reaction, proceed to the next step.

5) Open the bag more and repeat steps 3 and 4 above. Continue to no reaction. Proceed to the next step.

6) With the plastic bag fully open and crackling, repeat the process until there is no reaction.

7) Move to the face and repeat the progression.

8) Move to the ears and repeat the progression. The ears are always the most difficult area to desensitize to plastic bags (and clippers). Because the horse cannot see the offensive object, its brain is struggling to understand that there is no threat. As always, with a strong negative reaction, you will release pressure and begin at the previous step where no reaction was achieved.

The following photographic series is self-explanatory. No captions are required.

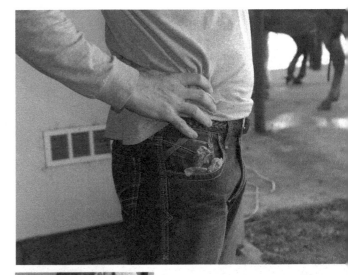

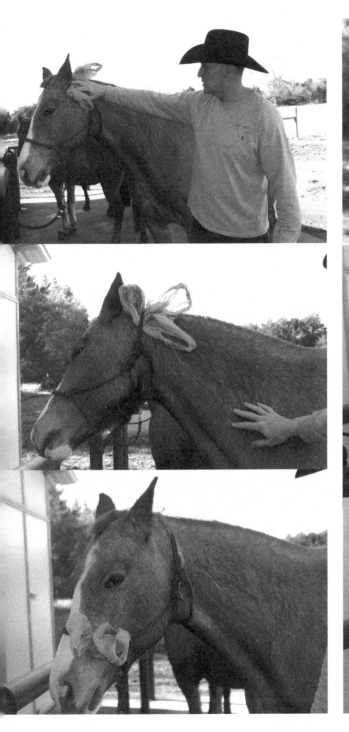

Once you have completed the above training session, you can consider your horse desensitized to plastic bags for that day. Repeat this process with each barn visit until the horse is thoroughly bored with the entire process.

Summary:

1. Start slowly, at 15-feet when releasing the plastic bag.

2. Slowly close the distance.

3. Allow the horse to smell the bag.

4. Touch horse on the shoulder.

5. Progress from the body to face to ears.

6. Back-off and restart at the last successful area.

Pre-purchase tips;

• Always take a plastic bag to a horse interview.

• Get the owner's permission to expose the horse to the plastic bag, or ask them to demonstrate the horse's tolerance to the test.

• Know that most horses can be desensitized to plastic bags rather quickly.

7

Ground Manners — Trailering

7) Trailering

0 – Will not load, becomes dangerous with pressure (needs sedation)

1– Requires 20 minutes or more to load (periodically dangerous)

2 – Requires 5 to 20 minutes to load (not dangerous)

3 – 1 to 5 minutes (needs slight encouragement)

4 – Loads immediately, but is slightly restless in trailer

5 – Readily loads, stands quietly

For trail riders, a horse that will not trailer easily may be the single most frustrating task in the sport. I have participated in and witnessed the dreaded, and sometimes all-day event of getting a horse in a trailer. Everyone that has experienced this, directly or indirectly, senses the frustration involved. Because this challenge can be so important in times of emergency or human safety, the scoring scale is expanded to 0-5.

This is a very sensitive and frustrating issue in my horse life. My first horse was "Sunny", a seven-year-old, 16.0 hand Tennessee Walking Horse gelding, and retired show horse. He was delivered to my house where I had two stalls in a detached barn. For a variety of reasons, Sunny was a terrible first horse. He was way too hot for a beginner, had never seen a trail in his life and, as it turns out, absolutely hated two-horse trailers, which was all I had. I cannot count the untold hours of coaxing, bribing, prodding, begging and attempts at intimidations that were wasted on that horse. Without a second person helping, I would have missed almost every trail ride in those first years of my horse hobby. Sometimes, I would have another person's help on the front end (leaving the ranch), but have no help when loading to return.

There were two incidents where I could have been badly injured trying to load that horse. Once he kicked very close to my head while I was trying to encourage him from behind; and the other time, he knocked me out of the trailer when frantically trying to escape. It is a very dangerous situation to attempt to load a frightened horse into any trailer. Very few of us can trail ride from our barn, so, trailering is of paramount importance.

There are situations where your horse may become sick or injured. What will you do if that horse will not load in a trailer? Veterinarians take vacations, can be too busy to make an emergency barn call, you may be out of town with your horse, etc. The need to load on a trailer may be a life or death situation.

Failure to load issues are not breed specific. However, perhaps because hotter breeds are more likely to react or because their flight instincts are sharper, they do not like the idea of containment in a trailer.

Trailering horses as early as possible in their lives is a big advantage. If the mother is a good loader, the foal can be taught to follow. Ramps certainly make it easier. With very young horses two people can physically pull and push them into a trailer, if need be. Once a horse gets in the trailer, a reward is recommended. Like so many other learned tasks, repetition is the key.

When possible, you can teach your young horse to eat from inside the trailer. The trailer must be connected to a solid object in case mom decides to enter the trailer. Connecting to a truck is ideal, but curious horses will almost always play with, chew and scratch a vehicle parked in their pasture. So, it takes considerable thought to make this training technique work. If pasture feeding, park the truck on one side of the gate and the trailer in the pasture. Use temporary fencing or gates to contain the horses. This allows stability of the trailer and safety for the truck. Place food in a ground bowl at the entrance to the trailer. Move the bowl back a few inches every day. Eventually, the horse will have no anxiety about entering the trailer. I tried this technique with Sunny's feed. He did not eat for four days. I gave up. This technique is much easier with young horses.

This is one very important evaluation category that MUST be evaluated before you purchase a trail horse. Or, if you have decided to purchase a particular horse and it will not load well, you should ask for a reduction in price so that you can have it trained to load. If you're buying from a ranch with trainers, you could even negotiate for them to fully train the horse to load before the sale is official. Trust me, it is THAT important!

Basics of Trailering

1) **Proper trailer connection**
   a. Trailer Terminology

   b. Confirm that your truck has a trailer braking system/ trailer brake controller. A brake controller is usually an Original Equipment Manufacturer (OEM) or aftermarket installed device or module. It is mounted to the tow vehicle's driver's-side dashboard area and engages a trailer's electrical braking system either time delayed, or in proportion to the tow vehicle's brake engagement when slowing down or coming to a halt.

Many new trucks have factory installed (OEM) trailer braking systems. This feature gives a cleaner look and is a seamless part of the truck's dashboard.

c. Insert hitch into receiver and secure locking pin.

d. Confirm that the receiver and the hitch ball are compatible.

   i. For bumper pull horse trailers hitch ball/receiver size is 2" or 2 5/16". The hitch

coupler (extension off trailer) will state the size.

   ii. A 2" coupler will not fit over a 2 5/16" ball so this connection will not be possible

   iii. A 2 5/16" coupler **will** fit over a 2" ball. This is the dangerous combination because the truck and trailer will appear to be securely connected when it is not. One bump in the road or the weight of the horse(s) can cause the coupler to slip off the ball and only the safety chains will be holding the trailer. Make sure the coupler and ball size are compatible.

e. Confirm that the locking latch is fully engaged. Some latches need special

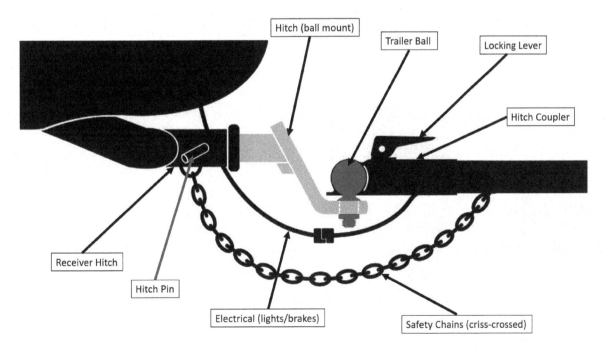

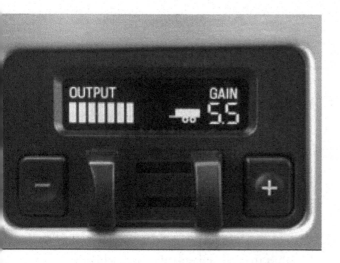

1-7/8"   2"   2 -5/16"   3"

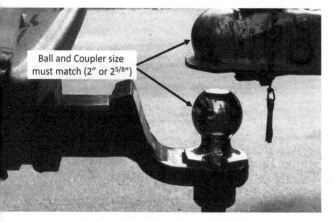

Ball and Coupler size must match (2" or 2⁵/₈")

attention to truly "lock" in position. Most locking latches also have a secondary locking pin. Insert locking pin.

f. Connect safety chains from trailer to truck. Criss-cross pattern is the law.

g. Connect trailer electrical (male) to truck electrical (female).

h. Test turn signals and lights.

i. Test brakes before horses are loaded. The truck's brake controller (a.) has a sliding lever that allows you to test the relative aggressiveness of the brake controllers' setting. For most situations the proper adjustment will give a slight "tug back" feeling to the trailer when light-to-moderate pressure is applied to the brake pedal. If the trailer brake is adjusted too lightly, the stopping distance will be increased as the truck and trailer will be relying mostly on the truck brakes for stopping. If the adjustment is too aggressive, the majority of the stopping will rely on the trailer brakes which may lock and cause jerking/violent moments to truck, trailer and horse(s).

The design of most trailers is front or front/slant load. Because horses carry 60% of the weight over their front legs, the best designed trailers are for hind quarters facing forward. In the event of a sudden stop, the horse doesn't crumple forward. Rear facing forward trailers require a longer and more expensive design.

j. It is advisable to double check all connections before pulling onto public roads, and at every gas or restroom break along the way. Not only is an improperly connected trailer a hazard to you and your horse(s), but also to other motorists and pedestrians.

2) Make the inside of the trailer as inviting as possible.
a. Brightness really helps.
  i. Park trailer so sun shines in.
  ii. Stall shavings are much brighter than a black mat.
  iii. Turn trailer lights on at night.
  iv. If no trailer lights, use secondary source (car headlights, flashlight, shop lights)

b. A larger, open design helps.
  i. Look for a tall, wide trailer. Remember, even if your horse loads well, you will be loading other horses, on occasion.
  ii. Open both doors of the trailer, even if it requires removing the tack hardware.
  iii. Start with someone else's wide trailer, first.

(If available, use a taller, wider trailer for early training. Open both doors to make the trailer as inviting as possible. Stall shavings can be added to make the black trailer floor even more inviting.)

c. Ramps are much easier for training.
  i. Purchase a trailer with ramps.
  ii. Ramps are much safer for the horse. Step up trailers can be very dangerous when unloading. Back legs can slip under trailer.
  iii. For training, borrow a trailer with ramps if yours doesn't have them.

3) Use stall shavings on floor of trailer.
a. Dry rubber mats are usually non-slip. Horse urine makes most rubber mats, especially worn ones, more slippery.

b. A moderate layer of stall shavings provides an additional shock absorber.

4) Handler's Responsibility.
a. Assume a matter-of-fact attitude. Do not anticipate problems until encountered.

b. Walk facing forward, as if you fully intend for every horse to walk right on.

c. Give the horse several opportunities to fail.

d. Do not lose your temper, be patient.

e. Read below for problem solving.

The remainder of the chapter addresses those horses we already own, and how to improve their willingness and style of loading. It is best to think of how we approach them as two different groups

Back trailer to paddock gate and open trailer doors. Secure trailer doors to the paddock posts so they cannot close in wind and so the horse is not tempted to squeeze through the opening.

Place food bucket/bowl at the back of the trailer.

Make trailer as inviting as possible with shavings. Once horse demonstrates that it will eat off trailer, begin moving bucket back.

Continue moving bucket back until horse must stand in trailer to eat.

Step 1. If available, use a taller, wider trailer for early training. Open both doors to make the trailer as inviting as possible. Stall shavings can be added to make the black trailer floor even more inviting.

Step 2. Handler always looks forward and expects the horse will follow.

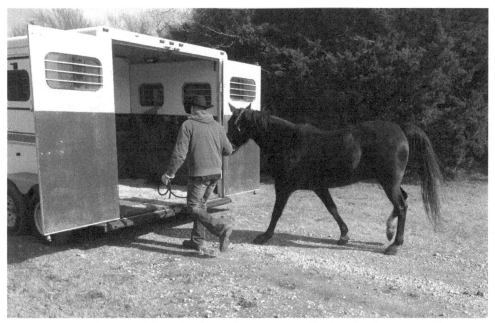

Step 3. Continue forward movement with eyes forward.

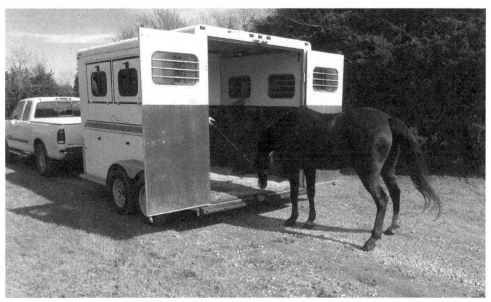

Step 4. Early in training it is acceptable for the horse to stop and investigate for a few seconds. After five seconds, verbally and physically encourage horse to load. Say, "load" and gently tug on lead rope.

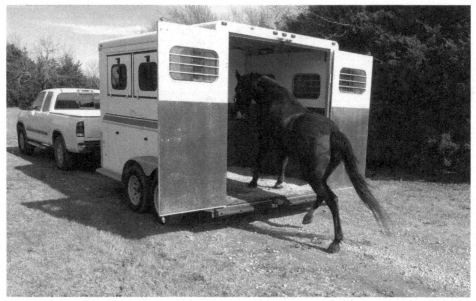

Step 5. Horse loading with only a slight hesitation.

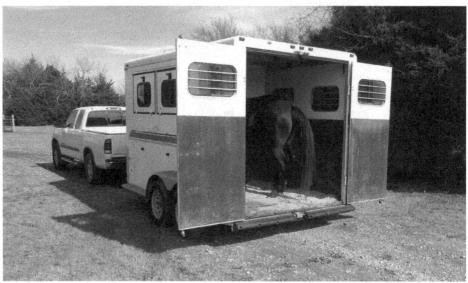

Step 6. Once in the trailer, release all pressure, reward with treat. Do not tie the horse. Allow the horse to relax while in trailer. Repeat.

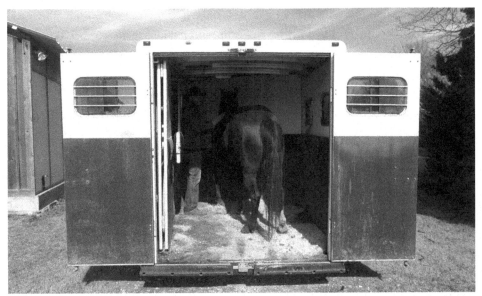

Step 7. Use the PR³ method. We want the horse to feel completely comfortable in trailer before we tie.

of horses:

Group 1 – horses scoring "0" or "1", "2".
Group 2 – horses scoring "3", "4" or "5".

Unless you are a moderately skilled and patient horse owner, those horses in Group 1 should be trained by a professional. They are too dangerous for the beginner or intermediate horse owners to train. For horses in Group 2, most horse owners should be able to improve their horses, themselves. With either category, repetition is the key.

GROUP 1— HORSES SCORING "0", "1" OR "2"

General premise: once the horse declares that it will not walk on the trailer, our goal is to make being outside the trailer more difficult than being inside the trailer.

This is where becoming an expert at line longeing will pay big dividends. Line longeing is the key to making conditions outside the trailer worse than inside the trailer. If you are not very competent at line longeing, you will have limited success in getting a stubborn horse on a trailer and should consider hiring a professional. A competent handler will make the horse move continuously near the outside, back of the trailer. Every few minutes, the handler will ask the horse to enter the trailer. Upon refusal, the horse will be sent back in motion. The pressure to load is continuous, and the cycle is repeated for as many times as it takes for the horse to enter the trailer. Small victories start by smelling or touching the ramp, standing on ramp, or partially entering trailer. These should be rewarded, but not accepted as success.

Once the horse fully enters the trailer, do not rush to close the door(s) unless you are short on time or are taking the horse somewhere. The reason for this is that we do not want the horse to feel trapped if it has already refused to load. Reward it with release of pressure, kind words or treats, but allow it to back out if it so chooses. The consequence of backing out without an invitation is more longeing. The reward for staying inside the trailer is rest. Repeat cycle until the horse loads with little encouragement.

Some trainers will declare success after one successful loading which is perfectly acceptable. The training can continue the next day or the next week. If you decide one loading is enough for that day, I recommend closing the door behind the horse when it enters. By this point, most horses will welcome the rest and be content inside the trailer. Leave the horse in the trailer for 5-10 minutes so that it begins to realize there is no threat inside the trailer.

GROUP 2 — HORSES SCORING "2", "3" OR "4"

Once the horse becomes an easy loader it is time to refine technique. These horses have now graduated to Group 2. Here is where almost any horse owner can refine technique, themselves. Most times, it is not of paramount importance that a horse scores a "4" or "5". However, there are times when it

is quite important. One of those times is during unexpected inclement weather. Practically all horse owners recognize that horses negatively react to climate change and become more excitable. In some parts of the world, harsh weather can roll in very quickly (tornadoes, lightning, flash flooding).

Often, when we are riding, we are not checking the weather forecast or for warnings and can be completely ambushed by inclement weather. Though rare, I can think of no better time to have a horse that scored a "4" or "5" in this category. Once a horse reaches a "3" on the scale, it takes very little time or effort to get them to a "4" or "5". Trailer training is a great time investment.

Trailer Unloading

While rarely discussed, there is a proper way for a horse to exit a trailer.

Train for these goals:

- Horses should back out of trailers. Many will try to turn around to come out head-first. Do not allow this unless the trailer is set up for pass-through loading and unloading. Some horses are too big to turn around and get stuck while trying to do so. Horse urine on the floor may cause dangerous slipping when they try to pivot on their back feet.

- Train the horse to exit slowly and with purpose. Horses that rush from trailers often slip or miss the ramp to the side. Physically slow them down by firmly holding the halter. Train your horse to understand the verbal cue "easy".

Step 1. Turning to exit, not acceptable.

Step 2. Say, "back-up" and gently push back on the lead rope to initiate unloading.

Step 3. Once the horse starts backing-up, release all pressure so that it focuses on the footfalls. We want this to be slow and purposeful.

Step 4. Upon exiting the trailer, the horse should calmly wait for the handler to exit.

Step 5. PR³

Summary:

1. Easy trailering is essential to a trail rider's horse ownership.

2. Start horses young when you can encourage them more.

3. Employ the help of professional trainers for highly resistant horses.

4. Refine the technique so you CAN expedite loading when necessary.

5. Don't purchase a horse that is unwilling to load in a trailer, unless you are willing to hire a professional who can train the horse for "drama-free" loading.

Pre-purchase tips:

- Ask the owner how well the horse loads.

- Ask the owner about the horse's loading history.

- Ask the owner on to which trailers the horse has loaded.

- Ask the owner to demonstrate loading the horse.

- Do not discount the importance of loading during the pre-purchase process.

- Do not purchase an older horse that refuses to load easily.

8
Ground Manners — Tarp Tolerance

8) Tarp Tolerance

0 – Terrified of non-moving tarp (pulls away, spooks at first sight, attempts flight)

1– Mild awareness of non-moving tarp (moves near, on/over tarp but mildly reactive)

2 – Indifferent to non-moving tarp (moves over tarp as if invisible)

Score the horse's reaction when it sees the tarp for the first time, from any distance.. We believe this test challenge to be one of the most suggestive of trail calmness. Tarps, especially moving ones, are one of the biggest challenges to a horse's perception of danger. Much like plastic bag tolerance, it is likely the unusual movement and sound that heighten a horse's danger perception. Therefore, desensitizing a horse to moving and non-moving tarps is a priority in your training regimen.

In this section we will train for tarp tolerance. Technique:

1) In a round pen, fold a tarp (plastic type, preferably a lighter color) into a small rectangle (12" X 36") and make it immobile by using bricks or rocks.

2) Always on a lead rope, start 180° (opposite side of round pen) from the tarp. Give the horse a chance to see the object before it becomes an imminent threat. DO NOT LOOK AT TARP! The owner/trainer's role is to pretend there is no object in the round pen.

3) How you proceed to lead the horse will depend upon the reaction:
   a. Strong, negative reaction to tarp: walk the perimeter of the round pen, but stop half

way to the tarp. Cut the circle in half, and walk past the tarp with plenty of room to spare. Continue walking closer with each pass. If the horse stops, reduce the pressure by allowing more distance until the horse passes without protest. Continue process until the horse is close enough to sniff the tarp. Once you're close enough for the horse to potentially sniff the tarp, stand there for as long as it takes to get the horse to sniff the tarp. Proceed to next step.

b. Attempt to get the horse to step over the tarp. Proceed to next step.

c. No reaction at or over tarp: unfold the tarp to make it twice the size. Prior to unfolding, tie the horse across the pen (if pen is sturdy enough to hold a spooky horse. If not, tie the horse to the nearest secure, safe spot. You could leave the horse loose in the round pen, but this is not recommended as the tarp may frighten the horse when being unfolded or may blow in the wind.) Proceed to next step.

d. Restart the test with the tarp unfolded to twice the size, secure with bricks or rocks. Repeat entire process until there is no reaction to the tarp.

e. Once the horse is standing at and sniffing the tarp, calmly attempt to get the

horse to step on the tarp with one front hoof. Proceed to next step.

f. Attempt to get both front hooves on the tarp. Proceed the horse to next step.

g. Attempt to get horse to step on and walk over the tarp without reaction. Proceed to next step.

h. Open tarp all the way, secure with bricks or rocks. Repeat process until the horse is calmly walking over the tarp without hesitation. Proceed to next step.

i. Remove a of couple bricks or rocks to allow one corner to move in the breeze. Of course, this step depends on the wind speed that day. Proceed to next step.

j. Continue to remove bricks or rocks until the tarp has a chance to flap or move on the ground. Proceed to next step.

k. Hang the tarp on a panel of the round pen and allow it to move in the wind. Repeat to indifference. Proceed to next step.

l. Once the horse has calmly accepted the concept that any tarp, moving or non-moving, is not a threat, it is time for the trainer to manually and slowly touch the tarp to the horse.

m. With the horse on a lead rope, fold the

tarp small enough you can hold it like a book. Place the tarp in front of the horse's face so it can be seen. Hold the tarp still and give the horse as long as it takes to sniff it. Proceed to next step.

n. Rub the horse at the shoulder with the folded tarp. Rub until there is no reaction. Proceed to next step.

o. Expand the area of rubbing until there is no reaction. If the horse moves its feet, go back to the area where there was no reaction and begin again. If the horse flinches but does not move its feet, continue rubbing until there is no reaction. Proceed to next step.

p. Increase the areas of the body where the tarp is being rubbed on the horse. Go down each leg, on the belly, and work your way back to the hind quarters (always stay out of the kick zone). Proceed to next step.

q. Most horses have a favored side. Go back to step "n" (above) and repeat for the opposite side. Continue to no reaction. Proceed to next step.

r. Unfold the tarp to twice the original size. Go back to step "n" and repeat all steps. Continue to no reaction. Proceed to next step.

s. Once your horse has mastered all of the above steps, it is time to completely unfold the tarp and train to no reaction, starting back at "n". Continue to no reaction. Proceed to next step.

t. Allow the full length of the tarp to flap in the wind. Begin shaking and popping the tarp. Continue to no reaction.

4) The goal is to train to the point of zero reaction to non-moving and moving tarps. Most horses become desensitized to tarp tolerance fairly quickly (within an hour if your technique of pressure, release and reward are correct). At any point that you think the horse failed the progression, go back to a successful step and begin again.

Tarp tolerance will go a long way in your endeavor to train fearless trail horses. This tolerance should be reinforced on a monthly basis. If your horse does not react to this test at the one month interval, you can lengthen the interval to two or three months until you find that interval that is right for your horse's reinforcement. Some veteran horses may only need yearly reinforcement. Test often enough that you know what's right for your horse.

More advanced, still, is the use of tarps while longeing and riding. In the most advanced form, tarps can be tied to the saddle while longeing to continue the desensitization process. For the most accomplished riders, managing a tarp while riding, is one of the most advanced desensitization tech-

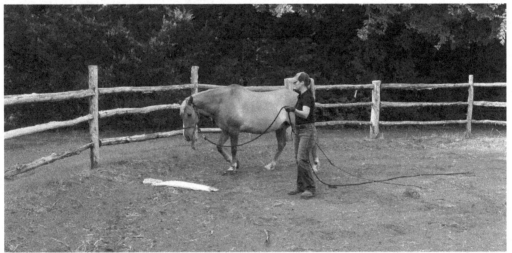

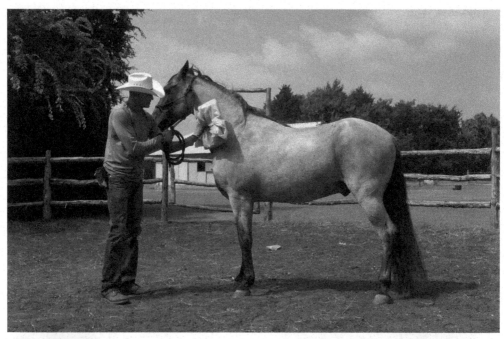

niques to attempt. Once the horse fully accepts the tarp, during longeing the rider can consider placing it on the saddle or wearing it like a cape. I am not recommending that anyone try this unless the rider is very confident of a positive outcome. If your horse has been desensitized to everything else and has not reacted to any challenge in many weeks, it may be a consideration. If you elect to attempt this challenge, start in a round pen or with a partner holding the horse on a longe line. Some horses will simply never get to the point of accepting this, and many riders should never try this. However, many trainers consider this the ultimate challenge for a trail horse. A horse that will accept being ridden while connected to a tarp flapping in the wind should accept almost any trail challenge they encounter.

Summary:

1) Desensitize the horse to tarps and plastic, often.

2) Start slowly and customize your training to the horse's initial reaction.

3) Desensitization to tarps is usually a fast process.

4) Customize your reinforcement to the horse's level of retention based on the first month's retest.

Pre-purchase tips:

- Tarp/plastic tolerance is a very easy test to administer at the pre-purchase interview.

- Bring a plastic bag and a small tarp to the interview.

- Always get owner's verbal consent.

- Request that the owner expose the horse to the plastic bag.

- Expose the tied horse to the plastic bag from a distance of 10 feet.

- Move closer to the horse with the bag moving and crackling in the wind.

- If you sense anxiety in the horse, stop.

- Retest from both sides.

- Repeat with tarp.

- The tarp can also be used in the round pen.

- While this is a category that can be improved very quickly, it is helpful to observe the severity of the reaction. A very severe reaction may indicate a horse that is moderately to highly reactive to every challenge. If nothing else, a poor reaction may give you some negotiating leverage.

9

Ground Manners — Walking over Ground Objects/Debris/Holes in Ground/Challenges

9) Walking over Ground Objects/Debris/Holes in ground/Challenges

- **0** – Will not walk over objects (refuses, walks around)
- **1** – Walks/runs over objects with head up
- **2** – Walks over objects carefully with head up
- **3** – Walks over objects while looking down and choosing footfalls

For trail riders, it is ideal to have a horse that is cautious and careful about where it steps (footfalls). Many trail horses do not pay any attention to the ground under their feet. Because they are so coordinated and are almost always on consistent footing, they do not need to evaluate the terrain they stand, walk, or run over. If they stumble, their athleticism allows them to recover. Natural selection has chosen those that can recover because those that couldn't were eaten by predators.

This can be a problem on the trail as some footings, crossings, or obstacles are different from their daily lives in the pasture, paddock, arena, or stall. Depending upon speed, terrain, and the severity of the stumble, the rider may not recover. Hence the need for this category.

The goal of training for this category is to teach the horse **purposeful footfalls**. Only when the horse visually identifies obstacles can it have purposeful footfalls. Ideally, the horse looks down at the path, identifies the obstacle(s), and either avoids them or carefully steps upon them. Therefore, we don't want to rush our horses over obstacles. Instead: stop, allow visual or smell investigation, time for the horse's small brain to compute the route, and gently urge forward movement. **A horse should NEVER race through an obstacle!**

It is simple to create an obstacle course. Arrange objects along a path about 4 feet wide and to 10 feet long. Length, of course, depends on the number of objects. Start with few and end with many. Gather any or all of the following:

- tarps (folded)

- rocks

- cans

- plastic bottles

- ropes, buckets

- spare saddle parts

- bags that can be weighted down

- fence posts

- tires

- logs

- sticks

- Etc.

Use your imagination to select any and all objects that will cause the horse to consider its footfalls. On a lead, introduce the horse to the obstacle course. Do not push him faster than his curiosity allows. Start with just one or two objects if you have any doubt as to the reaction of the horse. Remember: slow introduction to any challenge always yields the best results.

- Lead the horse to the obstacle course

- Allow him time to stop and recognize the challenge

- Move close enough for him to smell the first object

- Give time for him to investigate

- Stay beside not in front of, take a step forward while holding them in the middle of the course (some horses will want to jump over new obstacles)

- Observe reaction

- Retreat, hold the position, or continue down course, dependent upon horse's reaction

- Pressure, release, reward, repeat (PR3)

Scenarios:

RETREAT
If the horse refuses, shies, or pulls back, begin again by walking him backwards until he settles. Begin the challenge from the beginning. Even better, if the handler recognizes that the horse is going to refuse, intervene preemptively so that the "refusal" or reaction is prevented. This will expedite the lesson. The handler needs to monitor the horse to determine if it is better to retreat (before the horse decides to), to hold the position,

Simple obstacle course littered with debris that will be encountered on a trail.

Walk the horse through the obstacle course to teach slow, methodical pace. It is safer for the rider/handler to introduce the challenge from the ground. Add obstacles increasing the degree of difficulty with each successful crossing.

This horse demonstrates excellent obstacle recognition and careful footfalls.

This horse is recognizing obstacles and planning route around/through.

By adding obstacles to the course, the need for recognition increases.

or to continue. Remember, our goal is to build confidence.

HOLD POSITION

If the horse lightly refuses, but you think the re-action is mild enough to overlook, allow the horse more time to investigate. Retreat here if the horse was concerned but remained willing. Retreat to reward 'the try.' On the next approach, the horse will have more confidence to proceed further. After 30 more seconds, apply pressure by asking the horse to move forward. Now, you will either continue forward or begin again.

CONTINUE

If the horse calmly approaches the obstacle course and is willing to proceed, keep it moving down the course. One of two things will happen: the horse will finish the course without stress, or he will react to something further down the course. That reaction will dictate the handler's next move, either continue adding obstacles to the course and repeat, or begin again.

The great thing about this challenge is that you can continue to add obstacles and stress to the course for as long as your imagination will allow. A final goal might be to fill the entire course with tires. Leading up to the tires covering the entire course, you can distribute them randomly while the horse masters the challenge. Once you believe the horse is ready for the big challenge, place a dozen or more (as many as you can beg, borrow or steal) completely covering the course and lead your horse through them. This is an ultimate challenge as the horse must step in or on the tires with purposeful footfalls. The goal is for him to place each hoof inside the center tire opening for the entire length of the course.

Once you've trained the horse to complete the obstacle course with careful footfalls, it is time to mount and repeat the process. Remove the more complex obstacles and begin the mounted part of the challenge as you did the above.

Success is declared when you can cautiously ride through an obstacle course with a relaxed horse with purposeful footfalls. Most horses learn this challenge quickly.

Summary:

1. Purposeful footfalls are the goal for our trail horses.

2. By challenging the horse with ground obstacles, we can train for purposeful footfalls.

3. Add objects (stress) and length to the course as progress is made.

4. The goal is to have the horse look at each object and make good decisions on where to step.

Pre-purchase tips:

- In the pre-purchase bucket that you take to the interview, you can add empty cans and plastic bottles. You will already have a tarp.

- Ask the owners if they are comfortable with you testing the horse with a simple obstacle course.

- Find rocks and sticks at the barn where the horse lives.

- Ask the owner to tell you what you can use to create a makeshift obstacle course.

- Lay-out a simple obstacle course.

- Lead the horse to and through the course.

- Score accordingly.

10

Ground Manners — Saddling

10) Saddling

0 – Will not accept pad or saddle, becomes
dangerous if challenged

1 – Accepts saddle but nervous

2 – No visible reaction to saddling

The sooner you can start desensitizing a horse
to blankets and objects on its back, the sooner
you will be able to introduce a saddle and a rider.
Most horses purchased as trail horses will already
be accepting of the saddle. However, some horses
still flinch and move when a saddle is placed on
their back. One of my horses, Nash, a nine-year-
old Tennessee Walking Horse with thousands of
trail miles, still thinks it is a mountain lion, not a
saddle, you are attempting to place on his back.
On extended trail riding trips, it takes several days
of saddling and riding for him to stop reacting to
the saddle. If more than a few days go by without

saddling, we are right back to a pouncing mountain lion. The point here is that not all horses
become completely desensitized to the saddling
process. It hurts their T.R.A.I.L.S. score, but does
not make them bad horses. An odd fact about
Nash is that he does not move a muscle when
the rider mounts. He is my very best horse when
being mounted, but the very worst for saddling. It
seems to me that a human climbing on your back
would resemble a mountain lion more than the
saddle, but what do I know? Strange!

Like with all other new challenges, a slow introduction to saddling is ideal. Within the first few
days of a horse's life, you can begin placing towels,
bags, and pads on their backs. My first-born was
introduced to all these things and more. By a few
months old, we could place barn cats, toddlers, or
both on his back. He was so desensitized to things
on his back that he readily accepted a saddle and a
rider when the time came.

If a more mature horse is still skittish, further desensitization is in order to blanketing, saddling, or girth tightening. For a horse that accepts the saddle but does it in a less than graceful way, repetition is the solution. At your barn, tie the horse to the normal tacking area. Plan to spend as long as it takes to place your tack on the horse until no reaction is noted. Start with the blanket or pad. The process may take dozens of repetitions for the physical reaction to cease. Once you declare success, move on to the saddle. Again, this will take as many repetitions as it will take for any reaction to cease. Do not rush and do not become frustrated. Horses learn more slowly when they sense handler frustration. Frustration is a big distraction for their little brains.

To declare success, there can be no visual reaction to the blanket, pad, or saddle as it is lifted and placed on the back. Many horses regress overnight or over a week without reinforcement. Expect that perfect acceptance of the saddling will be an ongoing process. Each new saddling challenge should show a reduction in reaction to the stimulus. Many horse owners do not mind a little reaction to blanketing or saddling. If you fall into this group, there is no harm. If a horse's reaction to this challenge seems to be getting worse or they never really become desensitized to it, make sure they are not injured; or consider that your saddle may not fit properly. Consult your veterinarian if you have any suspicion that your horse may be in pain, causing the reaction to the saddle. Also, there are professional saddle fitters. They may be difficult to find in some parts of the country. Many large animal vets can help you with saddle fitting, as well. As most trail horses mature, they usually become completely accepting of the saddling process.

Some horses are surprised by the first cinch tightening. I have had one mare fall to her knees upon her first cinch tightening. It never occurred to me that this sensation could be so profound as my other horses barely reacted to their first cinch tightening. When she reacted this way, it made me consider that this first tightening compresses their lungs in a way that they feel like they cannot breathe. Many other horses with less handling often violently react by bucking and rearing when they feel that first bit of pressure compressing their chest. Any reaction to girth tightening usually wanes very quickly. However, many horses will bloat (expand their chest with air) to avoid girth tightening. To combat air-bloating, walk them a few steps, and retighten the girth. For some bloaters, you will be shocked that the girth can be tightened another 4-8 inches the second time when the horse is not air-bloating. From years of not being a well-balanced rider, I needed a very tight girth to maintain my balance. Even today, I keep my girths on the tight side.

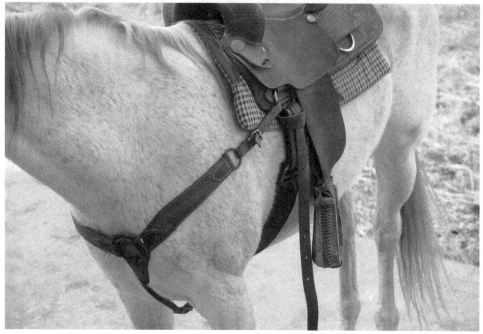

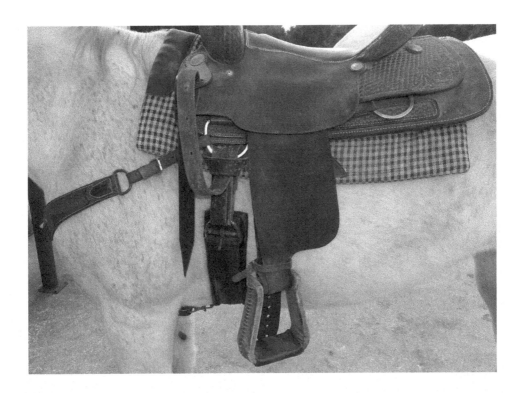

Summary:

1. While not of paramount importance, full acceptance of the saddling process is our goal.

2. Introduce tack slowly to a green horse.

3. Start as early as possible in the horse's life.

4. Repetition is the key to success.

5. Expect some regression for reactive horses.

Pre-purchase tips:

- Ask the owner to saddle the horse while you watch.

- Saddle the horse, yourself.

- Test the horse's reaction with a plastic bag, saddle pad, and/or saddle.

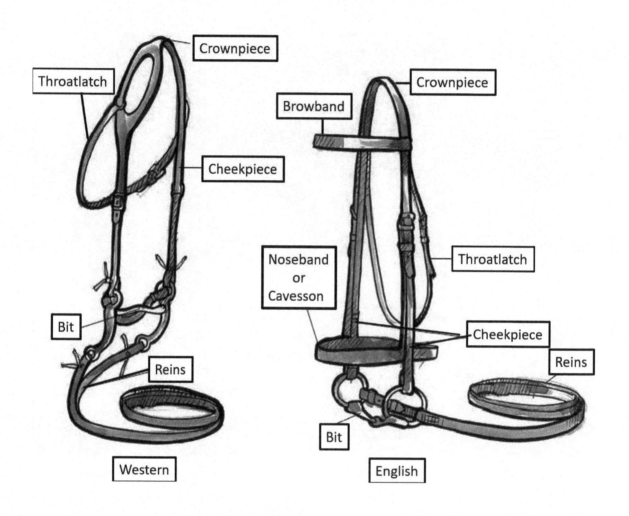

Crownpiece

Throatlatch

Cheekpiece

Bit

Reins

Western

Browband

Crownpiece

Noseband
or
Cavesson

Throatlatch

Cheekpiece

Reins

Bit

English

11

Ground Manners — Bridling

11) Bridling

0 – Will not bridle
1 – Accepts bridle but is slightly uncooperative, avoids bridle
2 – Bridles easily

I am always surprised and impressed at how easily most horses take to bridling. The above scoring explanations are self-explanatory. Unless the bit is too aggressive or the horse has tooth issues, most horses accept this challenge quickly. Once the bridle is in place, some horses appear to feel claustrophobic and move backward. As stated before, slow introduction of this new challenge is the best method for success. See opposite page for the parts of a bridle.

There are hundreds of bits available for purchase. Though there are only two basic categories, hundreds of variations have been invented for the wide range use between disciplines and preferences. There are several books dedicated to horse bits and

their uses. If you have an interest in this area, you will find more information than you will ever need in these books:

The Ultimate Book of Horse Bits: What They Are, What They Do, How They Work, Emily Esterson (2010)

The Complete Book of Bits and Bitting, Edwards, Elwyn H. (2004)

Mouths and Bits, Toni Webber (1998)

All horses need to be halter broken before introduction to the bit and bridle (See Part Four, Chapter One, **Haltering**). This category measures the amount of cooperation by the horse for bridling. Most horses require a human cue of the thumb in the mouth to initiate opening for the bit. The only difficult part of bridling is getting the bit in the horse's mouth. See the following pages for the proper bridling sequence:

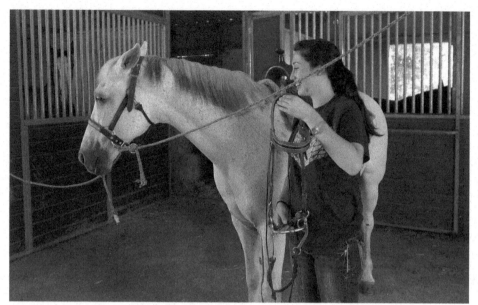

Step 1. Tie horse and ready the bridle.

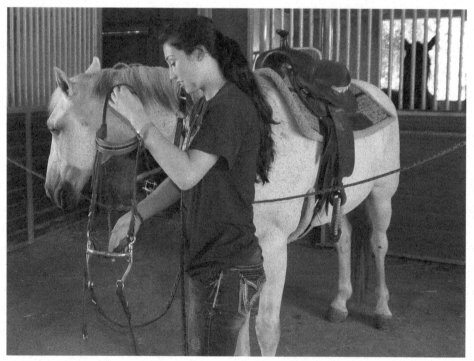

Step 2. Move halter down to neck.

Step 3. Position bridle and align head.

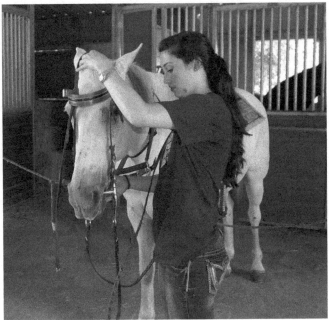

Step 4. Cue horse to open mouth, insert bit.

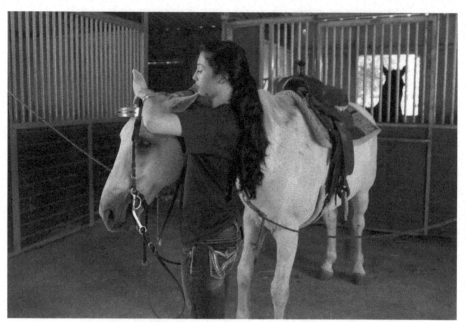

Step 5. Secure crownpiece behind ears.

Step 6. Position nose and brow bands.

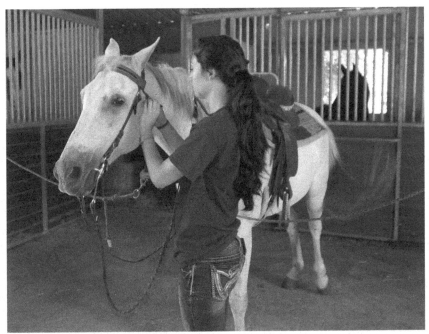

Step 7. Buckle the throatlatch.

Step 8. Bridling completed.

Types of Bits

1) Direct Pressure Bits without Leverage:

    a. Snaffle bit — Uses a bit ring at the mouthpiece to apply direct pressure on the bars, tongue, and corner of the mouth.

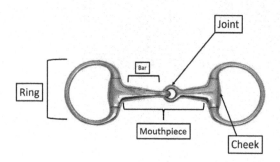

2) Leverage Bits:

    a. Curb bit — A bit that uses a type of lever called a shank that puts pressure not only on the mouth but also on the poll and chin groove. The longer the shank, the more the leverage.

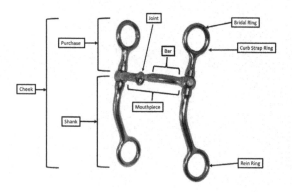

b. Pelham bit — A single curb bit with two sets of reins attached to rings at the mouthpiece and end of the shank. Partly combines snaffle and curb pressure. Often used for Polo horses. Trail riders should never need this bit.

c. Kimblewicke or Kimberwicke — A hybrid design that uses a slight amount of mild curb leverage on a bit ring by use of set rein placement on the ring. Often used in ponies with youth riders.

3) Accessory:

    a. Curb chain — a flat chain attached to the curb strap ring of the bit. Curb chains add additional control through applied pressure in the chin groove.

b. Curb strap — a thin leather or nylon strap attached to the curb strap ring of the bit. Curb straps add additional control through pressure in the chin groove. Curb straps are less aggressive than curb chains.

4) **Bitless:**
   a. **Hackamore or Bitless Bridle** — headgear for horses that exerts control with a noseband rather than a bit. Bitless bridles resemble halters.
   b. **Mechanical Hackemore** — only falls into this category because it doesn't have an in-the-mouth bit. This bridle has shanks for leverage and a curb chain to provide a squeeze between the noseband and the chain when the rider pulls back on the reins.

Most trail riders use a simple snaffle bit (see picture). It is the least harsh of the bits. One level up from this is the snaffle bit with a curb chain (see picture). Light pressure will only engage the bit while firmer pressure pulls the curb chain against the chin area so that more leverage is applied to the bit. For more spirited horses, a curb bit for additional control may be in order. The next level bit for even more control is the snaffle with a shank and a curb chain. This is all the control most trail riders will ever need. The shanks provide leverage that will apply pressure between the bit and the curb chain. It will require some experimentation to find the proper bit for your horse.

Those horses with a soft or sensitive mouth need to be brought along even slower. In extreme cases, some horses with soft mouths may be better suited to a Hackamore (bitless bridle) rather than even the lightest pressure bit. Many riders and experts believe a bitless system will yield better results while being kinder to the horse. The only disadvantage is that there is very little leverage for

stopping a runaway horse. I recommend whichever system that works best for each combination of horse and rider.

Summary:

1. Halter break before introducing a bit.

2. Introduce the least aggressive bit, first.

3. Through trial and error, determine what level of the bit is appropriate for the horse.

4. Experiment with a bitless headstall and evaluate the level of control.

Pre-purchase tips:

- Ask the owner to bridle the horse and observe.
- Bridle the horse, yourself (if the owner had success).
- Inquire about the horse's bit history.
- Ask about any past or present dental problems.
- Inquire about the frequency of tooth floating. Most tooth problems are easily resolved.

Rider at the "point of no return".

12

Ground Manners — Mounting Aids

12) Mounting Aids

0 – Will not approach mounting aid

1 – Will walk past mounting aid but will not stop next to it

2 – Impatiently stands near aid then moves away

3 – Stands next to aid until rider mounts block, then moves away

4 – Stands quietly at the correct distance, holds until released

Like the previous chapter, I believe this to be a very important category for anyone that struggles to mount their horse from the ground. There are numerous reasons you may need to dismount while on the trail: bathroom breaks, dropped glove, retighten saddle, adjust tack, another rider needs help, trail obstacles that prevent passage, water break, food break, etc. Of course, for some riders,

the issue of remounting creates great angst. Either solution from this chapter should prove to be very helpful.

I will use the term "point of no return" in this chapter. I define this as that moment when your leg (usually the right leg), not in the stirrup, crosses the horse's spine. From this point, you cannot abort the mounting process. Your momentum will carry you over the back of the horse and, aborting such an act is not possible. Just as you cross the point of no return, you are wholly dependent on all the training that horse has ever had, the mood that it is in that day, the weather, other animals and people, and about a dozen other factors completely out of your control. Of all the acts we do with our horses, this is the focal point. Except in unusual or extenuating circumstances, this is the most vulnerable time for the rider.

For this category, you will need to be somewhat creative as to what qualifies as a mounting aid. I

Mounting Block

Improvised mounting block- vehicle

Improvised mounting block- bucket

Improvised mounting block- picnic table

have seen people use a mounting block (preferred), curb, tree stump, rock, trailer fender, car bumper, picnic table, fallen tree, 5-gallon bucket, railroad tie, ATV, mounting stirrup (available in most trail riding magazines), etc. Any stable object that gives the additional height as an advantage to get up on a horse can be used.

This technique can be dangerous for rider and horse. Horses tend to shy away from these objects. And, it is dangerous for the rider attempting to mount when the horse moves away from the object at the point of no return. It can also be dangerous for the horse as some of the objects have sharp edges or points. Therefore, it is strongly encouraged to perfect the use of a mounting aid by using a plastic or rubber mounting block first.

Many times, it is the rider standing on the mounting block, being taller than the horse that frightens the horse. Other times, it is the mounting object itself. Of course, it can be both rider and object. Therefore, desensitizing the horse to the mounting block is a priority.

Spend the necessary time to get the horse to stand comfortably at the appropriate location next to the block. The correct position is as close to the block as possible without touching it. The correct block position is even with the left mounting stirrup.

Position the mounting block and slowly walk the horse towards it. If the horse hesitates, give it a few seconds to recover and attempt to move towards the block again. If continued reluctance is encountered, walk past the block several times. Each time walk a little closer until the horse is accustomed to walking past without hesitation or concern. Once

the horse is comfortable walking close to the block, stop them at or near the block. Continue introduction with this method until the horse will stand quietly beside the block.

Now, you will begin to step up on the first step of the mounting block. Usually, most horses will move away at this point. You will continue to reposition them at the proper location until they tolerate the handler being on all steps (mounting blocks usually have two or three steps). Once the horse has settled, it is usually easier to move the block into the perfect position rather than moving the horse to it.

Once the horse accepts and does not react to the rider on the top step, start putting a foot in the stirrup. Do not commit to your foot being all the way in the stirrup. Instead, just lightly allow the toes of your boot to be near the stirrup. Once again, the horse will want to move away during this part. The progression is to slowly place your foot in the stirrup and hold. Once the horse accepts and does not react to this, start putting weight in the stirrup.

Always be prepared to step off or climb on, whichever seems to be the safest decision. This decision will depend on your horse's tendencies towards flight in learning situations and upon your surroundings. It is always wise to use verbal commands while teaching your horse a new behavior. In this case, repeat, "stand." This will be the verbal cue to stand still. A horse that scores a "2" in this category will cooperate throughout the challenge and hold still until released after mounting.

One alternative way to start this process is to begin introducing the mounting block while the horse is tied for grooming. Start with the block at least ten feet away from the horse. Place it in

Step 1. Frightened horse moving away from the mounting block.

Step 2. Horse and mounting block properly positioned.

Step 3. Move the mounting block into the final position.

Step 4. Begin putting test pressure with foot partially in the stirrup.

Step 5. Horse stands still while rider mounts and finds right-side stirrup.

Step 6. Successful mounting, horse obediently waiting for the cue to move.

front of the horse, so it can be seen with both eyes. Slowly bring the block towards the horse. Once the block is close enough for the horse to smell it, leave it there during grooming. Later that day, or at another session, move the block to one side where it can be seen with one eye. If introduced slowly enough, the horse will quickly lose interest in the block. Be careful; if introduced too quickly, while they are tied, you could invoke a flight response making it dangerous for horse and handler. Mounting aid tolerance is usually a fairly fast process. Once the horse accepts the proximity of the block, you are halfway to your goal.

As always, some horses pick this up rather quickly, while others need constant reinforcement. Either through the "Park" position discussed below or through mounting aid tolerance, you will need to make sure the horse is consistently adept at either or both maneuvers if you plan to trail ride for any length of time.

Summary:

1. Desensitize horse to the mounting block

2. Desensitize horse to standing at the correct position

3. Desensitize horse to increased handler elevation on steps

4. Desensitize horse to rider putting weight in the stirrup

5. Use verbal commands

6. The horse is relaxed and holds the position until released

Pre-purchase tips:

- Ask the owner how easily the horse is mounted.

- Ask the owner to mount the horse.

- Mount the horse (if the owner was successful).

- Ask the owner to move a mounting block next to the horse and observe.

- A return, unannounced visit may reveal that the horse was exercised or drugged for the prior visit.

PARKING

Another very helpful method to assist in mounting your horse is teaching the horse to "Park." *Parking* is when a horse is trained to elongate or stretch to bring the stirrup closer to the ground for mounting and dismounting (see Part Four, Chapter 14, **Mounting**). Parking is unique to a couple of breeds. Mainly, Tennessee Walking Horse show horses were taught to park when evaluated by the judges. This elongated stance can be useful for riders who have difficulty mounting their horse without a block, tree stump, curb, or nearby picnic table. Because it is very difficult for many riders to dismount and mount on the trail, the "park" position can be very useful when you must stop on the trail and need to mount-up before continuing the ride. When done properly, this position brings the stirrup as much as six inches closer to the ground. Additionally, it places the horse in a position where it is more difficult for them to walk-off or move during mounting.

The technique can usually be taught in less than five sessions. Start with the horse's front legs. Stand adjacent to the front left shoulder. By pushing the horse's left shoulder to the right, it puts most of the weight on the right leg. Place your left foot against the back of the horse's left hoof. Push the horse's left leg forward a couple of inches, repeat the word "park" out loud and hold it until the horse puts weight back on the left hoof. The process will take a few tries to get the horse to leave its hoof in the slightly extended position. Once the horse submits to this extended left leg position, you will start to walk to the right side to repeat the process. Initially, the horse will reposition its leg back to a normal position while you start to walk around it. With persistence, you should be able to get your horse to assume this new position with front legs extended in less than an hour. This is a good stopping position for the first session. Reinforce this position in your second session. If your horse seems to be a fast learner, you can begin the back legs at session two or wait until session three. Be careful to mind your feet to avoid being stepped upon.

With each subsequent session, you should be able to extend the position of the front feet more forward. Some horses can be taught to stretch so far that you wonder if their feet will not slide apart like a person doing the splits.

To perfect the park position, the back legs need to be in the same general position extended backward away from the normal standing position. The horse will want to spread its feet from front to back to compensate for the change in balance you are introducing by manipulating their front legs. You will not obtain a lower mounting position if your horse has staggered back legs. So, when teaching the park position in later sessions, you should start lining up the back legs before you start extending the front legs. By moving the horse backward with the halter or bridle, you can stop them when the back hooves are on that same perpendicular plane. When you start with the back legs in later sessions, they must maintain that position while you are manipulating their front leg position. It is surprising how quickly they can learn this maneuver.

You may consider starting with the back legs during session one. There is no harm in this. It all depends on what sequence works best for your horse. Once the horse has achieved the proper position, say aloud, "stand." This will be the horse's verbal cue to hold that position.

Once the front and back legs are in the proper position, you can then encourage your horse to stretch further. Once they have perfected this position, you will move on to verbal commands only. It is acceptable to squeeze them at the withers and say "park," so they have verbal and non-verbal commands. Use this position when mounting on the trail. Most horses can be trained from the saddle to perform this maneuver, which facilitates getting out of the saddle and on to the ground more gracefully.

To score a "2" in this category, the horse must park on command and hold it until released. Some horse people believe this position to be a strain on the horse's spine and tendons. Unless the rider is over 30% the horse's weight (1000-pound

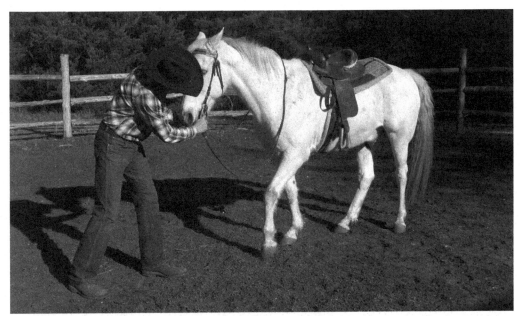

Step 1. Position back hooves, first.

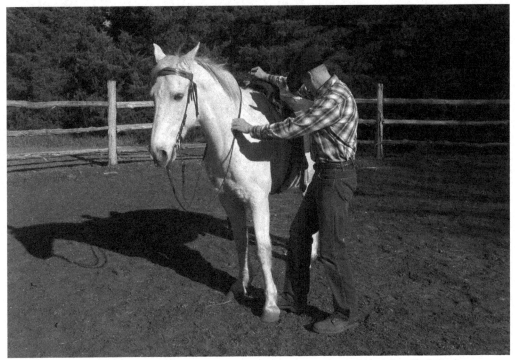

Step 2. Push horse away and extend left leg forward, say, "woah" or "hold".

Step 3. Once left leg is extended, pull horse towards you and extend right leg, say, "woah" or "hold."

Step 4. Continue that process while encouraging more stretch with both front legs.

Step 5. One a good extension is achieved, say, "woah" or "hold."

Step 6. Notice how much closer to the ground the mounting stirrup.

Step 7. Continue to say, "woah" or "hold" while starting the mounting process. Success is achieved when rider mounts and horse holds "Parked" position until released.

horse, 300-pound rider + tack), I do not believe this to be detrimental to the horse's musculoskeletal health. Moreover, male horses often assume this position to urinate while under saddle. Once your horse learns this maneuver, you may want to reinforce it a few times per week for the first month or two. After the horse perfects this, you may only need to use it on the rare occasions when on a long trail ride or when you must dismount to answer Mother Nature's calls. Using this position once or twice per month or even more frequently should be perfectly acceptable. Around your riding facility and at the trailheads, you should use a mounting aid when possible.

This technique may not be appealing to some horse owners. If you disagree with this category but still struggle to mount from the ground, you may consider an extension stirrup. The preferred brand is E-Z Up Extender Co. for its ease and safety. There are several others on the market, as well. These mounting aids place the extension stirrup three to four inches lower to the ground. For tall horses, you may need to use the stirrup extension and teach them to park for mounting on the trail. All riders who struggle with mounting from the ground know to what I refer!

Summary:

1. Start teaching the park position as early as possible.

2. Start with either front or back legs.

3. Teach the verbal command throughout the process by saying "park" aloud with each request.

4. Use with discretion as constant use may cause back issues with the horse.

Pre-purchase tip:

- Very few horses have been trained to park. Consider this a bonus if the horse can do it.

- With calm horses, you may be able to play with the position of their hoof position at the first visit. If a horse allows you to push on them and rearrange their hoof position using your feet, it is a good bet that they can learn to park fairly quickly.

13

Ground Manners — Readiness to Ride/Longeing

13) Readiness to ride/ Longeing (Lunging, Lungeing)

0 – Uncooperative after 30 minutes of longeing
1 – Requires 10-29 minutes longeing prior to riding
2 – Requires 5-10 minutes longeing prior to riding
3 – Requires 1-4 minutes of longeing prior to riding
4 – No longeing necessary, ready to ride immediately after saddling

As mentioned before, one aspect of trail riding rarely discussed is the actual act of riding. If your intention is to ride your horse, which I hope it is, how quickly it is "trail ready" for every ride is important. Whenever your horse is away from its barn or normal surroundings, it will be more anxious. Combine a new location with new stimuli, a good night's rest in the stall, perhaps cool weather, and some morning grain, and it is likely your horse will be in a highly excitable state. This is a point to strongly consider when interviewing horses for purchase.

I have owned horses that jig, prance, and crow-hop if you mount them before they have been exercised. This behavior improves with age, but the rider must be able to ride out the excitable state for a few seconds or minutes before the horse is reasonably calm. When owning younger horses (2- to 8-year-olds), this natural calming process may take years. It complicates the process if other horses in the group are in a similar state.

This chapter and the next (Chapter 14, Mounting) are dedicated to safe mounting practice and teaching the horse to cooperate with the process.

Longeing- def. (US English, classical spelling),

Excitable horse after mounting

Line Longeing

(Lunging- informal US spelling) or **lungeing** (UK English, informal USA) is a technique for <u>training horses</u>, where a horse is asked to work at the end of a long line and respond to commands from a handler on the ground which holds the line. Longeing is performed in a large circle with the horse traveling around the outside edge of a real or imaginary ring with the trainer in the middle.

Longeing can be a useful tool in preparing your horse to ride (see Longeing section below). However, if it takes an excessive amount of time (more than ten minutes) for the horse to be trail-ready, this can become a big problem. Horses are athletes. If you longe them for ten or more minutes a few times per week, they will become more and more fit, and the calming effect will diminish. Therefore, only longe the horse minimally to obtain the calming effect.

Longeing is considered an exercise in respect. Because, as stated above, most horses are so naturally fit that you cannot fatigue them in a longeing session, the longeing technique is a simple way to remind them of who is in charge. If I perceive them to be especially uncooperative during saddling or mounting, I lead them to the round pen for longeing. I keep heavy, constant pressure on them to canter or gallop for as long as it takes for them to stop and face me. If they have sufficiently disappointed me with unruly behavior prior to this session, I will firmly make them go around the opposite direction for the same amount of time. Depending upon my level of perception of their mood, this may continue for three or four directions. I can assure you that they are "fatigued" and "respectful" at the conclusion of the exercise. So, whether your goal is fatigue or respect, mission accomplished. Casual longeing can be considered a technique for respect, while aggressive longeing is more for attitude adjustment and fatigue. Please feel free to interchange the words "fatigue" and "relax" in the remaining paragraphs.

As trail riders, most of us want to ride at a variety of destinations. Many times, you will find yourself at locations where the footing is not good for longeing; you will not have access to a round pen, nor will you have enough room to longe on a line. In this situation, you will be unable to fatigue your horse enough to allow an easy beginning to the trail ride. Some horses are impossible to mount if they have not been adequately fatigued. This is especially significant for riders who need a horse to stand perfectly still when they mount. Then, even if you mount successfully, the horse is in such an excitable state that staying on may be a challenge. So, for the less athletic riders, you must find a horse that is calm enough or mature enough that they will stand still for mounting in all scenarios without the need for longeing (see Part Four, Chapter 14, **Mounting**).

Unless you have a consistently calm horse, it is highly advisable for all trail riders to learn the art of line longeing. Line longeing will allow you to fatigue your horse in almost any setting. When done correctly and safely, it will facilitate a more enjoyable trail ride. When available, round pen longeing is the most convenient for the average owner. However, to be prepared for any unforeseen event, it is advisable to become adept at line longeing (see Longeing Technique, on the following pages).

The ideal horse is calm right out of the pasture or stall and should need very little, if any, exercise before heading out on a trail ride. Younger horses and more spirited horses may need up to ten minutes of exercise before mounting and riding.

A horse that stands still for mounting is worth a higher price tag.

Most times, your trail horse will mellow with age, and this problem will be minimized. The main root of the problem with antsy horses is that they have never been trained to be patient. I am not a fan of tying up horses for extended periods. However, some high energy, impatient, poorly mannered horses need this technique (see Part Four, Chapter 3, **Tying**).

It is expected and appropriate for all trail horses to stand still until the rider mounts, places both feet in stirrups, gathers the reins, and is ready for the horse to move forward. Then, and only then, is the horse released with a verbal or non-verbal cue. If we agree that this is the goal, how do we get there?

Frequent saddling and mounting will help expedite your success at getting your trail horse trail-ready for each ride. I suggest having days where you do nothing but saddle and mount in a controlled environment (discussed, in detail in the next chapter, Mounting).

The owner/trainer must have zero tolerance for movement during the mounting process. Most horses will learn to stand still for mounting quickly if you take the time to train them. Again, consistency is the key. On your training day, you may mount and dismount dozens of times. Do not complete the mounting exercise if the horse moves at all. Tug or pull back on the reins and say aloud, "Whoa" or "stand" so that the horse knows the verbal cue for it to stand still. I suggest making the horse stand relaxed without movement every time you mount. During that minute or two of standing still, you can practice repeated flexion techniques (Chapter 15) before ever asking the horse to move forward. If you are not physically fit enough to complete this exercise, or any other training session, find a trainer or person in your horse community who can teach your horse to stand still for mounting. This is money well spent. I cannot reiterate enough that your personal safety is the primary focus here and throughout all horse-related activities.

Once your horse perfects the lesson of standing still for mounting, you can decide whether to teach it to "Park." "Parking" is an advanced technique to facilitate easy mounting on the trail. It is a rarely discussed horse training technique that can make trail riding much more pleasurable for our senior and less athletic riders (see Parking section in Chapter 12, Mounting Aids).

Summary:

1. Excitable horses are dangerous when being mounted.

2. Longeing is an effective means of fatiguing the horse enough to be quietly mounted.

3. Learn to line-longe before you need it.

4. Prepare your horse for quiet mounting long before you take them to a new location.

Pre-purchase tips:

- Ask yourself if the horse seems ready to go on a trail ride once it is saddled.

- Ask the owner to attempt to mount the recently saddled horse.

- Ask the owner to demonstrate longeing either on a line or in the round pen or preferably, both.

- Attempt to longe the horse yourself (if the owner has success).

- So, how do you ask the right questions or make the proper observations when interviewing a new horse prospect? Ask the current owner how long it takes the horse to be trail-ready. The previous owner may have never considered the above points or be such a good rider that they enjoyed the first few, frantic minutes on the trail with this horse. Again, I strongly recommend a potential buyer request the horse be left in their pasture or stall before they visit for the first time or subsequent visits. This will allow you the opportunity to see a variety of behaviors that have not been suppressed by exercise or drugs before you arrive. Unannounced visits will also give you more opportunity to evaluate the horse's true behavior. If the owner allows you to groom, saddle, and mount the horse, you will have a much better idea regarding the compat-

ibility of you and said horse. If the owner does not allow you to interact with the horse at this level, you may want to consider why. When shopping for a horse, review the entire interview process from Part Two.

Longeing Techniques

Longeing is a very useful training technique. This method uses the horse's natural flight instinct constructively. When the flight instinct is engaged, the horse will flee or avoid pressure by running from it. A horse owner or trainer can use longeing as a means of desensitizing a horse to challenges, teaching controlled gaits and transitions, fatiguing overzealous horses, safe saddle acceptance, verbal commands, submission, respect, lead changes and attention. This technique is part of "starting" a horse instead of "breaking" a horse. For most trainers and horse owners, it has become the preferred method of early training. It is a slower, safer process. In the past, it took a pretty brave and skillful rider to mount a green horse and ride out the bucking until it ceased. I do not know too many riders in the hobby world who would be capable of this endeavor. For trainers who are still capable, only a few will resort to this old-fashion method. Mounting an unbroken horse is a very dangerous technique. Even when done well, the rodeo style method will shorten a rider's career. Even the most accomplished cowboys have falls from horses. Aside from the concussion risks, the musculoskeletal system can only take so many accidents. So, longeing has all but replaced rodeo-style breaking of a horse. Most trainers will tell you it is the most used training method.

As with any technique, there is a right way to accomplish it. Inexperienced horses will not know to stay against the rail or at the end of the longe line, and may run towards the handler. I have seen some respond so intensely to the pressure that they try to jump out of the round pen. Some horses tend to kick when pressure is applied behind them. When first started in the round pen, most horses are predictably unpredictable. Therefore, understanding and practicing proper longeing techniques are imperative for safety.

Free Longeing – training or exercising a horse using a circular pattern, in a round pen without a line.

Line Longeing – training or exercising a horse in a circular pattern using a line of 20-30 ft in length (40-60 ft circle).

Short Line Longeing – training or exercising a horse in a smaller circular pattern using a line 6-14 ft in length (12-28 ft circle).

The basic technique for longeing is very similar for any of the three methods above (see description below, modify by method). Because longeing engages a horse's natural survival instinct, they usually learn it very quickly. Controlled longeing takes a little longer, but once the horse understands the drill, most are eager to participate. Longeing can be done on a line or in a round pen, or on a line in a round pen. Either way, the horse will be moving in a circular pattern. This

Honor the kick zone when short-line longeing.

allows the trainer to be in relative proximity to the horse at faster than normal speeds. Line longeing, especially on a shorter line, when done incorrectly, can be dangerous because the horse's hindquarters can be very close to the handler when changing directions.

Learning the art of line longeing can take some time to master. Because safety comes first, it is best to have someone show you the technique in person. Watching a DVD may be your only alternative, and there are plenty of those to purchase. However, unless you have great coordination and patience, it is best learned through a professional, as it can be a dangerous and difficult technique.

Line longeing begins with a horse and a longe line. A longe line is a line, tether, or rope of varying lengths. Most people start the longeing process with a fairly long line of approximately 25 feet. At one end of the line is a clip that is attached to the center ring of the halter. Begin by walking the horse around the circle that you want it to follow on its own. After a few circles, you can start to put some distance between you and the horse.

Step 1. Horse moves-off of hand signal.

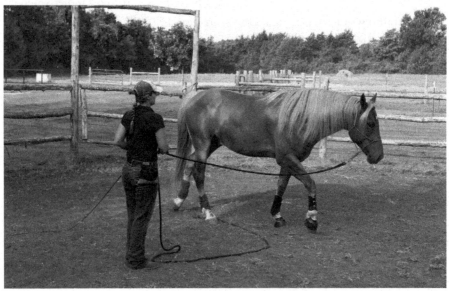

Step 2. Initiate left clockwise circle.

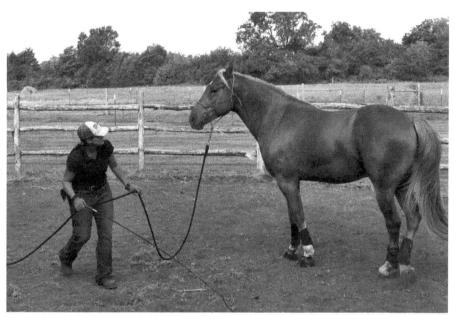

Step 3. Initiate with approaching hind-quarters

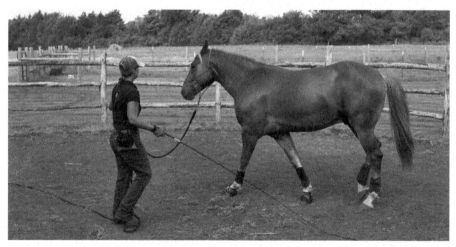

Step 4. Initiate counter-clockwise circle

Step 5. Once movement begins, encourage from behind.

Step 6. Horse at outer distance, continue

You will always keep the slightest pressure on the halter. This will keep the horse's head tipped towards you, and the hindquarters tipped away. At first, the horse will try to stay near your shoulder where you have trained it to be when leading. With an extended arm, create some distance between you and it. Walk in the same direction at the same pace as you did when leading the horse in a circle. Once the horse starts to follow at arm's length, you can begin to put a little more distance between you and it. Soon, the horse will sense that it is outside your control and will walk or run away. At this juncture, you will keep slight pressure on the halter to make it move in that same circular path. Horses that are veterans of longeing only need the slightest prompt from the trainer to head in the correct direction. The handler either points in the direction he/she chooses or looks at the hindquarters as a prompt for the horse to go one way or the other (see adjacent pages). For lazy horses, you may need to encourage them from behind by using a whip or a hand motion aimed at their hindquarters.

Whichever technique you choose, the fatigue process will not take long. Once fatigued, they are much more cooperative. Our goal is to get them to turn their attention on us and wait for cues for what we want them to do. When you see the inside ear turned towards you, you have their attention. Conversely, usually in the beginning and when excited, they will not be listening to you, literally or figuratively. Both ears will be forward or one ear forward while the other ear is turned outwardly. When not focused on you, they are listening for their pasture mates to cry out

for them, distracted by something near them, or scanning for predators. We want their focus on us. After they grow accustomed to the area of longeing or the process of longeing, it is much easier to get their focus on the handler.

Round pen longeing (free longeing) is safer and easier, but you give up some control. The initial learning process is similar. With a lead rope and halter, take the horse in the round pen and walk them along the rail. Use the same technique as when leading. Go in both directions. Like people, horses are right- or left-side dominant. Most horses will perform better in one direction than the other. Once you determine which direction the horse is weakest, work that direction twice as much as the dominant one. You want the horse to stay against the rail unless invited to come towards you. Early on, most horses will not know what to do when untied in a round pen. If they start to move away from you, you can allow them to continue in that direction. I have found that most horses need to be frightened into initiating the longeing process. Here is the technique:

1. Release horse from the lead rope.

2. The horse will either stay near the handler or start to move off.

3. If they stay near the handler, walk away. If they follow, turn back towards them and say, "whoa."

4. If they still want to follow the handler, you will need to discourage this by increasing the distance quickly or by making clucking sounds and/or hand/arm gestures shooing them away. This is usually enough to get the separation needed to begin the longeing process. Apply pressure to encourage separation in whichever direction they go. Proceed to #5, below.

5. Once the horse is moving away from you, apply forward pressure by following them at a safe distance from slightly behind. This is the forward motion from pressure that elicits the flight response. Some horses have been raised so gently and have so little fear or respect from their handlers that they may require pressure from a whip being waved behind them or some aggressive movement towards the hindquarters. For the lazy or fearless horses, constant pressure may be necessary. For spirited or easily frightened horses, no pressure is required.

6. Work the horse in that direction until they voluntarily stop to face you. This is the first sign of submission or an attitude change. Veteran horses may stop before the submission or attitude change because they learn that stopping and facing the trainer signals the goal or end of the longeing session. For these savvy horses, the handler must recognize the difference between an early, false submission and a real submission. Most

horses are lazy and learn very quickly that stopping is their goal, even if our goal has not been reached.

7. Once the horse stops and faces the handler, it is time to encourage them to go in the opposite direction. This can be accomplished with the same clucking sound, saying "reverse," or aggressive hand/arm gesture, as done in #5 above.

8. Work the horse in this direction until they stop and face you.

9. Release pressure by taking a few steps backward. If the horse starts walking towards you, it is a good indication that you have temporarily gained their attention and that they recognize you as their Alpha Leader. If they do not come towards you, start the longeing process over in the opposite direction. Continue until they stop and face you.

10. Eventually, the horse will stop and face you on its own, or you will need to decide how much longeing will produce the desired result. Experience is the best teacher, but because horses' cardiovascular systems recover quickly, err on the side of more longeing instead of less.

11. If the horse is anything other than calm and cooperative, the desired outcome has not been accomplished. Repeat the steps above until the desired outcome has been accomplished.

Step 1. Using the horse's flight response, push them to the rail of the pen.

Step 2. Many horses self longe. Once at the rail they will run for a short time. No pressure is required.

Step 3. Continue exercise until the horse stops to face the handler.

Step 4. The horse will eventually stop and face the trainer. The interval varies with each horse and can vary daily.

Step 5. Release pressure and invite the horse to come to the handler.

Step 6. After reward, begin walking away from the horse.

Step 7. A submissive horse usually follows the handler after adequate longeing. Give the horse two chances to fail. If it fails the second time, return to longeing.

Step 8. After proper longeing, the horse should follow you obediently.

12. Eventually, the horse will either tire or submit. When the horse has turned to face you, and you have decided that its attitude is correct, invite the horse to come to the middle of the round pen. Early in training, this may require that you back up a couple steps. Later, you will not need to back up to release pressure. A slight change in the handler's body language (aggressive to relaxed) is all that is necessary to give the cue to come hither.

13. Once the horse comes all the way to the trainer, reward the behavior.

14. Now, begin walking to the rail of the round pen. The horse should follow. If it doesn't, go back and reward then walk away towards the rail. The horse should follow. If not, more longeing is required.

15. At some point, the horse will submit completely and begin following the handler around the round pen. This is the goal, a fully relaxed, thinking, and obedient horse.

#15 is our ultimate goal for longeing. Anything less is not deemed a success. Early in training, you can stop at any time when you recognize a change in the horse's disposition.

Short line longeing (6-14') refines the technique further. When using a short longe line, the handler has more immediate and exact control of the horse. When trained properly, the horse is much more responsive to the handler's commands. By being near to the handler, the horse is forced to pay more attention. Instead of a gradual response as on a long line, the horse is expected to react to the handler's commands immediately. Experienced trainers and handlers shorten the longe line even more, sometimes down to 6'. At this distance, being in the wrong position (too close to the hindquarters) can be dangerous. Always use caution and do not shorten the line until you are confident in your skill level and the horse's behavior. There are common patterns for short longe line training (circles, figure 8, starts, and stops, etc.) where the horse learns immediate response from subtle cues, which leads to better communication with the rider. Well executed training on a short line is a beautiful thing to behold.

Free longeing in a round pen can make your horse more respectful and ready to ride. However, learning the art of line longeing may be the single best ground training exercise to learn. If you take the time to learn and refine your skills, it will pay huge dividends for your riding future.

There are numerous videos on the website, www.trails.horse.com

14

Riding — Mounting

14) Mounting

0 – Cannot be mounted

1 – Can be mounted but highly resistant, crow hops or bucks after mounting

2 – Requires two people (one holding, one mounting)

3 – Will not stand still for mounting, walks off, anxious

4 – Will stand for mounting but walks off immediately

5 – Stands for mounting, holds afterward, waits for release

This is a very important chapter for trail riders as we do not always have a place, on the trail, to mount in a controlled way or with a mounting aid. This category evaluates the horse's tolerance of mounting from the ground.

Mounting a horse from the ground should be a quick, fluid-like, and graceful endeavor. Ideal mounting would be described as:

"Place left foot in stirrup, build potential energy (momentum) by explosively pushing off the ground with the right leg, using said momentum to travel up and over the saddle, coming to rest squarely in the center of the horse and saddle, then finding the right stirrup with your right foot while controlling the reins before the horse moves."

Yeah, RIGHT! How many of us can pull this off? Very few! Below, alternatives to "ideal mounting" will be described and discussed.

A horse that is easily mounted, especially for the less athletic, is a great find. Most horses can be trained to be accepting and patient for the mounting process. In Part Four, Chapter 12, **Mounting Aids**, we discussed and defined the horse's behavior leading up to throwing the leg over the horse with the assistance of a mounting aid. This chapter evaluates the horse's behavior when being mounted from the ground, without aids. Once your leg leaves the ground or mounting block and travels over the horse's spine, you have reached "the point of no return." Your horse either stands quietly enough for your foot to find the other stirrup or it doesn't. It takes a pretty good amount of athleticism, coordination, or luck to find that stirrup if the horse is not standing still. Therefore, our goal in this chapter is to train your horse to score a "5" on this challenge.

Most of us have seen the struggles some riders have mounting a horse. For many riders, just the process of mounting can take 5-30 seconds of embarrassing gyrations to pull, climb, shimmy, hoist, crawl, and wiggle onto the saddle. The task is difficult enough when the horse is standing like a statue, but practically impossible if the horse is not cooperating. Each side of a horse's brain is processing information at different speeds and in different ways. When the image of the rider passes from the left eye to the right eye, the brain has forgotten what was happening on the left side. Suddenly, there is something on its back that was not there a few nanoseconds earlier. The severity of the reaction to this event is different for every horse. Some will simply stand and look back until the right brain catches up with the left brain. Mildly reactive horses will start to walk off. Highly reactive horses may explode and enter full rodeo mode. Trainers know this and are always ready for an explosion, especially on a green horse.

That moment called the "point of no return," mentioned above, is a rider's most vulnerable moment. In addition to the visual disparity where the left and right brain are conflicted, there are a number of physical things, especially when mounting from the ground, that can cause a horse to react negatively during mounting: the right foot may brush the rump on the way over, the toe of the right foot may poke the horse on the right side, the heel of the right foot may thump against the right abdomen or hip, the weight shift may startle the horse, the right stirrup may contact the rib cage, and the list of unintentional stimuli goes on. Therefore, it is important that we judge each horse in two different mounting categories (Chapter 12, Mounting Aids, and this chapter, Mounting).

Mounting from the ground for many people over the age of 30 is very difficult. For this reason, I discuss parking at the end of Part 4, Chapter 9. Parking is a very effective technique to help riders mount without a mounting aid. Another solution, an extension stirrup is available, which will bring a secondary stirrup up to four inches closer to the ground. Several brands are available from an actual stirrup that extends and retracts (**E-Z Up Extender Co.** – highly recommended for ease and safety) to add-on stirrup extenders (less costly but

Ground Mounting

Step 1. Place left foot in left stirrup.

Step 2. Build momentum with the right leg to propel yourself over saddle.

Step 3. Allow momentum to carry you to the middle of the saddle.

Step 4. Settle into saddle and find the right stirrup with the right foot.

Step 5. Reposition the reins and situate yourself to release the horse.

potentially dangerous). If you are in a situation where you must mount from the ground, without an aid, try to position your horse in a depression or mount from the downhill (higher than the horse) side.

Horse selection, going back to Book One, is worth mentioning. For many trail riders who struggle with mounting from the ground, it is wise to consider a shorter horse. I would recommend a horse under 15.0 hands. Perhaps even one closer to 14.0 hands may be in order.

Rarely, is enough time spent teaching a horse to stand still during mounting. A horse that has been taught this lesson well is a great horse to find.

Fortunately, teaching a horse to stand only takes persistence.

Whether you dedicate a day to mounting or just have a daily steadfast determination that your horse will stand still for every mounting, it should not take long to teach. Any horse that has been mounted more than a few times quickly recognizes the rider's body language when they decide it is time to mount-up. Some horses flatly refuse and begin turning or side-passing away from the would-be rider. Horses that misbehave during attempted mountings need more time for desensitization to mounting. Several methods will yield good results. The first method is an entire day/

session dedicated to mounting only. This practice should be done in a round pen, arena, or even a smaller pasture. Below is the technique:

1. Saddle the horse as usual. The saddle will need to be tighter than normal.

2. Place nylon halter and lead rope, not a bridle.

3. Tie the horse to a sturdy post or object, preferably on grass or dirt. If concrete is the only option, progress through the challenge slower.

4. Approach horse from the mounting side (Horse's left-side).

5. Use a mounting block if necessary. This will help desensitize the horse to the mounting aid, also.

6. Place your foot in the left stirrup. Observe the reaction. If any movement, say, "whoa." Wait until the horse is still.

7. Repeat step #5 until there is no movement. Begin placing more weight in the stirrup. Observe behavior.

8. Once the horse has demonstrated that it will stand still with a foot and weight in the stirrup, place more weight in the stirrup and lift the other foot off the ground. At this point, the rider's entire weight will be on the horse. If any horse movement, go back to #5 and begin again.

9. Once you can stand in the stirrup without any movement, it is time to throw your right leg over and mount. Do not attempt to place your right foot in the stirrup. Be prepared to dismount quickly if there is any negative reaction. Be judicious with dismounting-without-cause as this can unintentionally train the horse use movement or negative reaction to cause you to dismount. In other words, it is better to stay mounted and allow the horse to settle than to dismount too soon.

10. By this time, the horse should understand and obey your request to stand still. Once the horse has demonstrated that it will stand still while you are mounted, stay mounted for a few minutes. Repeat "stand" to verbally reinforce the horse's need to stay still.

11. Repeat the full mounting process another dozen times to reinforce the positive behavior.

Step 1. Approach horse from left, stand on the block until horse relaxes.

Step 2. Place and hold the foot in stirrup until no reaction.

Step 3. Transfer all your weight to the stirrup and hold. Allow the horse to balance and relax.

Step 4. If horse moves, hold your position until the horse settles or you feel unsafe. You can always repeat the process until horse settles.

Step 5. Once horse settles, maintain your position, then dismount and reward. Repeat this part of the training until there is zero movement.

Step 6. Once you are very confident that the horse understands that you will not tolerate any movement, it is time to mount. If you are athletic enough, you can hold the above position without mounting as an intermediate step in this process.

Step 7. Full mount. Do not enter the right stirrup until you have had repeated success with this step.

Step 8. Once perfected from the left side, repeat for the right side

Step 9. The process is the same without a mounting block.

Step 10. Success is declared when the entire mounting process is completed
without horse movement.

The other methods described below will also reinforce proper horse behavior for mounting:

1. Longe the horse until mild to moderate fatigue. Place saddle and tie the horse somewhere safe. For as long as you can stand it, mount and dismount until no visible reaction is noted.

2. Longe the horse in a round pen until mild to moderate fatigue is noted. In the same round pen, without tying, begin mounting and dismounting. Every time the horse moves or reacts to mounting, longe it around for a minute or two. Repeat until no visible reaction to mounting is noted.

3. Go on a trail ride, or ride away from the barn with the intention of stopping to mount and dismount every five minutes. Spend the entire ride repeating this exercise until no visible reaction to mounting is noted.

4. In an arena, you can line longe to moderate fatigue. Begin a normal arena workout but stop to mount and dismount every time around. Repeat until no visible reaction to mounting is noted.

For impatient riders or refractory horses, you might consider the "short left rein" technique. If you simply can't or won't teach your horse to stand still, a short-left rein will give more control. Just prior to mounting, pull the left rein so

This training technique can be done while riding in a round pen, arena, or on a trail ride.

that your horse's head is turned halfway to the saddle. Alternatively, you can tie the rein to the saddle horn (if you have one). Should the horse decide to move while you are mounting, it will be in a tight left circle, which, while not being ideal, is, at least a "controlled" mounting. This is a potentially dangerous technique that should be practiced prior to mounting.

One other useful technique when you have no other mounting technique options is to mount from a downhill position. Usually, there is a depression in the trail or road where you can position the horse while you mount from a higher

Step 1. Pull horse's head off-center to the left with the left rein.

Step 2. Keep pressure on the left rein while finding stirrup.

Step 3. Continue pressure throughout mounting

Step 4. Do not release pressure until you are settled in the saddle and ready to move forward.

Mounting from an elevated position.

Note the difference of six inches higher when compared to the above
photo.

elevation. In some cases, you can gain six to eight inches of advantage. Conversely, if you attempt to mount uphill (below the horse), you can lose that same amount.

———

I understand that many riders do not have the endurance or athleticism to complete any of the above. This is a time to ask a friend or trainer to help with one or more of the above methods. Especially for the less athletic, a horse that stands still for mounting is very important for safety and convenience. Once a horse develops bad mounting habits, it becomes the norm. It may take a few long sessions to break those old habits. Do whatever it takes to form new, good habits for your mounting ease.

Goal: No matter what technique is used for mounting, the horse should stand completely still; then wait for a verbal cue to release when the rider is ready. Nothing less should be accepted.

Summary:

1. Horses need to be taught to stand still for mounting.

2. Mounting from the ground is one of the most physically challenging tasks for many riders.

3. Spend as much time as necessary to teach this valuable lesson.

4. Accept nothing short of the goal for each mounting.

5. Repetition is the key to success.

Pre-purchase tips:

- Ask the owner to mount the horse.

- Mount the horse (if the owner was safely successful).

- Make an unscheduled visit to see the horse. Ask if you can halter, saddle, bridle, and mount the horse. This will rule out any chance the first visit involved any foul play (exercising or drugging the horse).

- Take a trainer or friend with you if you are unsure about your ability to ride an unfamiliar horse.

15

Riding — Neck Flexion

15) Neck Flexion

0 – No flexing in any direction
1 – Braces against rider's request to flex
2 – Requires two people (one holding, one mounted)
3 – Flexes slightly while turning circles
4 – Flexes well to both sides without moving, but rider must hold with pressure
5 – Flexes well to both sides, holds head passively until released

"Lateral Flexion" is the term used to describe the bending of the horse's neck to either side, towards the shoulder. Most horse trainers and enthusiasts believe that lateral flexion is a primary key to mounted respect and control. The more supple the horse's neck, the more control you have over said horse. Every horse can learn to bend around to the shoulder. Not only does lateral flexion give the rider more control over the horse, it is also another method of getting the horse to submit to the wishes of the rider.

When a horse braces its neck to lateral bending, it is much more difficult to steer, control, and stop. Bracing is the horse's way to refuse your intentions. Lateral flexion is a behavior that is usually learned in less than a day. Really supple and enthusiastic lateral flexion may take some weeks to perfect, but it is one of the easier behavior modifications we teach. Lateral flexion should be practiced, repeatedly each time you are working the horse on the ground or under saddle. Make it a habit to practice and reinforce lateral flexion.

Lateral flexion technique from the ground:

1. Place a saddle (optional), halter, and lead rope. A bridle may also be used but may be a little too aggressive in the early stages of training for lateral flexion.

2. Hold the saddle horn (the saddle provides you with some leverage from which to start applying pressure to the right or left side). While standing on the same side as you will be making the request, start pulling the lead rope towards the same side shoulder. Most horses will want to turn towards the pressure with their body. This is where you must be mindful of your own feet. It is very easy to be stepped upon in this position with this pressure angle. Move with the horse to avoid being stepped upon. One main key to success is to make small requests. Horses with no previous experience will not know what you want. Therefore, when you reach down the lead rope to make your initial request, only ask them to move their head a couple inches to that side.

3. Keep constant pressure on the rope until you feel them relax (submit). Reward each small submission with a release. Once they submit, even a little, release the pressure on the rope quickly and completely, reward, repeat (PR3).

4. After each successful repetition, you will ask for more bending. Most horses will be better on one side as opposed to the other. Spend more time on the weaker side.

5. Continue training until the slightest pressure causes the horse to immediately and softly turn towards the side of the request.

6. Success is declared when the horse can touch its nose continuously to either shoulder with muscles relaxed.

Lateral flexion from ground

Step 1. Initiate the lateral flexion request with pressure to one side. For leverage, push against saddle horn.

Step 2. Early in training, the horse will always want to yield to the pressure by turning with it. Repeat "Whoa" while following the horse as it turns.

Step 3. Continue to follow and repeat "Whoa" until the horse stops turning.

Step 4. Once the turning stops, immediately release the pressure and reward.

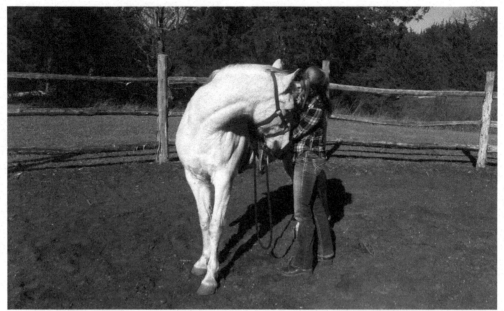

Step 5. With practice, the horse will understand the request to turn and touch the stirrup.

Step 6. Immediate, supple neck flexion to both sides is the goal.

Lateral flexion training is easier from the saddle because of the mechanical advantage (leverage) gained. The other advantage realized from the saddle is not having the horse step on your feet. Lateral flexion technique from the saddle:

1. Place saddle and bridle. If using a bit, be very gentle.

2. Reach down the reins as far as you can while keeping a solid base in the saddle.

3. Pull on one rein with very little pressure initiating the request to bend its head toward that side. Again, the horse will want to turn its entire body. This is a common response.

4. Keep constant pressure on the rope until you feel him relax (submit). Reward each small submission with a release. Once it submits, even a little, release the pressure on the rope quickly and completely, reward, repeat (PR^3).

5. After each successful repetition, you will ask for more bending. Most horses will be better on one side as opposed to the other. Spend more time on the weaker side.

6. Continue the training until the slightest pressure causes the horse to immediately and softly turn towards the side of the request.

7. Success is declared when the horse can touch its nose continuously to either shoulder with muscles relaxed.

Lateral flexion from saddle

Step 1. Start neck flexion training from a stop.

Step 2. While saying "Whoa" pull rein firmly to one side.

Step 3. Early in training, the horse will always move towards the pressure.

Step 4. With minimum but constant pressure while repeating "Whoa", the horse will begin to understand and slow its movement.

Step 5. Eventually, the horse will stop turning, but the lesson is not complete until the nose touches the rider's knee.

Step 6. As soon as the nose touches the rider's knee, the pressure is completely released.

Step 7. Both sides should be immediate, complete, and supple.

As the horse learns what you want, you will ask for more bending (increase the distance their nose travels towards their shoulder). Keep adding distance as progress is made. Eventually, you will be able to request that the horse touch its nose to your knee or your stirrup. In the beginning, make small requests and allow the horse to turn the entire body until they tire or submit to your request. When enough repetitions have been completed, you may decide to hold the rein to your knee and allow them to struggle for as long as it takes to stop turning their body and simply leave their nose against your knee or stirrup. Finally, to complete the lesson, the horse must keep its neck in this position until released. Once most horses learn lateral flexion, they will easily and smoothly turn back at the slightest request without resistance.

"Vertical flexion" or the exercise of requesting the horse to move its head towards its chest is a similar technique. This is an even easier technique to teach from the saddle as the request from the rider is the same as a halt or backing-up. Use equal pressure on both reins and ask the horse to yield its head to the pressure without backing up. Like with lateral flexion, at first, the horse will resist by bracing itself against the pressure. Secondly, the horse may want to back-up whether they have been taught to do so, or not. Vertical flexion can be taught from the ground with a food reward. This helps differentiate vertical flexion from backing up. The key to teaching this technique is to reward with a release of pressure as soon as you feel even the slightest submission by the horse. With each slight submission, release the pressure, verbally praise the horse, and give it a short break, a few seconds (PR³).

Many trainers suggest using lateral and vertical flexing exercises at every stop. It is okay to use the same pattern each time (right, left, vertical), but we really do not want the horse to anticipate our request, so I recommend making the request in a random sequence each time. This reinforces that the rider is making all decisions.

To differentiate between a vertical flexing cue, and a backing-up cue, do the following (see Chapter 14 on Backing up):

1. A slight weight shift in the saddle towards the back is the cue for backing up.

2. Use the verbal cue "back" for backing-up.

Goal: Immediate, supple response to the request to flex the neck, and hold, to either side and vertically.

Vertical flexion

Step 1. Initiate the vertical flexion request with a pull towards the chest with the lead rope.

Step 2. The horse will either back-up or brace the neck.

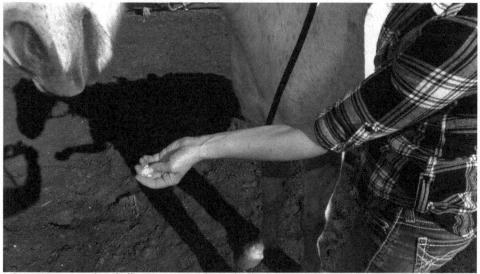

Step 3. Because this challenge is so similar to backing up using a treat to teach the difference.

Step 4. The horse's head immediately comes back when a treat is recognized.

Step 5. It is amazing how supple and cooperative they can be when searching for the treat. Use the verbal cue, "flex," when teaching this maneuver.

Summary:

1. Teaching a horse to flex in both lateral directions and vertically is great for respect and control.

2. Best started in young horses from the ground.

3. For under saddle horses, teach from the saddle with bridle.

4. Release at the slightest submission.

5. Lesson is complete when each request is fulfilled with immediate, smooth turn and hold.

Pre-purchase tips:

- Ask the owner to demonstrate lateral and vertical flexion from the ground.

- Ask the owner to demonstrate lateral and vertical flexion from the saddle.

- Attempt to get the horse to flex in all directions on the ground, yourself (if the owner was successful).

- Attempt to get the horse to flex in all directions from the saddle yourself (if the owner was successful).

- If the horse cannot perform or poorly performs upon this request, it can usually be taught very quickly (less than a day in most cases).

- Take a trainer or friend with you if you are unsure about your ability to ride an unfamiliar horse.

16

Riding — Backing Up

16) Backing Up

0 – Will not back

1 – Will back up one step with much pressure

2 – Backs with moderate pressure but throws head

3 – Backs well but requires significant rein pressure, may throw head

4 – Backs well but only straight backward

5 – Backs well in patterns as directed by rein and leg pressure

Teaching a horse to back up from the mounted position is pretty fast and easy because of the leverage afforded by the rider's position and the stability of the saddle. Always use the verbal cue "Back" when teaching a horse to back up. Shift your weight back in the saddle while subtly moving feet and stirrups forward and away from the body and say aloud, "Back," then begin pulling directly back on the reins. Pull slightly downward as we want the horse to back with its head down, not up. Some people use alternating right and left pressure instead of equal pressure. Either technique is acceptable.

Backing can also be taught from the ground. By standing in front of the horse and using the reins for leverage, push back on the bridle while pushing against the chest as a second cue. This physical presence of a person in front of them makes them want to back up, anyway. Either from the saddle or the ground, the horse usually takes a step backward within a couple seconds. Before they know the command, all horses will brace against the pressure to back up. At the slightest sign of submission, reward them with a release of pressure, praise and repeat (PR3). Once they take their first step and are rewarded, they will learn much more rapidly. For more stubborn horses, once they understand the re-

Step 1. Initial backing request, weight back, legs forward, down and back pressure on reins, verbal cue "back." (Intermittent pressure with reins, weight and verbal to continue to back up).

Step 2. Continued backward rein pressure and verbal cues.

Step 3. Release of pressure when the desired result is achieved.

Step 4. From the ground, initiate the request with backward pressure on lead rope or reins.

Step 5. Early in training, the horse will refuse by bracing the neck.

Step 6. The better cue is using tying the lead rope to both sides of the halter to simulate the reins and bridle. Use equal pressure with each hand.

Step 7. For more resistant horses, you can use the tip of your thumb at the pressure point on the sternum.

quest, continue to apply the pressure until they comply.

A two-person technique usually takes less time. With a person in the saddle and a handler on the ground (in front of the horse), there can be little confusion for the horse as to the meaning of the request. Training is not complete until the horse calmly backs up with minimal encouragement. Like lateral flexion, this is another exercise that should be reinforced many times per ride.

Most horses can be taught to back up in less than an hour. With two people, one on the ground and the other in the saddle, it can take less than 20 minutes. Well broke horses are pretty receptive to backing up. Horses that brace themselves against the bit and refuse to step back may require more time and patience, or anoth-

er handler on the ground. Backing up is a very handy technique for a horse to know when on the trail.

Summary:

1. Teaching a horse to back is fairly easy.

2. Shift your weight back in the saddle, subtly move legs, and stirrups forward and away.

3. Use the verbal cue, "Back."

4. Begin applying steady or alternating pressure until a backward step is taken.

5. Reward any backward movement with a release.

The two-person technique is faster.

While the rider pulls back and says, "back," the handler pushes back on the muzzle or reins.

Both rider and handler release as soon as the first step is taken.

6. Do not stop training to back up until they do it calmly and willingly.

7. Repeat frequently.

8. Once the straight back-up is mastered, begin teaching the horse to back up in a pattern based on your rein cues.

Pre-purchase tips:

- Ask the owner to demonstrate the horse backing from ground cues.

- Attempt to get the horse to back-up from ground cues (if the owner is successful).

- Ask the owner to demonstrate the horse backing from the saddle.

- If you consider the horse to be "safe," experiment with backing in a pattern.

- Take a trainer or friend with you if you are unsure about your ability to ride an unfamiliar horse.

17

Riding — Side Passing

17) Side Passing

0 – Will not side pass

1 – Baby step to one side with much encouragement

2 – Baby steps to each side with much encouragement

3 – Side passes well to one side, poor to other with mild encouragement

4 – Side passes well to both sides with continuous leg/heel pressure

5 – Side passes to both sides with light or no pressure (verbal commands)

Side passing is an invaluable technique for trail riding. Whether it is to allow other horses to pass on a narrow trail or to open and close a gate from the mounted position, side passing is a must for an enjoyable trail ride. Expect to spend at least double the time training a horse to side pass when compared to backing. Training the horse to understand that the rider wants it to move directly sideways is confusing. Most horses have been taught that leg or heel pressure means to go forward or to go forward, faster. Therefore, they are conflicted when leg pressure doesn't mean the same as it has previously.

Much like backing up, the leverage from the saddle helps hold them from going forward as the request is made to go sideways. Also, like backing up, a shift of weight will be the differentiating cue to move sideways instead of forward. In addition, uneven pressure can be placed on the bridle to encourage movement in the proper direction. The hardest step is the first one. The technique for a right lateral movement is:

- From a complete stop, touch the heel on the opposite side (left side, just behind the girth strap), direct the horse's head slightly to the same side (left side). Upon refusal, you will begin tapping that same side heel with increasing pressure.

- Hold the reins firmly to prevent forward movement. You may even tip the head slightly towards the side of the heel pressure (left side), as this discourages forward movement even more.

- Say aloud, "right."

- Continue to apply increasing pressure until the slightest movement to the intended side is noted, then release.

- Continue the training until only the mildest pressure or just the verbal command is all it takes for the horse to willingly and immediately step laterally.

- Reverse the technique for "left" lateral movement.

Most horses fight this by shaking or swinging the head because they are confused about the request. Be patient and persistent. Side passing can be introduced in one session of an hour. It takes several sessions to perfect. One lateral step per session can certainly be considered a success. Add one step per day or week, and you will be side passing like a champ in no time! If you and your horse are overachievers, there is no reason it cannot be learned in a day. Some trainers like to start by placing the horse up against a gate, fence, or wall. With this modification, the horse cannot move forward which is always their tendency when learning to side pass. This lesson goes faster with two people, with the second person encouraging from the ground.

Early side passing can be taught from the ground. Using the verbal command, "pass," "right," or "left" while applying hand pressure (where your heel will eventually give the cue) can get the horse started in the right direction. A fingertip placed between the ribs gives a little more stimulation for the horse to move away from the pressure. Side passing training from the ground is difficult as there is little mechanical advantage to be gained. From a mounted position, you will have much better leverage to execute the maneuver (described below).

Why is this important to trail riders? There are frequent trail situations where you cannot maneuver through an obstacle; you must open and close a gate; change the order of the horses in line; or with a severe terrain change, side passing is an incredibly important technique.

Step 1. Left heel to lower left ribs, tip nose slightly to left, say, "right".

Step 2. Upon any right movement, release pressure, reward, repeat.

Step 3. For continuous side passing, continue pressure without release.

Step 4. The side passing exercise ends when the rider decides.

Step 5. Tip head towards you, press at lower ribs, say "right".

Step 6. Upon the first sideways step, release pressure, reward, repeat.

Step 7. Release of pressure, prepare for the next step.

Step 8. In later stages of side passing training, continuous pressure for continued sideways movement.

Summary:

1. Side passing is not a necessity, but every trail horse should do it.

2. Side passing is more difficult to teach than backing up.

3. Have patience and be persistent.

4. A second person on the ground makes the lesson go faster.

Pre-purchase tips:

• Many pleasure horses do not know how to side pass.

• Ask the owner if the horse knows how to side pass.

• Ask the owner to demonstrate side passing from ground cues.

• Attempt to get the horse to side pass from ground cues (if the owner was successful).

• Ask the owner to demonstrate side passing from the saddle.

• Attempt to get the horse to side pass from the saddle (if the owner was successful).

• Take a trainer or friend with you if you are unsure about your ability to ride an unfamiliar horse.

• Expect to pay more for a horse that can side pass well.

18

Riding — Reining/Steering

18) Reining/Steering

0 – Very difficult (barely able to be ridden)
1 – Difficult (slow reaction to turning or stopping)
2 – Will direct (bridle) rein but takes time to respond
3 – Direct reins well and/or early neck reining
4 – Almost automatic response to neck reining, weight and leg cues
5 – No visible need for any reining, all leg and weight cues

Being able to guide a horse in the direction you would like to go is desirable. Generally, a horse will only go in the direction to which its head is pointed. This category measures the horse's ability to respond to those requests from the rider. Teaching a horse to steer is not too difficult, but it does take time. Most horses are started through a process called *direct reining*, which uses both hands. With this method, the reins are usually attached directly to a simple snaffle bit. When the rider pulls right or left, it is intended for the horse to turn in this direction, hence the term "Direct Reining." Another name for this method is "Bridle Reining," but it is not an accepted or accurate term. "Bit Reining" is a more accurate term.

Horses learn this relatively quickly as it is intuitive because the head is pulled to the right or left, then the body follows. English style riders (Hunter/Jumper, Dressage and Saddle Seat) use direct reining.

The more advanced steering method is "Neck Reining," which is an indirect reining method. The horse is trained so that light pressure on one side of the neck is the cue for turning the other direction. For example, the rein touching the

Bridle reining:

Step 1. Initiate turn with head turn, weight shift, and leg pressure.

Step 2. Use a loose outside rein and a tight inside rein.

Step 3. Release pressure between turns.

Step 4. Initiate next turn with head turn, weight shift, and leg cues.

Step 5. Close-up showing inside rider's head turning inward, right leg moving back, weight shift toward the barrel, loose outside rein, and tight inside rein.

Step 6. Opposite turn. Rider should release outside rein more.

horse on the left side of the neck is a signal for it to turn right and vice versa. Neck reining is used in "Western" style riding and is desirable for trail riders as it only requires one hand.

Neck reining:

Steering can be taught to young horses, prior to riding age, by using a harness or light saddle and longe lines which serve as long reins. The more you teach and desensitize them early, the easier it is for you to ride them later.

When teaching moderately trained horses to steer, it is simple to get them to go where you want from the saddle through "trial and error" along with repetition. In an arena, barrels, blocks, cones, or even chairs can be set-up so that the horse has a visual target on which to focus for direction and turns. Following other horses or on a well-defined trail gives the perfect opportunity to teach or reinforce whichever method we choose. While teaching a horse to steer, it is critical to "release" the pressure as a reward as the horse makes any attempt to comply or submit to the request (Pressure, Release, Reward, Repeat = PR3). Because horses learn through conditioning, they quickly realize that cooperation will result in a reward (less pressure or release of pressure); so, it is in their best interest to cooperate immediately and completely. Always use the minimum amount of pressure to initiate the request. Additional pressure is always an option. Endeavor to find the correct amount of rein pressure that is necessary to obtain the desired result.

Teaching a horse to turn with weight and leg cues is ideal. These cues are an extension of and should eventually replace either form of reining (bridle or neck reining). To teach these cues for steering, begin incorporating them from the very beginning of reining training. Horses are so sensitive to movement and slight pressure that in the final stages of training, you should be able to simply turn your head to the side you want to turn towards and the horse will know what you want from this most subtle cue. Below is a training progression:

While teaching the horse to steer with either method of reining:

1. Right turn – slightly rotate your body and head in a clockwise manner while slightly touching the left foot to the left side of the horse.

2. Left turn – slightly rotate your body and head in a counter-clockwise manner while slightly touching the right foot to the right side of the horse.

Another finesse point of reining is "Timing." As you refine your technique of leg cues, weight shift, head turn, and rein pressure, make sure that you are consistent. As the horse learns, make sure that you are not changing the timing of your requests. Give the horse the chance to do the right thing through the most subtle cues. For example, you are coming to a turn in the trail, use the following progression of cues:

1. Turn your head in the direction you want to turn, observe if the horse recognizes your cues, if not:

Neck reining:

Step 1. Initiate request by turning head, shifting weight, and leg pressure while placing the rein against the opposite side of the neck. Note loose inside rein.

Step 2. Better angle to view the rein pressure. Against neck on opposite side as turn, loose inside rein.

Step 3. Continue technique through the turn during training.

Step 4. Reverse technique for right turn.

2. Ever so lightly shift your weight, observe if the horse recognizes your cue, if not:

3. Give the appropriate leg cue, observe if the horse recognizes your cue, if not:

4. Then and only then use the reins.

If you're patient, persistent, and consistent, you will soon have your horse responding to the most subtle cues, and the reins will only be a last resort. If you can continue to reinforce weight and/or leg cues, your horse will keep getting better. Eventually, these cues become unnoticeable to the casual observer. A horse that steers almost from reading the rider's mind is a true joy to ride! All movements should be soft and fluid.

In many situations on the trail, precise steering is critical for precision riding in potentially dangerous situations like bridge crossings, water crossings, washout areas, larger rocks and boulder crossings where exact footfalls are necessary. Imagine traversing the Grand Canyon on a narrow trail with a few thousand feet drop to the bottom of the canyon, you would probably want perfect steering and a horse that is very precise in picking its footfalls.

Safety Discussion

A "One-Rein-Stop" can be the emergency brake for horses. This is an invaluable technique for safety, especially on younger and green horses. This technique is a last resort if a horse is badly misbehaving, attempting to run-away with a rider, or you lose your stirrup(s) at a canter/lope/gallop. This technique should be initiated well in advance through lateral flexion training (Part 4, Chapter 15, **Neck Flexion**). We want our horses to have a supple neck. Meaning, when the request is made to turn its neck to one side, it is done immediately, without resistance or hesitation and completely (nose touches the rider's knee). Once perfected, a one-rein-stop can be a lifesaving technique. The technique should be practiced frequently (multiple times per trail ride or training session) when the horse is cooperative. Remember to use the absolute minimum amount of pressure when training for this maneuver, especially when performing it with a bit. Many riders believe this technique to be too aggressive and one that can hurt the horse. First, it is very difficult to hurt horses. Second, if we do injure the horse, it will heal — OUR SAFETY IS MUCH MORE IMPORTANT. This is no time to be sensitive. For those of you who read the introductory chapters, this technique would have saved Donna from her horse incident, riding-ending fall.

When riding or training, this technique requires some space as the horse will need to yield to the request while moving towards the side of the request. The use of the word "Whoa" should ALWAYS accompany the physical request. Here is the technique:

1. Start training with a halter with reins or a bitless bridle. As the horse learns and becomes more willing and supple, progress to a less aggressive bit (simple snaffle).

Step 1. The lost stirrup causes loss of control and a run-away horse. Tug firmly on one rein to regain control.

Step 2. Horse begins to yield to one rein pressure and slows.

Step 3. Rider regaining control but continues pressure until horse completely stops.

Step 4. Rider does not release pressure until the horse is still and rider regains stirrups, composure, and control.

2. While traveling in a straight line, in this order, shift your weight backward and to the side of the request (because the horse will be performing a sharp turn, the rider will need to counter-balance the momentum with a preemptive weight shift).

3. The horse will sense the two-way weight shift in conjunction with the verbal cue "Whoa" as a strong message to stop. This "Whoa" should be spoken louder and more aggressively than any other "Whoa" used for regular stopping.

4. If used for training, the severity of the rein pressure can be mild to moderate.

5. If used in an emergency stopping situation, the severity of rein pressure is intense and continuous until the horse stops. It is AN EMERGENCY as you have lost control of the horse!

Summary:

1. Most horses learn basic steering very quickly.

2. Direct reining is usually taught first.

3. Neck reining for trail horses is highly desirable.

4. Work towards weight shifting and leg cues as the goal for steering.

5. Always reinforce weight shift and leg cues in every turn during a ride.

Pre-purchase tips:

- Ask the owner to demonstrate what type of reining the horse knows.

- Ask the owner if the horse knows leg and weight shift cues.

- Ask the owner if the horse knows the one-rein-stop.

- Attempt to ride/steer the horse yourself (if the owner was successful).

- The current owner may not be an accomplished rider. The horse may know more than the owner can demonstrate. If you consider the horse to be "safe", you can experiment with direct and neck reining during your test ride.

- Take a trainer or friend with you if you are unsure about your ability to ride an unfamiliar horse.

Additional pre-purchase comments:

If you are riding a new horse during a test ride, these are some signs that the horse needs reining work:

- The horse raises its head and neck and "hollows" its back

- The horse pulls or braces against pressure

- The horse opens its mouth in resistance

- The rider must use significant pressure or pulling to get a response

During a test ride, if the horse is properly trained, you should feel / see:

- A yielding horse who is soft and responsive to the slightest cue

- The horse never braces or resists against reining pressure

- An immediate response

- The horse will not raise his head and neck against pressure

- The horse will not open his mouth in resistance

Warning: If a horse is being ridden in an ill-fitting bit or an otherwise inappropriate bit for the training the horse has received, you will notice discomfort and resistance from the horse. It doesn't necessarily mean that the reining or steering is poor. Prior to assigning a low reining score, it may be worth asking the Seller if they have experimented with other bits. In most cases, it simply comes down to training, but proper bit selection should not be dismissed.

Herd bound horses will begin looking back at barn almost immediately when separated.

19

Riding — Alone on Trail

19) Alone on Trail

0 – Will not allow mounting without horses nearby, extremely uncooperative

1 – Will not trail ride alone (dangerous, spinning, refusing, running back)

2 – Extremely anxious, frequently spooks, ignores rider, refuses

3 – Reluctant alone, spooky, stops, frequently refuses, slowly recovers

4 – Goes alone, mildly spooky, occasional refusals but recovers

5 – Goes alone, mostly willing, infrequent refusals, won't hold gait

6 – Calm, no issues, attentive to the rider, holds gait

Horses find safety in a herd. Before the equine species was domesticated, individuals had the best chance of survival in a herd. Centuries after their domestication, this herd mentality persists. This instinct is counterproductive for our enjoyment as trail riders. The vast majority of hobby trail horses simply will not safely go out on the trail alone. If you force them, you will likely regret it as you will fear for your safety, and the trail ride will end just after it starts. Even if you *always* ride in a group, this category is important because many herd-bound horses do not allow enough space between themselves and the horse ahead of them.

When they are too close to the horse ahead to see the ground, it can be unsafe for the rider as they frequently stumble and can even fall on uneven terrain. With a faster pace, the chance of stumbling and/or falling increases. Frequently, on group trail rides, riders and horses get separated. If you must stop to pick up a dropped item, relieve yourself, or adjust tack, you may fall behind the group. With each passing inch of separation, the solo horse becomes increasingly agitated. During

This mare is rarely ridden alone. Her protests escalate as the distance from the barn increases.

mounting or just after mounting, the horse's urge to be reunited with the herd is so intense that it may sprint back, buck while running, or take shortcuts. This is a very dangerous situation. I have known two trail enthusiasts who have broken bones in this very scenario. DO NOT UNDERESTIMATE THE INTENSITY OF THE REACTION TO HERD SEPARATION! Teaching your horse to be less anxious on the trail alone will also have significant benefits when riding in a group.

Many riders will never experience this emotion as they never leave the arena or ride alone. It continually frustrates me when even my best, most fearless trail horses refuse or highly protest, leaving their barn or group. Once they realize the

distance between them and their herd has reached a tipping point (this distance varies for each horse but may be as little as 10 feet), they will start to look back, whiny, refuse, pull or rear. The degree to which they react is directly related to their degree of barn sourness. Horse that have been separated from their herd more frequently don't react as much. Those that have little or no experience with separation react the most intensely. See the pictures on the start of this chapter: the black mare is looking back within 50 feet of the barn. The white mare has had a little more recent experience leaving her barn. If any of the stalled horses call out to the one leaving, this usually created a choir of cries from both sides.

Many of these fearless trail horses (when in groups) act like they've never been on a trail ride if you ask them to go alone. The white mare on the previous page is very unhappy to be ridden away from her herd.

The explanation is obvious through understanding "herd mentality" or just logical reasoning; from foaling to weaning to adjacent stalls to group pastures, **they have NEVER been alone**. It is crystal clear why they have such a strong aversion to being alone. This does not make it any less frustrating. Even on a 100-acres ranch with four different barns, we have trouble getting any horse to go alone from one barn to another. Most of the time, rather than riding, we must walk them on a lead between barns. In my twenty years of trail riding, I have only had one horse that had no issues with being alone on the trail.

Cisco, my second horse to whom the book is dedicated, had not a care in the world about being on the trail alone. Even on group rides, he would lag behind, casually picking-off leaves of trees while passing by, allowing the distance between him and the herd to widen and not be disturbed, in the least. Often, when the distance became so great that the person riding him felt compelled to catch up, Cisco would still need a couple kicks in the ribs to catch up. Even then, he would pick up a comfortable little cantor and slowly catch the herd. Once the herd was visible again and the rider's pressure released, he would begin a slow walk, and the herd would slowly disappear in the distance. These horses are exceptionally rare.

Separation anxiety, instincts, and human-imposed habits are the cause of many problems with the human-horse interaction (see Parts 1 and 2). The solution for this issue is to remove your horse from the herd often, for as long as time and money will permit. This requires access to or ownership of a truck and trailer. Many horse owners don't have either. Therefore, it will take some creativity to decrease your horse's herd bound tendency (See Part Two, Chapter 4, **Desensitization**). The Desensitization chapter may be the most important chapter in the book. Please reread it.

If the need or desire to ride alone occurs, know that it does put even more responsibility on the rider to be the true "leader." This demands that you are even more keenly aware of potential hazards such as wildlife encounters, unsafe trails and footing, and weather issues.

Summary:

1. If possible, take your horse on a long trip away from its herd. It is not even necessary to ride, just get away.

2. Be creative when attempting to increase your horse's willingness to be away from the herd.

3. Even walks, with halter and lead, away from barn and herd, are helpful.

4. Frequency is the key to success.

5. Reward your horse with grazing or treats when it allows you to calmly separate it from the herd.

Pre-purchase tips:

- Endeavor to find a horse with "boldness." Review, "Boldness" section in Part 2, Chapter 2, **Herd Mentality**.

- Ask the owner to walk the horse away from its barn.

- Walk the horse away from its barn.

- Increase distance until horse is uncooperative.

- Ask the owner if the horse has ever been ridden alone.

- Ask the owner to ride the horse away from the barn/herd.

- Ride the horse away from the barn/herd (if the owner was successful).

- Take a trainer or friend with you if you are unsure about your ability to ride an unfamiliar horse.

- Most horses will fail this test.

- If you plan to ride alone, do not settle for anything below a 4 in this category. One exception may be a young horse that can be retrained to be alone.

- Expect to pay more for a horse that shows little or no separation anxiety.

- In some cases, it may be possible for the owner and prospective horse to meet you at a trail where you can ride together. If all goes well, you may be able to ride the prospective horse and experiment with many of the above reactions/situations to observe how the horse handles separation. Ask the owner or try to ride the horse away from the group (exercise extreme safety). There is no better pre-purchase due diligence than to observe or ride the horse on a trail.

20

Riding — Trail Responsiveness/ Trail Pace

20) Trail Responsiveness/ Trail Pace

0 – Will not move any faster than a slow walk

1 – Sluggish, lazy, may have attitude when asked

2 – Sluggish, needs kicking, spurs, crop

3 – Willing but lacks enthusiasm

4 – Requires minimal encouragement, maintains speed

5 – Responds immediately when asked, maintains speed

Trail responsiveness measures a horse's enthusiasm while on the trail ride. For some riders, it may be considered a desirable attribute, but for me, "laziness" may be my biggest pet peeve about trail horses. Because most horses desperately want to be in close proximity to their equine counterparts (see Part Two, Chapter 2, **Herd Mentality**), most of them will keep up with the horse in front of them. This category does not give credit for responsiveness to keeping up with the horse in front of them because it is a negative habit. Instead, this category measures their responsiveness to the rider's requests. It can be measured in a round pen, arena, around the barn or on the trail when your horse is leading. It measures the horse's response immediately after you ask to increase speed.

For many riders "laziness" is a wonderful attribute as a lazy horse is usually a safe horse. So, if you like slow, peaceful trail rides with no drama, a score of "0", "1" or "2" may be ideal for you. A high score in this category is better suited for riders who want to "go" or expect some versatility in their horses. Even though this book is targeted at the trail riding discipline, most trail riders do spend time in play days, arenas, trail challenges or occasionally like to canter, lope or gallop. I, for one, want my horse to be as versatile as possible. Use this category for what best suits your riding

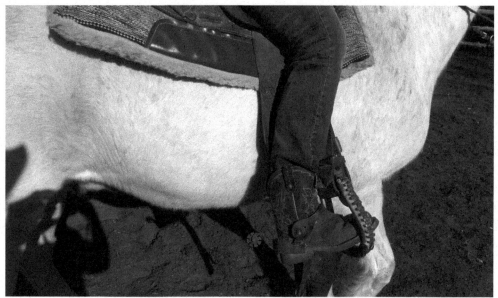

Spurs can be motivational for lazy horses. When used properly they only touch the horse when the riders wants to encourage forward movement.

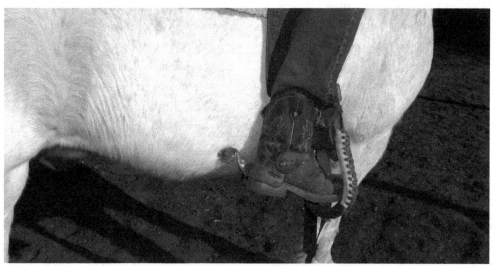

Use only the lightest spur pressure necessary to get forward movement.

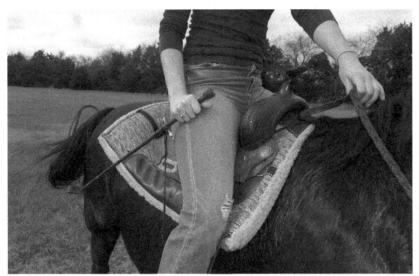

Crops can also be used to encourage forward movement. Many horses are motivated by the rider carrying a crop and never need it to touch them.

goals and personality. Though it can be heartbreaking if your horse's responsiveness, whether too much or too little, is not aligned with your desires, consider selling the horse and finding another better suited to your riding needs or ambitions.

My collection of trail horses runs the entire spectrum when it comes to "responsiveness". One of my favorites, "Sport" wants to go all the time. He needs to be held back 100% of the time. If you are not controlling his speed through constant, moderate bit pressure, he will pick up speed until he is in a full gallop. It can be a little burdensome to hold him back all the time, but I wholeheartedly appreciate his attitude. His "5" in this category is what makes him one of my favorite horses. His responsiveness, enthusiasm and willingness make him the poster child for this category.

Conversely, I have Cisco and Beauty who are the opposite of the poster children for this category. For both these horses, I use a crop and spurs. Cisco was the classic "dead head." Even in a group, he happily traveled at his speed, dining on anything green along the way. When he lagged behind the group by 100 yards, you could usually get him to canter to catch up. Once caught up, he would start to lag behind, immediately. He was the poster child for the previous chapter, "On the Trail Alone." Beauty, on the other hand, is herd bound and will not allow any separation between her and the horse in front of her. However, when you ask her to lead, she is almost a statue. If she does move forward it is at a pace that only a statue would admire. She is very tolerant of the crop and spurs, also. "Dead-sided" is the term that describes a horse that ignores/refuses to be influenced by negative stimuli like crops and spurs, when asked to move faster. I do not enjoy riding either Cisco or Beauty, but I am grateful to have both as they will safely babysit beginners and novices perfectly. In fact, both horses have made first-time riders look like seasoned veterans on many occasions. So, even though their score in this category is low, they are perfect for novices and, thus, very valuable horses to me!

The contrast between Sport and Beauty should help you understand this category. It's the only category where a bad score can be desirable. Motivational devices like crops, spurs and whips can improve a horse's responsiveness, but not significantly. On occasion, sluggish horses are simply not getting enough protein. Know that many horses "for sale" are often undernourished or have parasites. Once fed and dewormed properly, they can be completely different horses. I have seen dead-heads turn into rodeo horses with proper care and nourishment. Consult your vet before adding more grain or protein to your horse's diet. If you want a responsive horse and enjoy the versatility therein, you should seek one out from the beginning. This is another category where breed and temperament should be strongly considered during your research (see breed and temperament sections, Part Two). In general, people should want a horse that mirrors their own personality. Good riders with hyper personalities want a spunky horse. Average to poor riders with laid-back personalities may be better suited for calm, laid-back horses. Of course, exceptions do exist!

Summary:

1. Decide early what riding style you plan to pursue and find a horse whose responsiveness best suits that style.

2. Horses can be motivated to be more responsive but they may always be frustrating for a rider that desires more spunk.

3. The use of motivational devices (crops, spurs and whips) usually is not a long term solution.

4. Do not hesitate to trade a too spunky or too lazy horse in for one better suited to your riding style.

5. If you aren't sure you can accurately identify your riding style, consult a trainer and ask for their input regarding the relative abilities and the type of horse personality that might best suit you.

Pre-purchase tips:

- Try to accurately determine the amount of horse responsiveness that best matches your personality and riding style.

- If you plan to ride with friends, evaluate their style of riding and match it.

- Pay closer attention to the temperament rating given by the owner. Scores from 0-3 are more likely to be low energy. Scores from 4-6 will be much more spunky. Scores 7-10, DO NOT EVEN LOOK AT THESE!

- If you're athletic enough to improve your riding skills, a slightly more energetic horse than you are comfortable on today might be in order.

- Ride the horse as many times as possible before you purchase.

- Have a trainer ride the horse as many times as necessary and receive their feedback regarding how well-suited you are to its level of energy, responsiveness and willingness. A person with a non-emotional perspective is in a much better position to give advice.

- I cannot stress how important the match of personalities is in choosing the best horse.

21

Riding — Quietness at halt

21) Quietness at halt

0 – Will not stand still, at all
1 – May stand but moves often
2 – Stands when tired but is restless otherwise
3 – Stands still but requires tension on reins
4 – Usually stands for tack/ clothing adjustments, photographs
5 – Stands quietly at all times on loose or no rein

One of the most frustrating characteristics horses have is an inability/unwillingness to stand quietly at a halt. Whether you are trail riding or training, we want our horses to stand quietly when we want to rest, eat, drink, take pictures or visit with other riders or pedestrians while still mounted. Usually, this restlessness will wane with age, but there are some methods we can use to quiet a restless horse at the halt.

There are many reasons this is important to trail riders:

- Quietness while waiting your turn to execute a trail obstacle translates into a more careful, purposeful and successful completion of the challenge.

- Patiently waiting as another horse/rider handles issues, adjustments, bathroom breaks, traffic, etc.

- Waiting for a hazard to pass, i.e., traffic, a train, other horse groups, wildlife, etc.

- Waiting on slower horses/riders.

Observing a horse's behavior when tied will give a strong indication as to their tendencies under saddle, at a halt. Horses that are restless when tied are usually restless at a halt. Many of these ten-

Quietness at the halt is desirable.

Horses that paw when tied are likely to paw under saddle.

With any break in the action, some horses will paw out of separation, impatience or frustration.

dencies are breed specific. Hot horses are bred to move and have a much higher tendency to move when we don't want them to move. Warm bloods are less likely, and Cold Bloods are the least likely to move at a halt. Breed selection vs. your abilities/desires should be considered at purchase.

Tying a horse for extended periods to teach patience is a good start (Part Four, Chapter 3, **Tying**). Many people do not assess this virtue when buying a horse, but many people very much dislike when a horse will not stand quietly. Here are the reasons for restlessness at a halt:

Age: Age is the most important factor with this topic. Young horses (1-5 years of age) have more energy, curiosity, less patience, and less discipline than older horses. When you purchase a young horse, this is a factor you should consider. While

restlessness can be dangerous, it is more annoying than anything else. I take many pictures of friends while I am on horseback. My picture taking frustration is largely dependent upon which horse I am riding. Not everyone photographs from horseback, but most riders want to stop and eat, drink, rearrange clothing, look at a map, look at your phone, talk, etc. (activities that do not require dismounting). For those riders who have difficulty mounting and dismounting, it is always inconvenient to dismount for any or all those activities. This should be considered in your purchase and training.

Fatigue: After any given amount of time and fatigue, most horses will gladly stand quietly at the halt. For good riders you may canter, lope, and/ or canter or lope in circles to expedite the fatigue factor for quietness. For beginner or moderate riders, those accelerated fatigue activities may not be possible. For many horses, only heavy fatigue will cause them to want to stand quietly.

Breed: As previously discussed, breed behavior varies greatly for many categories. Energy level and restlessness are no exception. Many breeds have been bred "hot". Because the uses of different breeds require more energy or more forward motion, some breeds will be more challenging in this category. Even with hot breeds, age will usually solve this frustration. Depending upon your riding level and your patience, breed should factor in the purchase.

Heat: In hot weather, horses will have less energy. They will likely start out with less energy or, at the very least, fatigue much faster. You may not want to ride in hot weather, but summer riding usually involves less horse restlessness than cool weather riding.

For the least athletic riders (those of you who have trouble mounting and dismounting), this can be an important category. Trying to mount or dismount when a horse won't stand still is at the least, frustrating and at the worst, dangerous (see Part 4, Chapter 14, **Mounting**). The good news is that most horses, when they sense that you are going to dismount will stand still because they suspect that the ride is over and that they can go back to being lazy. The level of tolerance is at the discretion of the rider.

Summary:

1. Be aware that different breeds have different energy levels.

2. Young horses (1-5 years old) have more energy than older horses.

3. Tying a horse for extended periods develops patience.

4. Fatigue is the best solution for restlessness.

5. Most horses do mature out of this restlessness. During the pre-purchase phase, consider if you are willing to wait for them to age out of it, or not.

Pre-purchase tips:

*   Observe the quietness of the horse when tied.

*   Ask the owner to ride the horse then halt. Observe quietness at halt.

*   Ride and halt the horse yourself. Observe quietness at halt.

*   Most horses have an acceptable level of relative quietness at the halt. This is a category that improves with age and miles.

22

Riding — Opening and closing gates

22) Opening and closing gates

0 – Afraid of gate, will not approach

1 – Approaches gate but will not stop next to it

2 – Will approach gate and stop but moves when rider leans

3 – Will stand for untying of gate but unable to close

4 – Completes task but poorly

5 – Completes task but more than one minute

6 – Completes task in less than one minute

In order for horse and rider to successfully negotiate passing through a gate (the proper way), the horse must be capable of backing and side passing, easily and smoothly. It's almost comical to watch a rider try to direct a horse to open and close a gate with little prior training. This is not a skill where luck will prevail. The challenge is way too complicated to accomplish without preparation. Once learned it is easy, but this task takes longer to train than any other one in trail riding. Gate obstacles are a common challenge in trail riding. The vast majority of trail riders simply dismount, open the gate, walk the horse through it, close it behind them, mount and go. This is perfectly acceptable if you can mount from the ground. None of my horses have been trained to properly open and close a gate, so, I dismount. I admit, I do feel like a loser each time I must do this, but I have never been willing to take the time to teach them. If you have trouble mounting from the ground, this is time and/or money well spent to teach them the pattern. While there are many ways to accomplish the opening and closing of a gate, there is but one acceptable proper technique. In addition to ours, there are many Internet videos to view this pattern. So, let us assume your horse can back up and side pass. Let us also assume that it is not afraid of gates. Here are the basics of gate opening and closing:

- Approach the gate so that the horse's head is on the same side of the gate as the handle,

latch, rope or chain (fastener).

- Bring the horse up alongside the gate so that your hand on that side is even with the fastener.
- Side pass towards the gate so that you do not have to lean to reach the fastener. From this point until the gate is latched closed, your hand should not lose contact with the gate.
- Unlatch or untie the gate fastener.
- Once the fastener is disengaged, without letting go of the gate, ask your horse to back up enough for it to be able to turn through the opening as you push the gate away from you.
- Stop the horse when you are through the opening while their hind quarters are still between the opening and the gate.
- Ask the horse to pivot away from the opening to create room for the gate to close.
- Take a step forward, then ask it to side pass towards the gate as you close and latch it.

The picture series on the previous pages demonstrates the above bullet points.

The horse should remain calm and stand still when asked. Points are deducted if the rider must lean away from horse to reach the fastener. An exception exists when the gate has a low chain fastener, where a tall horse and rider must lean down to reach it. Standard ranch gates are manufactured this way, but are often raised on horse trails to accommodate the average height of horse and rider.

Summary:

1. Learn the prescribed pattern to open and close a gate.

2. Horse must back up and side pass to accomplish this task. It is helpful but not necessary that the horse pivot while in the middle of the gate opening.

3. Opening and closing a gate should be a great obstacle and exercise for refinement of backing and side passing.

4. The horse must remain calm throughout the challenge by standing still as rider manages gate fastener.

Pre-purchase tips:

- Very few horses have been trained to open and close a gate.

- A horse must be quite good at smoothly backing-up and side passing to begin the training for this pattern. You should be able to evaluate the speed at which a horse can learn this task based on their scores in the backing-up and side passing tests.

- It is not the end of the world if your horse never learns this skill. It is not a deal breaker.

Expose horses to water as early as possible.

23

Riding — Crossing Water

23) Crossing Water

  0 – Will not approach water
  1 – Very anxiously approaches water with
     much encouragement
  2 – Will approach water, but will not cross
     under saddle
  3 – Approaches, enters with front feet only,
     will not cross
  4 – Will cross with pressure, may not lead
  5 – No hesitation through any water challenge
     as leader

Horses struggle to cross water because of limited forward vision, and the lack of depth perception confuses their small brains. Therefore, the new challenge is assumed to be an unacceptable risk.

Some horses that cross water on a lead will refuse to cross under saddle. Many horses will not be the first in a group to cross a water obsta- cle. Only speculation exists in the explanation of this phenomenon. Some people believe the horse interprets the water as a hole into which they will be swallowed. Others believe it is their primitive survival instinct that predators are lurking in and around the water. When viewing documenta- ries on nature channels, all prey animals are in a heightened state when near a body of water.

Watering holes are the site of many predator ambushes. When the prey animal lowers its head to drink, it is vulnerable. This predator/prey dynamic has existed for millions of years and we have only domesticated horses for a few thousand years, so it seems likely that this is a residual, primitive survival instinct. Zebras still face this challenge in Africa. Whichever theory you choose to believe, know that most horses struggle to learn to feel comfortable around water.

Once most horses become accustomed to water and crossing it, they seem to rather enjoy it. For

water-experienced horses it represents thirst relief, body cooling and rest. I have three creeks on my property and my young horses are led across those creeks from the time they are halter broken. In spite of this early introduction to water, they still struggle to feel comfortable crossing any water the first dozen times. Many horses will reluctantly follow a lead horse across water. This is where their herd instinct will cause them to follow the horse in front of them rather than be left behind. However, when you ride them across in this manner, they tend to cross in a less than graceful and careful way. Be prepared for them to jump across a small stream or creek. For larger water crossings, they may cross with reckless abandon. Rarely, do they fall but it can be a harrowing experience. Hang on!

Preparing them to cross water takes time, patience and water. This process is much easier if you start with a young horse that is halter broken.

Start with puddles and work your way up from there. Even small puddles can scare many horses. With a hose and any depression in the earth, you can create a water crossing if one does not exist. Try to get the horse to stop in the water if you can. This helps show them that there is no danger. If you do not have access to a water crossing, it will be quite a challenge to desensitize your horse. In this situation, you will have to be creative or trailer out to find some water.

The process can be a little dangerous as you cannot force a horse across a water crossing, even if it's shallow. If you finally get them to cross the water, they often want to jump. And, they are much more preoccupied by the water below than the human in front of them. Watch out for flying horses! So, it is very helpful to have another horse, handled by another person who is calm at crossing water. Using that horse as a leader creates a better dynamic for a reluctant horse.

This is another time when longeing is a great training technique. If you have developed your skills at line longeing, you will be better able to get your horse to cross water. Using a 12-14' longe line, you will begin longeing the horse close to the water challenge. Once the horse is respectfully honoring your request to longe both directions, you can slowly move it closer to the water. With time, persistence and patience you will be able to get them to run through the water obstacle. It is best to begin with a small puddle and work your way up to larger and deeper water obstacles. When the horse stops in the water, reward it by removing the longeing pressure. Eventually, and many times quite quickly, the horse realizes the water is its friend. Often, you will need to repeat the process from the saddle.

No matter what method you decide upon, it will take time and energy to make your horse into a water crossing machine. The good news is that once they learn, it is usually a lifetime lesson. We rarely see veteran trail horses balk at a water crossing. Occasionally, certain veteran trail horses will not be the *first* to cross. Further investigation usually reveals that this particular horse has always been the follower across water.

Summary:

1. Introduce young horses to water obstacles as early as possible.

2. Attempt to get any horse to cross water on a lead, first. Take care not to be jumped upon.

3. Get the horse to stop in the water once it enters. This reinforces that there is no danger.

4. Use a more seasoned lead horse to cross first, thereby taking advantage of your horse's herd instincts.

Pre-purchase tips:

- Your trail horse will be called upon to cross water frequently. It is nearly unavoidable.

- Ask the owner how often the horse has crossed water.

- Ask the owner how the horse reacts to water crossings.

- Ask the owner to demonstrate a water crossing from the ground and the saddle.

- There are some horses that never get comfortable crossing water. It may not be easily discovered that any particular horse won't cross water before finalizing the purchase.

- If you have any doubt, try to arrange a situation where you can observe the horse crossing water.

- Hire a trainer to help you determine the answer.

- If the owner is reluctant to give a specific answer or arrange a demonstration, move on.

- Failure to cross water is a deal breaker.

Swimming with Horses

Near my ranch in southern Dallas County we have a small lake where we can take the horses swimming. There is a large parking lot for the horse trailer, a grassy area, a decent little beach and easy entry to a gently sloping and shallow lake. All of my horses are very familiar with water as they have been exposed to water and water crossings since yearlings. And, there is almost always water on the trails we ride. If your horse has no experience with water, it is best not to try to swim with it as it will constantly turn back towards shore. However, we have found that most horses only need a mild exposure to water to want to enter. All it takes is a halter, lead rope and a swimming suit (for handler, not horse!). It only takes a little coaxing, especially if it's hot weather.

Most horses have never been separated from Mother Earth, and it is a very comical experience when they get far enough out where their hooves are not contacting the lake bottom. The look on their faces will make you laugh, I promise! Horses are natural swimmers, and many don't mind having their entire body submerged. It might surprise you that it is very safe to be in the water with horses. The water slows down movements, and you can float beside them while holding on to the lead rope. The only hazard is having your feet stepped upon. This lake bottom is very soft and even if they step upon your foot there is little chance for injury. Because the water buffers your fall, it is a great place to desensitize, work on horsemanship, work on bareback balance and play with your horse. Swimming with horses is a grand experience. Should you have the opportunity, I highly recommend it.

24

Riding — Plastic Bag Tolerance Under Saddle

24) Plastic Bag Tolerance Under Saddle

0 – Highly reactive when bag removed from gullet (spooks and moves)

1 – Moderately reactive when bag removed from gullet (spooks in place)

2 – Mildly reactive when bag removed from gullet (ear(s) turns back)

3 – No reaction until bag placed on lower neck

4 – No reaction until bag is placed on ear(s)

5 – No reaction to bag in any position or to increased sound

The sound and movement of plastic bags present a real challenge for horses. Plastic bags will be encountered on the trail, so we want our horses desensitized to them. This is one of our easiest challenges as it can be done on any or every trail ride with relative ease if you remember to place the plastic bag in the gullet of the saddle each time.

The gullet of a saddle is that opening below the saddle horn or pommel. All saddles have enough space in the gullet for a plastic bag to be placed for a future test. The bag can be placed once you have desensitized the horse to plastic bags from the ground (Part 4, Chapter 6, **Plastic Bags**). After the saddling process, place the plastic bag in the gullet of the saddle. Do this with as little sound as possible. Have the crumpled bag in your hand and compress it into the gullet as quietly as possible. Leave it there until you are ready to perform the challenge. If your horse is not desensitized to plastic bags in the Ground Manners section, you should not attempt this challenge. Plastic bag tolerance under saddle is much more of a surprise for the horse as it cannot see the challenge coming. With Plastic Bag Tolerance from the ground, we give them some warning, by way of distance, when the bag is exposed. Study the technique below and follow it exactly to minimize risk of

Plastic bag training/scoring in round pen or arena.

Step 1. Remember to place the bag in the cantel.

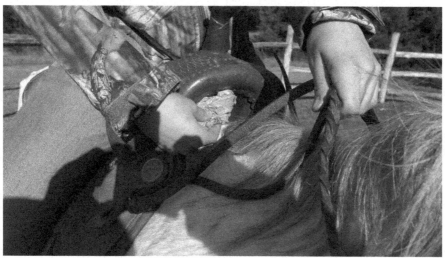

Step 2. Lightly rustle the bag while still contained.

Step 3. Slowly remove the bag and allow the horse to recognize it.

Step 4. Once the horse relaxes, allow the bag to move in the breeze.

Step 5. Once the horse relaxes, rub the bag on its shoulder.

Step 6. Continue rubbing the bag on neck and progress to ears.

Step 7. This horse is desensitized to plastic bags under saddle. Reinforce often.

injury from a frightened horse that may spook.

The entire challenge will take less than 5 seconds. Here is the technique:

1. For safety, lightly rustle the bag while still in the gullet to test for reaction. If horse's reaction seems acceptable, move on the #2 below.

2. Once you reach this point in your T.R.A.I.L.S. scoring, you will simply remove the bag from the gullet while mounted.

3. Note the horse's reaction when the bag is completely out of the gullet, and when it is moving in the breeze.

4. Remember score; document at the conclusion of the ride.

Score the horse for its reaction to the initial recognition of the bag. Once the horse has a repeatedly perfect score to the plastic bag ground training, it should only take a few minutes to train for a perfect score under saddle.

Proceed slowly and always be prepared for a spook. After the test is complete, you should

Plastic bag training on the trail:

Step 1. Trail training progresses the same as above.

Step 2. Introduce bag slowly.

Step 3. Continue pressure.

Step 4. When the horse is this desensitized, you can consider leaving the bag on for the trail ride.

continue desensitizing the horse by rustling the bag ever so slightly during the trail ride without removing it from the gullet. Place your fingers inside the gullet and slightly move the bag to elicit a subtle sound. You will then increase the sound by pulling more of the bag out and crinkling it in your fingers. As the horse becomes more tolerant of the bag, you can remove part or all at the pace you feel the most comfortable. Within minutes, with most horses, you should be able to train to no reaction. Your goal should be to have no reaction to sight, sound or touch to any part of the body.

Summary:

1. Perfect the Ground Manners test, first.

2. Rustle the bag while still in the gullet for early desensitization.

3. Partially remove the bag for further desensitization.

4. Proceed slowly under saddle.

Pre-purchase:

- Test the plastic bag tolerance on the ground (Part 4, Chapter 6, **Plastic Bags**).

- Ask owner to test under saddle.

- Test under saddle if owner was successful.

25

Riding — Cantering

25) Cantering

0 – Refuses to canter

1 – Dangerous canter/ gallop

2 – Canters but uncontrolled, not comfortable

3 – Willing to canter but unbalanced, doesn't know leads

4 – Solid, balanced canter but does not know leads

5 – Solid departure/transition, well-balanced, knows leads

Cantering is one of the most exhilarating experiences that most amateur riders can enjoy. When done properly it is comfortable, graceful, and rewarding. Teaching a horse to canter is important because the need or desire to canter is frequent. Due to lack of proper training, many hobby horses do not canter well mainly because their canter is rough; they tend to go too fast or accelerate into a lope or gallop. **The goal is to have a smooth, well-balanced canter, initiated by the rider on the proper lead.**

Let us start with a score of **"0"**, "refuses to canter". A refusal can come in a variety of forms: balky, cranky, crow hop, buck or other protest thereby threatening the rider's safety should the rider continue to pursue the canter. Horses that do not canter well are either disrespectful or untrained to canter, or both. On rare occasions, some horses have injuries or are so out of shape that it is physically difficult to depart into the canter.

A score of **"1"** means the horse will break into the canter, but it's more of a reaction than purposeful, meaning this is just their next gear as they increase speed much like they do in a pasture when moving at different speeds. For example, when coming to the gate at feed time, blowing off steam, playing or fighting with other horses. It is not a purposeful act. The horse is unwilling to slow down or stop, and the rider has no control. Horses that exhibit this behavior are either frightened due to bad experiences, or have never been trained to canter.

A score of **"2"** is where most horses start, naturally. These horses haven't had the training to learn body control and position. They typically 'run into' the canter, meaning they do an accelerating trot before breaking into the canter. The fast trot can be quite uncomfortable unless the rider is posting. Once the horse finally breaks into the canter, it is fast and unbalanced. More specifically, these horses typically raise their heads, do not travel straight and hollow-out their backs, all of which results in an uncomfortable ride. These horses may also show some signs of disrespect or resistance such as head shaking, a crow hop, buck or pinned ears. Additionally, any issues that were evident at the walk or trot, always get worse at the faster gait. So, if, at the trot the horse doesn't steer well, steering is exponentially worse at the canter. A slow, controlled canter requires practice, physical fitness and patience. Cantering does not come naturally for many horses.

A score of **"3"** typically indicates the beginning of canter training. The horse will transition cleanly into the canter after a little trotting and have no resistance with the canter request. The horse has not learned leads as of yet, but in the beginning of canter training that is okay. The goal at this point is a compliant horse who responds to your request to canter. This horse may also still be learning how to stay in the gait without falling into the trot.

A score of **"4"** is a horse who is in advanced canter training. They understand the concept of picking up the correct lead, but do not pick the correct lead all the time. They may require a couple of trotting steps before they transition to the canter, but they do not run into the canter. There are still occasional mistakes, but they are learning. The horse is compliant and has learned body control. They now know how to slow down without falling out of the canter, round their back and neck, and stay soft in the bridle. This horse has a comfortable canter that any rider will love!

A horse who scores a **"5"** can transition to the canter, on the correct lead from a stand-still or walk. They have no resistance to the canter request. Once in the gait, they are soft, relaxed, rounded and oh so comfortable! It takes many miles to achieve this, but it is worth it!

The good news to all horse owners is no matter what your horse scores, it can get better! Other than physical limitations such as old injuries, there is no reason a horse cannot have a solid score of 5. Here is how to do it:

Step 1: Start on the Ground

- Allow the horse to figure out where his feet need to go and what you are expecting, without a rider. With a longe line or in a round pen, from the trot, cluck twice to your horse (which will be the same cue when you are eventually riding the horse). If the horse does not canter, use a whip to whip the ground to create some energy. Once the horse breaks into the gait, back the pressure off and stop whipping the

ground and clucking. By removing this pressure, you are rewarding your horse for breaking into the canter. If he falls out of the canter, repeat the 'pressure and release'. Your horse will soon learn it's more comfortable to stay in the canter than to fall out of it. When the horse slows without breaking into the trot or shows a sign of relaxation, let the horse rest. Each day build on the slowing down without stopping, and reward him by letting him rest. The horse will soon learn to conserve energy and maintain the canter.

- Starting from the safety of the ground will give the handler insight as to whether there will be issues associated with the transition, such as bucking or bolting.

- If your horse bucks, quickly make the horse move his feet faster, change direction, speed up, etc. Do not let your horse rest until the bucking has stopped. Bucking demands more work without reward! Again, you want your horse to figure out that a slow relaxed canter is the best option. Anything other than a calm, compliant horse means they will be required to work.

- If your horse bolts, let him run. Let him run until he wants to stop and get air. Continue applying pressure until it is clear the horse wants to stop. Then, with your permission, by slowly backing off the pressure, let the horse stop. He will soon learn that he may have to canter 10 or 15 minutes, so it is much better to conserve energy and go slowly.

- The transition to canter is typically where

things can go wrong. Here, you will discover if there are underlying issues that need to be addressed. Again, starting from the ground is always advisable.

- If this ground-work, canter exercise is part of your regular pre-ride routine, the horse learns on its own how to slow down and maintain its gait.

Step 2: On the Horse

- At the absolute minimum, your horse should be able to flex laterally and stop when asked before cantering. The ground work above should also have been started so you have a base line for its behavior and so the horse understands the concept of cantering and your expectations.

- Never expect perfection at first, but do demand good behavior.

- Start at the trot and stay in the trot until the horse is responsive and relaxed. Once you achieve a good trot, ask for the canter with the following steps:

    - Sit deep in the saddle.

    - Outside leg reaches back slightly and at the same time, the inside leg is positioned near the girth. At the same time, squeeze both legs and cluck twice. If your horse responds, 'release'

the pressure (similar to the round pen exercise) so the horse is rewarded for moving out. If the horse increases speed, but does not break into the canter, increase the pressure with your legs and cluck and keep with it until the horse breaks into the canter. Do your very best not to stop squeezing until after the horse canters. Reducing speed after you ask for the canter, but before the horse canters, will only reward the horse for not cantering!

- As the rider, it is your duty to avoid hanging on the horse's mouth for balance.

- In the beginning, less rider interference is best. Let the horse figure this out and give them the time and space to do so. Once they understand the concept, then you can start getting picky about direction and leads.

- Soon, the horse will be conditioned to canter from leg cues and with practice, the canter response and timing will continue to improve.

So, what is a lead? When a horse is cantering, one side of legs (left front and left rear, for example) will literally be in the lead and reach out further forward than the opposite side. For a balanced canter, if you are traveling in a left circle or arch, the horse should be on the left lead. If

Step 1. Left lead cantor. Note, three hooves on ground.

Step 2. Note, one hoof on ground.

Step 3. Go back two pictures, pattern repeats.

Step 4. Go back two pictures, pattern repeats.

you are cantering around to the right, the horse should be on the right lead. If you are traveling in a straight line down the trail, it typically does not matter what lead the horse is on.

A Few Tips

- If your horse consistently shows signs of resistance, it is always a good idea to have a vet examine the horse for pain, discomfort or lameness.
- Additionally, poor saddle fit can often cause resistant behavior. Once you remove the saddle from after a work-out, if there are any dry spots on an otherwise sweaty back or uneven sweat marks, that is a sign of poor saddle fit.

- If you have access to a well-trained horse proficient in cantering, try to take lessons on it so the horse can teach you the cues. It is always easier to learn something new on a trained horse.

Summary:

1. Start the training process from the ground.

2. Use verbal cues to ask for the canter.

3. Refine for a slow, balanced canter.

4. Under saddle, use leg pressure and verbal cues to ask for the canter.

5. Refine for a slow, balanced canter.

6. Begin training for proper leads.

Pre-Purchase Tips:

- Ask the owner if the horse knows how to canter.

- Ask the owner to demonstrate the horse cantering in a round pen.

- Ask the owner to demonstrate cantering under saddle.

- Canter the horse in the round pen.

- Canter the horse under saddle.

The website will have videos that will be much more informative. Find them at www.trail.horse

26-1

Riding — Alternative Test 1
Trail Willingness

Trail Willingness

0 – Will not lead, cannot be encouraged to lead

1 – Will only lead under much duress, very reluctant

2 – Will only pass obstacles with other horses near

3 – Crosses most but not all obstacles as leader

4 – Crosses all obstacles with slight hesitation

5 – Crosses all obstacles without encouragement, leader

6 – Fearless

If this test were not so difficult to administer at the pre-purchase or early in horse ownership, it would certainly be in the main book. In fact, it may be the quality I am most passionate about in horses. Not everyone or every horse wants to lead a trail ride, but a horse and rider to lead a trail ride is a necessity. As discussed in previous chapters, most horses follow well because they have "separation anxiety" or are "herd bound" meaning they simply match the speed of the horse ahead of them through survival instincts (see Part Two, Chapter 2, **Herd Mentality-Understanding Separation Anxiety**). This category measures the horse's willingness to be a leader.

In Part Four, Chapter 20, Trail Responsiveness, I told the story of "Sport," one of my favorite horses. He is a favorite because he is the poster child for "responsiveness." He wants to go forward all the time and needs held back, to prevent him from going too fast. He scores a perfect "5" in the "Responsive" category, but vacillates between a "2", "3" and "4" in "Trail Willingness" depending on the day and his mood. This can be wildly frustrating because he is often called upon to be the leader. We will be chugging along down the trail, and without notice, he senses a threat and stops.

Lead horse, many obstacles. We want an alert but willing leader.

His will is so strong that he cannot be made to go forward no matter how much encouragement. Here is where my other favorite horse is called to the rescue. Diesel's trail willingness is a "5" on most days and a "6" on great days. It is such an honor to have or be in the presence of a horse that will think through its fears, if it has any, and decide that there is no threat that prevents it from respecting the human's decision to pass through an obstacle. Diesel has saved the day more times than I can count. Some good leaders enjoy it so much that they are not great followers and are constantly trying to get to the front. This can be frustrating, but I admire these horses. As the saying goes, "If you're not the lead sled dog, the view is all the same!"

I believe all horses should develop some level of trail willingness and the ability to lead. They do not need to be stellar, just mildly willing to lead a trail ride. This attribute is paramount for a horse to learn to be on the trail alone. Again, many trail riders will never need this virtue, but there are scenarios where you may need to ride off alone to get help for an injured horse or rider, be separated from the herd by happenstance, or simply want to ride alone. Being the lead horse sets the tone for the group. Crossing obstacles, discovering abandoned cars and machinery, and wildlife encounters are all reasons to have some experience for leading. The last thing any group of riders wants is for the lead horse to spook and bolt. Scoring a "3" here should be our minimum goal.

Another important point about developing a horse to be a leader is that, in general, a herd of horses follows the reaction of the lead horse when a potential threat is perceived. Meaning, most times, if the lead horse is calm through perceived threats, the others will likely follow that behavior. Conversely, if the lead horse is spooky (spooks at more perceived threats), the others will likely be more spooky/reactive.

The only way to build trail willingness is to lead as often as possible or to go on trail rides alone. With each successful trail ride, your horse should improve its confidence. It may take months, but most horses will eventually be willing to lead a trail ride. And, then there is "Nash". I have mentioned Nash before. He is a nine-year-old Tennessee Walking Horse gelding with thousands of trail miles. He has trailed far and wide, been ridden in five different states, and still is absolutely convinced there is a pack of wolves around every corner and lurking in every bush. He can spin like a reining horse, without notice. He scores a "0" in this category. He will never get better. Some horses simply cannot handle the pressure of leading. For many horse owners this is acceptable.

Summary:

1. A confident lead horse is imperative for an enjoyable trail ride.

2. Horses can be conditioned to lead through repetitive leading.

3. Some horses are forever unwilling to lead.

4. Some great leaders are not great followers.

5. A fearless leader is a great find.

6. Expect to pay more for a great leader.

Pre-purchase tips:

- Ask the owner about trail experience.

- Ask the owner if the horse is willing to lead a trail ride.

- Ask the owner how often the horse has led a trail ride. If none, what does the horse do when asked to lead?

- Ask the owner about the tolerance of trail obstacles.

- Ask the owner about the tolerance of trail obstacles as the leader.

- Attempt to arrange a trail ride with the owner and the horse prospect before you purchase.

- Hire a trainer to take the horse on a trail ride, if the owner permits.

26-2

Riding — Alternative Test 2
Tolerance of unexpected trail challenges

Tolerance of unexpected trail challenges (vehicles, dogs, livestock, wild animals)

This extra category can be substituted for any of the other categories where testing is not possible for a variety of reasons… no trailer, no gate, no water, etc.

Vehicle

0 – Spins, attempts to flee
1 – Spooks at non-moving, non-running vehicles
2 – Nervous around non-running; spooks at running vehicles
3 – Stops, looks, snorts, will not pass running and moving vehicles
4 – Aware of running and moving vehicles, but does not react
5 – Oblivious to all vehicles

Dogs

0 – Spins, attempts to flee
1 – Spooks, spins, rears, runs from dogs
2 – Very nervous and preoccupied in company of dogs
3 – Tolerates but does not like dogs, charges or kicks
4 – Accepting of dogs, but neutral towards them
5 – Accepting and friendly towards dogs

Farm Animals/Animals in the Wild

0 – Terrified of and spooks badly
1 – Frightened of and refuses to pass
2 – Frightened, but will pass with encouragement
3 – Tolerant of but mildly preoccupied
4 – Notices but no reaction
5 – Oblivious to all animals

Hikers

0 – Terrified of and spooks badly
1 – Frightened of and refuses to pass
2 – Frightened, but will pass with encouragement
3 – Tolerant of but mildly preoccupied
4 – Notices but no reaction
5 – Oblivious of hikers

Many horses have a low tolerance to vehicles, dogs and other farm animals. Score your horse on whichever of the three categories are available that day.

Only through constant, repeated exposure can they be desensitized. Horses acclimate to those things they are around daily. If those things are moved or are unexpected, they will likely react to it as if it were new. In a way this is true for most animals, even familiar objects in a different place is a noteworthy change. Consider the tractor that sits outside their barn every day. The absence of that tractor on any given day is unexpected. The same tractor now on the other side of the barn is new. Because their brains are so small, each situation presents a new threat even when a nearly exact same situation presents itself. They are genetically programmed to recognize subtle changes in their environment in the event a predator is responsible for that change. This explains why they are so reactive to change and can spook at things they have seen thousands of times, it's the mechanism that kept their ancestors alive.

Horses get accustomed to dogs and other farm animals quickly, especially when they are raised in close proximity. Both dogs and farm animals can be introduced to horses later in life, but acceptance can take longer. Please review Part Two, Chapter 4, **Desensitization**.

This may be the single most important action in forging the best possible partnership with your horse. It is most certainly the single best way to increase rider safety. The pictures below demonstrate just a scant few of the objects and techniques for which we can perform desensitization training:

Farm equipment, hay bales, ladders, ATVs, manure spreaders, other horses in stalls.

Farm equipment.

Trail obstacle training. Teeter-totter for horses.

The teeter-totter is an excellent training obstacle as it moves when the horse crosses the halfway point.

Horse stairsteps is another way to desensitize and teach purposeful footfalls.

This picture may represent my favorite desensitization scene. Leading a young horse in and around a party with numerous guests of all ages, bounce houses, a petting zoo and a live band. Wow, what an opportunity.

Most horses are exposed to dogs early in their lives. There is nothing better than to be on a trail ride with a loose dog running every which way to investigate nature. It is truly the definition of "trail desensitization", when the dog(s) crosses the trail in front of and behind the horses, rustles the underbrush from all directions, and chases a rabbit or bird.

Any and all vehicles can be used for desensitization.

Use your imagination to create as many obstacles possible to which to expose the horse.

Any water challenge should be utilized for desensitization.

Deer.

Windmills. Yes, windmills!

One never knows…

Summary:

1. Desensitization through multiple methods is an ongoing process.

2. Time permitting, desensitize your horse to any negative reaction as it happens.

3. Use your imagination to come up with fresh techniques.

4. Allow desensitization to occur naturally when possible in the stall or pasture.

Pre-purchase tips:

- What a horse is desensitized to depends on the conditions where it lives.

- Ask the owner what objects or situations the horse has been exposed and desensitized to in the past.

- Ask the owner if the horse has any issues with any particular objects or situations.

- Ask the owner if you can test the horse with items from the barn and items you have brought for testing purposes.

- There are so many man-made items that can challenge a horse's calmness that no horse can be desensitized to them all. The more stimuli that the horse ignores the better chance there is that it will be less reactive to new challenges.

Our pre-purchase list of items to take to the interview will help you understand the level of reactivity and the range of tolerances of any horse (Part Three, Chapter 4, **Prepare for the Interview - Interview Checklist**).

If you come across a horse that is moderately to highly reactive to objects around a ranch or barn, move on. Things like bags, tarps, ATVs, manure spreaders, rakes, wheelbarrows, etc. are common objects on a ranch to which they should have long since adjusted.

Riding — Alternative Test 3
Unintentional Dismounts

Reaction when rider falls off (unintentional dismount, rider loses reins)

  0 – Spooks and runs as rider loses balance (can't catch afterwards)

  1 – Spooks and runs after rider is on ground (difficult to catch)

  2 – Spooks and runs but comes back to rider and/or group

  3 – Surprised by seeing rider on ground, but only moves a few steps away

  4 – Does not move or react

  5 – Senses when rider is off balance and stops, stands, waits for recovery

This seems like a very odd category, I am sure. However, some of the most severe accidents happen when a rider loses balance, struggles to regain it, but ultimately comes off the horse. This occurrence has dire consequence as many horses spook at the sight and chaos of a rider coming off their back and want to run from the commotion. Being dragged by a frightened horse will almost always leave physical injuries (or worse), but will certainly result in permanent emotional scars. Training to score well in this category may just be the best training we ever do. Consider using a trainer for this challenge.

There are a handful of preparatory issues to address:

• Match the horse you buy to your personality and riding style.

• Make sure your tack is sized properly for you and your horse.

• Make sure your tack is adjusted and tightened properly before each ride.

- Make sure your boots are smaller than your stirrups or stirrups larger than your boots.

- Improve your horsemanship continuously.

One of the most common causes of unintentional dismount is when people forget to tighten or retighten the girth. Many horses learn to inflate themselves with air to avoid the mild discomfort of the girth being tightened. Therefore, retighten the girth several times for these horses. A rider's shifting weight causes the saddle to rotate, rider comes off, saddle ends up on the side or underneath horse. Not good!

Reread the section on "Desensitization". This is the main solution to this and most other spooking issues; but, here, I am suggesting specific desensitization to just this challenge. As odd or obvious as it may sound, a horse does not expect to see a rider half on and half off their back; nor do they expect to see one on the ground at their feet. There are specific techniques that we can employ to reduce their reaction to either scenario.

When desensitizing a horse to any stimulus that can cause an explosion (severe reaction), it is best to do it in an old saddle. Most barns and boarding facilities have old saddles that are prefect for this. You should be able to purchase an old saddle for a nominal price. Do not use your good saddle. I prefer a western saddle for training for this category. You can start training for unintentional dismount at any stage of training.

However, the horse must be saddle-broke and tolerant of mounting, dismounting and riding.

Otherwise, this category could teach the horse that spooking will get us to dismount and that is counter to our goals.

It is imperative that each new challenge/ stimulus (each bullet point below) be applied, repeatedly, until the horse has no physical reaction to it. Some of the challenges below take strength and athleticism. Solicit the help from someone capable or skip these exercises. Be patient. Go slowly.

On the following pages are techniques to increase your horse's tolerance to unintended dismount:

Desensitize the horse to counterbalancing:

Halter and lead rope only.

- Push and pull the horse in all directions.

- Hang on their neck.

- Jump/lay across their back. Use mounting block if necessary.

- Mount them bareback.

- Wave hands and feet from all positions.

- Slide off in all directions.

Be as creative as your coordination will allow to teach calm counterbalance from weight shift.

In preparation for your unintended dismount training, expose the horse to partial dismounts.

Desensitize the Horse to Weight Shift:

These exercises are done in a round pen or small paddock with a saddle, halter and lead rope. Hold on to the lead rope throughout.

- From the ground, push and pull on the horse in all directions to begin getting it accustomed to counterbalancing.

- Mount and dismount repeatedly from both sides.

- Practice partial mounting from both sides.

- Tighten the girth firmly enough that you can stand in one stirrup making the horse counterbalance your weight.

- Lay all the way over the saddle.

- Rock your weight back and forth while lying over the saddle.

- Wave your hands and feet.

- Mount the horse and sit.

- Rock your weight in all directions while mounted.

- Wave your hands and feet.

- Lean forward putting weight on their neck.

An old, children's saddle is ideal for training for unusual saddle positions.

Desensitize your horse to saddle movement:

These exercises are done in the round pen with a halter and lead rope.

It is best to use a youth saddle so you can lift it easily. Holding on to halter and lead rope is optional if the horse is calm.

- Begin by pushing and pulling on the horn, fenders, leather and stirrups.

- Completely untie girth and begin sliding it on and off the horse in all directions.

- Place and hold the saddle all over the neck, torso and legs.

- Loosely tie the girth and rotate the saddle slightly to one side then the other.

- Increase the degree of rotation until the saddle is under the horse. If you have previously desensitized the horse to all other odd saddle positions, it should tolerate this one. If the horse explodes, make sure you are out of the way. The loosely tied girth should allow the saddle to come off within a few steps.

Fast, unannounced dismounts will continue the training.

Practice the right side as much as the left. Unintended dismounts are not biased to one side.

Desensitize your horse to atypical dismount:

Use a saddle with a tight girth, halter and lead rope. Hold on to lead rope throughout.

- Partially mount the horse from both sides. Stand in stirrup then step down quickly.

- Partially mount the horse from both sides and jump down.

- Mount horse from one side and immediately dismount from the other side.

- Mount horse from both sides and quickly dismount without stirrups.

- From a mounted position dismount by leaning forward, holding on to the neck of the horse and slide off.

- From a mounted position dismount with or without stirrups and go directly to a squatting position beside the horse. Repeat to other side.

- From a mounted position dismount with or without stirrups go directly to a lying position beside the horse. Repeat to other side.

Desensitize your horse to seeing you on the ground beside it:

Perform with a saddle. A halter and lead rope are preferred, but a bridle is acceptable. This is a training exercise where allowing the horse to calmly graze while you are assuming the below positions is a great positive reinforcement.

- Kneel beside the horse.

- Squatting (catcher's position) next to the horse.

- One knee on the ground.

- Both knees on the ground.

- Lay beside horse.

- As the horse becomes desensitized to each position, you can reach up and move the saddle, push or nudge its legs, give slight yanks on the lead rope, etc. We are trying to simulate an extraordinary situation where you have just landed next to the horse in an unintended dismount. Any odd sensation you can think of is possible if you have lost your seat. Be creative. Proceed slowly. Be safe.

Step 1. After dismount, squat beside the horse. The very best scenario is that the horse calmly looks at you.

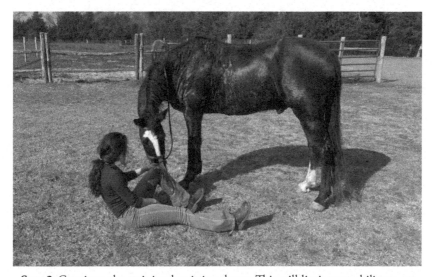

Step 2. Continue the training by sitting down. This will limit your ability to escape should the horse move towards you. However, most always a horse will move away from a potential danger.

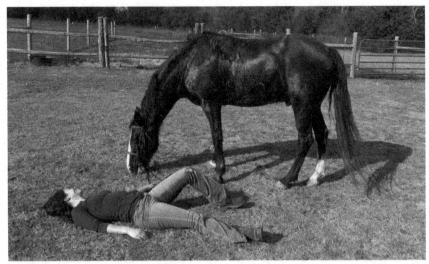

Step 3. Demonstrated here is the perfect result. Rider on ground and vulnerable, horse calmly grazing.

Step 4. As the horse becomes more accustomed to this desensitization exercise, you can become more creative. Here, we replicate what can happen in the worst unintended dismount scenario: foot stuck in stirrup. Again, get help from a veteran horse person or training if you have any doubts about your horse's reaction or your ability to escape this situation while training.

Now, I do understand that many observers of these exercises will declare you insane. However, as repeated throughout this book, "Safety, safety, safety!" I believe we would all agree that being safe and considered crazy is a way better outcome than being injured or dead!

Summary:

Desensitize the horse to:

1. As many saddle positions as possible.

2. As many rider positions as possible.

3. As many dismount positions as possible.

4. Squatting beside it.

5. Lying beside it.

Pre-purchase tips:

1. Ask the rider if they have ever had an unintentional dismount with this horse. If yes, ask them to describe the horse's reaction.

2. Ask the owner to ride the horse.

3. Ride the horse.

4. If the horse seems very calm and you are athletic enough, you could attempt a very quick dismount.

5. If this goes well, you may try a more aggressive dismount and land in a squatting position.

6. Take a trainer, good rider or more athletic person with you and see how the horse does with a quick dismount and a quick dismount landing in a squatting position.

7. Of course, this can be a very dangerous test, and it will not be for most riders/buyers. Use this test with great caution.

26-4

Riding — Alternative Test 4
Initial 10 Minutes of Trail Ride

Initial 10 minutes of trail ride

0 – Bucks, rears, refuses, bolts

1 – Starts trail ride but is highly reactive, mildly reluctant to leave barn/trailer

2 – Mildly reactive, leaves barn/trailer reluctantly, turns back toward barn

3 – Willing horse in group, reluctant alone

4 – Willing alone, no issues

A well-broke, calm horse is invaluable to your trail riding experience and overall riding joy. Many horses are not willing or able to start a trial ride calmly. This chapter deals with the issue of the first ten minutes after you mount the horse for a trail ride. Whether it's at the trail head as you begin a trail ride or on your own property, the first few minutes after mounting can be a very difficult time for you and your horse.

Initial trail calmness is dependent upon many factors:

1. **Temperament.** Relative genetic disposition of the horse. Many horses, such as Arabs, Tennessee Walking Horses, and Thoroughbreds are bred "hot". For the moderate to experienced riders, this is a positive attribute. Hot breeds will be much more excitable during the initial ten minutes on the trail.

2. **Weather.** Cold and cool weather will give your horse more energy than usual. This is particularly true in warm climates where the turning of seasons brings relief from moderate to oppressive heat.

3. **Turnout.** The frequency and duration of turnout will affect your horse's relative en-

When you mount-up, the horse should be calm. As other riders mount, all horses should remain calm.

ergy level. If you ride early in the morning and your horse is stalled during the night, they will likely have higher energy and excitability. Bad weather may keep your horse stalled for extended periods, and will also result in an increase in energy.

4. **Wind.** Horse's survival instincts are piqued during moderate to high winds. Because their hearing is impaired, thereby making them more vulnerable to predatory attacks, horses are on high alert during windy conditions.

5. **Feed.** Because most horses get a jolt of energy from high calorie meals of sugar and protein (grain) and alfalfa they can be more energetic after a meal. Much like a child on a sugar high, this can impact their energy level and excitability.

6. **New surroundings.** When trailering to a new area, the horse will be subject to different smells, sounds, animals, manmade objects and vegetation. This will heighten their flight response thereby increasing their excitability.

7. **Other horses.** Whether you meet up with friends or simply cross paths with other riders, your horse will be exposed to other horses. Many mares will be in season on the trail, and we know that many geldings still have enough testosterone to believe they are stallions. It only takes one horse in a group to spook and cause a herd reaction.

8. **Separation anxiety.** If you are taking your horse away from its pasture mates, it will have anxiety about leaving safety. All herd animals are "herd bound" for safety reasons. Survival of any one individual is profoundly increased when living in a herd. When removed from the herd, all herd animals' senses will be in a heightened state. A solitary herd animal will be solely responsible for its own survival thereby making it more reactive.

9. **Miscellaneous.** In one broad category we can list many other stimuli that will increase the horse's excitability: bicycles, kids, dogs, vehicles, wildlife, domestic animals, sirens, trains, tarps, barrels, pavement…and the list goes on.

It is rare that only one of the above factors exists singularly when you try to start a trail ride. Frequently, it is the majority of these factors that exist on every trail ride.

Another trick to make your horse more docile is to dramatically decrease grain and alfalfa consumption for the day of and the day before you trailer out. You may safely substitute grass or hay for grain as a method of reducing energy levels. Consult your veterinarian before you change your horse's diet.

Summary:

1. Choose the horse with the appropriate temperament that matches your riding skill and style.

2. Control the environmental factors for safety, but don't take it too far.

3. Modify your horse's routine to encourage its confidence and security.

4. Modify feed for reduced energy, if appropriate.

Pre-purchase tips:

1. Ask the owner how the horse is for the initial ten minutes of a ride.

2. Ask the owner to mount the horse while you observe the horse's behavior.

3. Mount the horse and observe behavior.

4. If you are unable or fearful of performing this pre-purchase test, take a friend or a trainer who is not afraid.

5. Pass on horses that are unruly or excitable for the first ten minutes after mounting.

26-5

Riding — Alternative Test 5
Drag a log

Drag a log

0 – Will not approach log or rope

1 – Will not allow rider to handle rope

2 – Spooks badly at sound of dragging log

3 – Completes task with much duress (hops, lunges at sound)

4 – Drags log cautiously but no spooking

5 – Will drag log at various speeds

The ability of the horse to tolerate dragging a log is an important challenge to desensitize the horse to potential trail issues. Namely, we want to prevent an intense reaction when the horse gets a branch tangled in its tail or when it may be caught up in weeds, vines or wire. This challenge allows us to prepare them for inevitable occurrences where they may otherwise react with an intense spook with potential, severe consequences for the rider.

Horses do not like unidentified sounds behind them especially when it appears to be following or gaining on them. They are keenly aware of the location of each of their trail buddies and any new sound is cause for concern. When something is caught in their tail or legs, it can have the same sound and effect of something chasing or attacking them. It triggers an alert that makes them want to take flight. As always, the hotter the breed the more likely and severe this reaction. By teaching them to drag a log, especially at different speeds and with starting and stopping, they will become more tolerant of this challenge and be safer trail horses.

On even rarer occasions, horses can get their feet caught up in or tangled in ground cover weeds, vines, and sometimes old fencing that has found its final resting place near our trails. This is most common when we decide to leave the beaten trail to explore, or when we must go around a downed tree or errant boulder which is crossing the path. The last thing we want them to do is become entangled and attempt to power their way out of it. This situation can endanger us and injure them. It is a far better outcome when they stop, stand calmly and allow us to dismount to untangle the impediment.

As always, desensitization is the key to success. It is best to begin this process after the horse has been ridden, when it is somewhat fatigued and less reactive. The desensitization can be done from the saddle or the ground. Starting from the ground is safest. A round pen is best, but a small paddock or arena will work. In the event the horse spooks and breaks free, it is best to have it contained. Follow the instructions below:

From the Ground:

- Attach a long rope (lariat) to a log weighing approximately 50 lbs.

- Prepare your horse with a saddle and firmly tightened girth.

- Lead the horse around the log and rope to desensitize it to them.

- Hold the lead rope with one hand and reach for the log rope with the other.

- Begin pulling the log towards yourself and the horse.

- Begin leading the horse and dragging the log with ropes separated.

- Wind the rope around the saddle horn, do not tie it. If you use a saddle without a saddle horn, simply squeeze the rope to the front of the saddle so the horse can start to sense that there is pressure being applied from the rope/log. NEVER TIE THE ROPE TO THE SADDLE!

- Begin walking the horse until there is tension on the rope and stop. Allow the horse to feel this new sensation. Once they seem comfortable, ask them to take another step.

- Repeat this process until they understand there is something back there and that it makes a noise.

- Once you believe the horse is desensitized to this new sensation and sound, you will ask it to begin walking a few consecutive steps. Once they master this, it is time to ask them to walk half way around the pen.

- Begin increasing distance until there is no reaction to the challenge.

- Once you believe the horse to be completely tolerant of the challenge, you are ready to stop or continue the training with you in the saddle.

Step 1. Allow horse to recognize object (log) and investigate.

Step 2. Thoroughly desensitize to the rope. We do not want the horse to be more concerned with rope than object.

Step 3. Begin the dragging process by pulling object, not using saddle while walking the horse.

Step 4. Place rope around saddle horn without wrapping.

Step 5. Twist rope around saddle horn, once. Allow horse to feel full weight of object while walking.

- By holding the free end of the rope, you will always have the option to drop it in case of panic by the horse, or you.

- If you have desensitized them well from the ground, the mounted part should come quickly.

From the Saddle:

- Attach a long rope (lariat) to a log weighing approximately 50 lbs.

- Prepare your horse with a saddle and firmly tightened girth.

- Ride or lead the horse around the log and rope to desensitize him to it.

- Have a person on the ground hand you the rope, if available.

- If alone, place the end of the rope on a fence or gate so that you may ride to it and take ahold without dismounting. You can mount with the rope in your hand if you are athletic enough.

- Once holding the rope, you can begin to ask your horse to move away from the log. Most horses will be well aware of the rope and log, so expect the first few steps to be a little frantic. Some horses will want to turn around to look at the log. It's okay to allow this in the beginning. Once they settle, you can ask them to back up. Once they see that the log doesn't gain on them, they usually settle down quickly. Once they are comfortable seeing the log with both eyes, they are ready to turn and pull it the proper way.

- As long as the horse is under control, you can stop and start to show it that there is no threat behind them.

- By holding the free end of the rope, you will always have the option to drop it in case of panic by the horse, or you.

- Finally, attempt to ride at varying speeds to complete the task.

Step 1. If the horse will not approach a post to grab the rope, a second person is necessary to hand the rope to the rider.

Step 2. Begin the dragging challenge by holding rope for quick release should there be a spook.

Step 3. Once the horse has demonstrated calmness with the above challenge, loop the rope around the saddle horn.

Step 4. Begin dragging object at a slow walk. Increase and decrease speed for final training.

You may decide to take the challenge to the next level by dragging other objects. A tree limb with branches and leaves is a great next challenge. The sound is much more intense than a dressed log. This more closely mimics what will happen on the trail if a branch or vine becomes entangled in their tail or wrapped around a leg. Our experience is that when the horse becomes desensitized to dragging something, they are moderately tolerant of dragging anything. I believe they quickly recognize that when said object is not gaining on them it is not a threat. This is exactly our goal in "desensitization training!"

Summary:

1. Introduce the challenge of dragging a log in an area no smaller than a round pen and no larger than an arena. It is nice to have containment fencing should the rope snag on the saddle, instead of releasing when dropped, or if the horse and rider become separated.

2. Introduce the weight and the sound of the log behind, slowly. Literally, one step at a time.

3. Do not mount the horse for this challenge, until you believe it to be fully desensitized from the ground.

4. Never tie the rope to the saddle.

Pre-purchase tips:

- This will be a difficult test to administer at a first visit.

- If additional visits are planned, try to make sure they include someone riding the horse. Make the request to test this challenge, in advance. If the owner doesn't have the interest in setting up the challenge, you can bring something as simple as a small piece of lumber or newspaper attached to a long piece of string. This will allow you to evaluate the tolerance of the horse to the sound and the object following it.

- Most horses build a rapid tolerance to this challenge. Don't place too much emphasis on it at the pre-purchase.

27

Riding — My Perfect Trail Ride

I park my truck outside the barn. I walk into the barn to grab a halter and lead rope. From 80 yards away, my horse recognizes me and begins to walk towards the gate. Many days, the horse recognizes my truck and meets me at the gate. The horse backs away from the gate as I open it inward. His head comes down as I extend the halter towards him.

While standing perfectly still, he bends his neck and changes the position of his head in concert with my placing, buckling and securing the halter strap. I turn to move in the direction of the barn and he obediently follows behind and right of my right shoulder on a loose rope. He maintains that position no matter my walking pace. We arrive at the hitching post where he stops 18" from the post and patiently waits for me to tie a quick-release knot.

I walk away from the horse to gather my grooming supplies. He stands statue still, patiently waiting for me to return. I begin by cleaning the hooves. As I approach each hoof, the horse shifts his weight away from the leg I am approaching and begins to lift the hoof as I reach for it. Each hoof is completed, and I use a broom to sweep away the debris. The broom travels under and around the horse without reaction.

I then begin to groom the body, mane and tail while the horse lowers its head to allow me to groom the top of the head and upper mane. Fly spray is then applied without reaction. I start the clippers and begin trimming the body, face and finish with the ears, without reaction. The horse lowers his head to facilitate clipping the ears and bridle path.

The horse remains quietly tied while I connect the trailer to the truck and move it to a location for loading. I load my tack and mounting block, checking twice for completeness. I open the trailer doors and secure them. I check the trailer for safe footing, foreign objects and old grain or hay. Once I am confident that the trailer is safe for horse and human, I fetch the horse. The horse stands quietly for untying. I move off towards the trailer and the horse obediently follows allowing a respectful 18" of space between us. His pace mirrors mine. I look forward into the trailer as we approach. He continues to follow me, without hesitation, up and into the trailer. Once we arrive at the proper position in the trailer, he stands quietly as I secure the trailer tie to the halter. I double check that the horse is safely tied to the trailer. As I depart the trailer, the horse moves away from my path to allow safe exiting. I close all dividers or restraints, then close and secure the trailer doors. Throughout the drive to the trailhead, the horse is patient and quiet in the trailer.

Once we arrive at the trailhead, I unload the tack while the horse is quiet and patient. I open and secure the trailer doors, open any dividers or restraints and approach the horse to untie. He moves away to open space for my approach and stands still while I untie the trailer tie. He does not move until I say, "back". Upon this prompt, the horse slowly and carefully moves backward until he encounters the step or gate. At this point, he carefully and fluidly measures each footfall for a safe and graceful exit. I follow from inside the trailer as the horse slowly exits and waits for me to exit. Once both of us are outside the trailer, the horse waits for me to declare which direction we will move. I move to secure the horse where I have positioned the tack. We walk to that side of the trailer and I tie the horse to the outside while he stands quietly. I complete any additional groom-

ing and begin the saddling process. I remove the mounting block from the trailer and position it in a safe place for mounting.

As the horse stands quietly, I place the blanket, followed by the saddle. Once in position, I tighten the girth without protest. Once secure, the halter is loosened, placed around the neck and I then place the bridle, while the horse assists with well-timed head movement, mouth opening and cooperation. The throat latch is secured, and the reins managed. The halter is then unfastened and left behind.

I lead the horse a safe distance away from the trailer to an area for mounting. I position the horse next to the mounting block. The horse stands perfectly still while I climb the mounting block, position my left foot in the left stirrup, push off the mounting block, throw my right leg over the horse, coming to rest on the saddle, reach down to place my right foot in the right stirrup and raise up to gather myself and the reins. The horse stands statue-still until I give a slight leg squeeze and cluck with my voice at which time he moves forward in a slow, purposeful way.

We encounter a gate at the entrance to the trail. With leg pressure, only my horse side passes, moves forward, backs up, passes through the open gate while I hold the gate continuously with one hand. He backs up, side passes and stands quietly as I latch the gate. We move off at my decision.

The initial few minutes, under saddle are calm and controlled without drama. We continue the trail ride at various controlled gaits. The horse is responsive to my requests to change speeds between a walk, trot and canter. Though alert to danger, there is not a moment of separation anxiety or spookiness. Turns only require a slight turn of the head and subtle leg cue.

A neighborhood dog rushes across our path. My horse stops then quickly identifies that there is no threat and continues forward without concern. We come to a water crossing, which we enter without hesitation. I allow the horse to stop to drink. Once I am satisfied, he has consumed enough water, I squeeze, cluck and we continue through the water. After about 30 minutes, I see my friends approaching on their horses. My horse recognizes other riders and familiar horses but does not change speed to join them. We proceed at this pace until we meet-up with them. Once in their company, my horse does not engage with the other horses but stands quietly while the riders visit.

It's time for a break, so, through weight shift, I signal my intention to dismount. My horse stands still while I dismount. The other riders dismount, and we take a ten-minute break. I tie my horse to a nearby tree where it stands quietly for the entire break. When our break ends, I gather my horse and place it in a low spot on the trail. I prompt it to park and the horse stretches out to lower the stirrup. I place my foot in the stirrup which is now six inches lower and proceed to mount. The horse maintains this position until released with a squeeze and a cluck.

We ride with the group for another half-hour. My horse leads willingly and follows patiently as riders and horses switch places throughout the trail ride. Eventually, we come to a fork in the trail where we depart, alone from the group without protest. There is no desire to return to the group as the distance increases between us and them.

We navigate the gate in the opposite direction, in the same pattern as we did on the way out. We arrive back at the trailer. The horse is tied to the outside and stands quietly while I remove tack. At this trailhead there is a rinsing station. We move to the rinsing station where the horse stands still while I rinse the sweat from its fur and allows me to soak its head without protest.

As earlier, the horse follows me onto trailer where it is tied for the ride home. We arrive back home where I park in a safe area for unloading. We unload, uneventfully. I walk the horse to its paddock where it respectfully waits for me to open the gate. We walk through the gate then close it behind me. I turn the horse away from the gate and begin to unbuckle the halter. The horse lowers its head to assist and stands completely still during the process. Once the halter is removed the horse stays in place as it waits for a food treat. Once the treat is given, the horse slowly ambles away. I return to the chores of tack and trailer management.

This uneventful and rewarding scenario is our goal in horse ownership and trail riding. The T.R.A.I.L.S. system provides a rational basis for purchasing and training your trail horse to achieve this type of performance. I wish you much success in your journey!

Bibliography

L. Briard, C. Dorn, O. Petit. *Personality and affinities play a key role in the organisation of collective movements in a group of domestic horses.* Ethol, 121 (2015), pp. 888-902

Casey, R. et al. *Clinical problems associated with intensive management of performance horses. The Welfare of Horses.* Kluwer Academic Publishers, Dordrecht, Boston, London, 19-44, 2002.

Chitnavis, J. et al. *Accidents with horses: what has changed in 20 years?* Injury 27, 103-105, 1996.

Christy, G. et al. *Horseback riding injuries among children and young-adults.* J. Fam. Pract. 39 (2), 148-12, 1994

Croweel,-David, S., Weeks, J. *Maternal behaviour and mare-foal interactions.* In: Mills, D.S., McDonnell, S.M. (Eds), The Domestic Horse: The Origin, Development and Management of its behaviour. Cambridge University Press, Cambridge, 126-138, 2005.

de Pasille, A.M.B. et al. *Dairy calves' discrimination of people based on previous handling*, J. Anim. Sci. 74, 969-974, 1996.

Estep, D.Q. *Changes in the social behaviour of drafthorse (Equus caballus) mares coincident with foaling.* Appl. Anim. Behav. Sci. 35, 199-213, 1993.

Grogan, E.H., McDonnell, S.M. *Mare and foal bonding problems.* Clin. Tech. Equine Pract> 4, 228-237, 2005.

Hama et al. *Effects of stroking horses on both humans' and horses' heart rate responses.* Jpn. Psychol. Res. 38, 66-73, 1996

Hartmann, E., et al. *Dominance and Leadership: Useful Concepts in Human-Horse Interactions?* J. Equine Vet. Sci. 52, 1-9, 2017

Hausberger, M et al. *Experiences precoceset developpment du comportement chezle poulain.* In: Compte-rendu la 30eme Journee de la Recherche Equine, 3 mars 2004, Paris, 155-164, 2004.

Hausberger, M et al. *Interpaly between environmental and genetic factors in temperament/personality traits in horses (Equus caballus)).* J. Comp. Psychol. 118, 434-446, 2004.

(NOTHING YET)

Hausberger, Martine et al. *A review of the human-horse relationship.* Applied Animal Behaviour Science, 109 (2008), 1-24

Hayes, K. *Temperament tip-offs.* Horse and Rider, 47-84, 1998.

Hemsworth, P.H. *Behavioural responses to domestic pigs and cattle to humans and novel stimuli.* Appl. Anim. Behav. Sci. 50, 43-56, 1996.

Henry, S. et al. 2006b. *Influence of various early human-foal interferences on the subsequent human-foal relationship.* Dev. Psycobiol. 48, 712-718.

Henry, S. et al. *Human-mare relationship and behaviour of foals toward humans.* Appl. Behav. Sci. 93, 341-362, 2005.

Hinde, R. *Towards Understanding Relationships.* Academic Press, Londres, 1979.

Houpt, K. *Formation and dissolution of the mare-foal bond.* Appl. Anim. Behav. Sci. 78, 319-328, 2002.

Jago, J. G. et al. *The influence of feeding and handling on the development of the human-animal interaction in young cattle.* Appl. Ani. Behav. Sci. 62, 137-151, 1999.

Janczak, A.M. et al. *Relation between early fear- and anxiety-related behaviour and maternal ability in sows.* Appl. Anim> Behav. Sci. 82, 121-135, 2003.

Jezierski, T et al. *Effects of handling on behavior and heart rate in Konik horses: comparison of stable and forest reared youngstock.* Allp. Ani. Behav. Sci. 62, 1-11, 1999.

Keeling, L. et al. *Horse-riding accidents: when the human-animal relationship goes wrong.* In: 33rd International Congress of the International Society for Applied Ethology, Agriculture University of Norway, Lillehammer, 1999.

Lansade, L. *Le temperament du cheval. Edute theorique. Application a la selection des chevaux destines a l'equitation.* These universitaire en Sciences de la Vie, Tours, 2005.

Lose, M. Phyllis. *Blessed are the Brood Mares,* Howell Book House, New York, NY (1991).

Mal, M.E. and McCall, C.A. T*he influence of handling during ages on a halter training test in foals.* Apl. Anim. Behav. Sci 50, 115-120, 1996.

McCall, C. A. et al. *Locomotor, vocal and other behavioral responses to varying methods of weaning foals.* Appl. Anim. Behav. Sci. 14, 27-35, 1985.

McGreevy, P.D. and McLean, A.N., 2009. *Punishment in horse-training and the concept of ethical aquitation.* J. Vet. Behav: Clin. Applic. and Res. Vol 4, Issue 5, 193-197.

Miller R.M. *Imprint Training of the Newborn Foal,* Western Horseman, Colorado Springs, CO (1991).

Moons, C.P.H. et al. *Effects of short-term maternal separations on weaning stress in foals.* Appl. Anim. Behav. Sci. 91, 321-335, 2005.

Morgan et al. *Rider's personality and the perception of the co-operation between rider and horse.* In: 51st Annual Meeting of the European Association for Animal Production (abstract), 2000.

Munksgaard, L., et al. *Discrimination of people by dairy cows based on handling.* J. Dairy Sci. 80, 1106-1112, 1997.

Reinhart, V. T*raining adult male Rhesus Monkeys to actively cooperate during in-homecare venipunc-*

ture. Anim. Technol. 42, 11-17, 1991.

Rivera, E. et al. *Behavioral and physiological responses of horses to initial training: the comparison between pastured versus stalled horses.* Appl. Behav. Sci. 78, 235-252, 2002.

Rossdale, P.D. *Clinical studies on the newborn thoroughbred foal.* I. Perinatal Behaviour. Br. Vet. J. 123, 470-481, 1967.

Rushen, J. et al. *Domestic animals' fear of humans and its effect on their welfare.* Appl. Anim. Behav. Sci. 65, 285-303, 1999.

Seaman et al. *How reliable is temperament assessment in the domestic horse (Equus caballus)?.* Appl. Anim. Behav. Sci. 78, 175-191, 2002

Sondergaard, E., Ladewig, J. *Group housing exerts a positive effect on the behavior of young horses during training.* Appl. Anim. Behav. Sci. 87, 105-118, 2004.

Ueeck, B. et al. P*atterns of maxillofacial injuries related to interaction with horses.* J. Orl Maxillo. Surg 62, 693-696, 2004

"University of Connecticut's College of Agriculture, Health, and Natural Resources."

van Dierendonck, M.C. et al. *Differences in social behaviour between late pregnant, post-partum and barren mares in a herd of Icelandic horses.* Appl. Anim. Behav. Sci. 89, 283-297, 2004.

Visser et al. *Heart rate and heart rate variability during a novel object test and a handling test in young horses.* Physiol. Behav. 76, 289-296, 2002.

Visser, E. et al. *Quantifying aspects of young* horses' *temperaments: consistency of behavioural variables.* Appl. Anim. Behav. Sci. 74, 241-258, 2001.

Waran, N. and Casey, R., 2005. *Horse training.* In: Mills, D.S., McDonnell, S. M. (Edsa, The *Domestic Horse: The Origins, Development and Management of its Behaviour.* Cambridge University Press, Cambridge, 189-195.

Waran, N. et al. *The Welfare of Horses*, Springer Publishing, 2007.

Waring, G.H. *Horse Behavior.* Noyes Publications, New York, 2003.

Winkler E. et al. *Adult sports-related traumatic brain injury in the United States trauma centers.* J. Neurosurg. 40, E4, 2016.

Index

Contributors

No book can be written without collaboration.
   I would like to thank the following parents,
   coaches, experts, trainers, riders, models,
   artists, contributors, friends, editors, publishers
   and horses:

David H. and Sarah "Betty" McFadden	"Cisco"
Kathryn Roan	"Sport"
David Lyles	"Seven"
Glee Hastings	"Eeyore"
Rachel Winnenberg	"Diesel"
Glenn Fox	"Ace"
Donna Seeds	"Nash"
Barbara Paradis	"Jewel"
Melina Inmon	"Beauty"
Sierra Hartman	"Gal"
Kim Chelius	"Boni"
Carl Pierce	"Lydia"
Kelley McPherson	"Doubler"
Lisa Gratz	
Lori Ericson	
Alan Paradis	
Kathryn Ingley	
Laura Hildreth	